GUARDIANS AND ANGELS

GUARDIANS AND ANGELS

Parents and Children in Nineteenth-Century Literature

by

DAVID GRYLLS

FABER AND FABER
London & Boston

First published in 1978
by Faber and Faber Limited
3 Queen Square London WC1
Printed in Great Britain by
The Bowering Press Ltd Plymouth
All rights reserved

British Library Cataloguing in Publication Data

Grylls, David
  Guardians and Angels.
  1. Parent and child in literature 2. English
  fiction – 19th century – History and criticism
  I. Title
  823'.8'092355   PR830.P/

  ISBN 0-571-10919-5

TO MY MOTHER AND FATHER

CONTENTS

A*

PREFACE

When, from the last quarter of the twentieth century, we look back on Victorian parents and children, we tend to imagine a stereotype. Surely those families were exceedingly strict—the fathers despotic, unbending, sententious, the mothers deferential, devoted to duty, the children repressed or ignored. The household seems thick with hypocrisy, a compound of canings and family prayers; real affection, we feel, could not live in this climate; young and old were estranged by fear. Of course, we admit, there were certain exceptions, but mostly the parents were stern and unsmiling and the children were deplorably treated: belittled, kept under, deprived of their freedom, compelled to be seen and not heard.

The stereotype is not completely false. The truth it contains is that since the nineteenth century a regard for childhood has steadily increased—but the crucial word is *increased*. What if we compare the Victorian situation, not with the assumptions of the twentieth century, but with those of the centuries before? And what if we consider, not only the history of discipline, but several other symptoms of the adult view of children: the books they were given, the discussions about them, their rights and duties as portrayed in fiction, the treatment they received at work? What, finally, if we drop our untenable assumption that the Victorian period was all of a piece, and begin to acknowledge the changes that happened in the course of the nineteenth century? In this case, our certainties start to dissolve: the stereotype prints in reverse.

This book is a study of parent-child relations in nineteenth-century literature; its theme is the growth of childhood independence and the decay of parental power. It is, essentially, a *literary* study, not a work of sociology or social history: its data are literary documents, and its intention is rather to detect and trace attitudes—values, assumptions, popular notions—than establish facts about social behaviour, or specify how families lived. It is, necessarily, a *selective* study, for the relevant materials—on this topic, for this period—are so great, so extensive in both variety and quantity, as to force some narrowing-down of interests, some exclusion, some delimitation. This superabundance of relevant evidence is, incidentally, not only a problem: it speaks for the case that the book is making; it is part of the argument.

The chief concern, then, of the following chapters is the development of thought in the nineteenth century on the subject of parent-child relations. But since changes in thought are so often connected with changes in society and in economics, the discussion (especially in the first two chapters) is not always confined to literary history or to literary criticism. It incorporates the findings of several other disciplines, ranges over several subjects. However, though the plunder from these excursions is a necessary basis for the later chapters, it is always subordinate to them: the ultimate object of the book's enquiry is the study of literary texts.

I should like to express my thanks to those people who have helped me in various ways: to Professor John Carey, for his useful comments and his friendly encouragement over several years; to Keith Thomas, for a number of valuable suggestions as to relevant further reading; to Judith Stinton, for support, for many discussions, for her long-standing, generous and kindly interest; to Patricia Feeney, for protecting me from exhaustion, from typist's cramp and emotional despair; finally my thanks to Peter Kemp, whose suggestions, arguments and stylistic sensitivity, a blend of enthusiasm and critical rigour, have not only helped to sustain the author but have certainly improved the book. Needless to say, as everyone says, the errors are all my own.

Chapter I
PARENTS AND CHILDREN

'He who sees a child, sees nothing.'
LATE MEDIEVAL PROVERB

(i)

At the end of the nineteenth century the most popular novelist in
Great Britain was probably Marie Corelli. She was a woman both
eccentric and commonplace: while suspecting herself to be Jesus
Christ, and indeed implying as much in her books, she was
nonetheless able to furnish her readers with sentiments of flawless
banality. Her fiction was a medley of popular prejudices, a
symphony of fashionable talking-points. She exposed the vices of
high-society—the absinth orgies, the shameless amours—while
acknowledging the benefits of gentle birth. She warned against
atheism and other French failings and demonstrated the necessity
of religion and fresh air. Above all she extolled romantic love and
—which was more or less the same thing—the essential truth of
Christianity, a gentle, uplifting and beautiful creed which should
be universally imposed.

In 1900 Marie Corelli published a book called *Boy*. As with all her
books, its theme was didactic, its message very clearly pronounced;
the idea she had got hold of was the iniquity of parental neglect.
The story is intended to prove beyond doubt that whenever a
young person goes astray, his parents are wholly to blame. Too
many parents fail to meet their obligations, too many allow their
offspring to sink into sorrow and vice. Such is the lamentable
fate of Boy, young Robert D'Arcy Muir. A sweet child with a
'lovely far-away look in his dreamy blue eyes', Boy is shackled
to incompetent parents. His mother is a fat, conceited slattern
and his father, now an habitual soak, quite ignores his angelic
potential. 'As for any sacredness in the life of a child, or any idea
of grave responsibility resting upon him as a father, for that child's
future, such primitive notions never occurred to him', comments
Miss Corelli, bitterly. From first to last the hero is inadequately
reared. His mother brings him up on doses of medicine and

leaves him to his own amusements: '. . . a child of the gutter had the same sort of maternal care.' She fails to instruct him in the truths of the gospel and, what is more, lets his clothes become so grubby that at last 'there was very little difference in appearance between him and the common boys of the village'. Nor is he allowed to receive the salvation of attendance at a British prep school. Instead he is shipped away to France, stuffed with facts in a pretentious crammer, and exposed to the unspeakable, or at least unspecified, horrors of Gallic morality.

In contrast with the monstrous D'Arcy Muirs are a couple of alternative parents. These are Miss Letty Leslie, a saccharine spinster with private means, and her platonic paramour, Major Desmond, a bluff and basically kind-hearted man, although he gets 'satisfaction' from thrashing philandering actors and says he would like to see whipping brought back to punish adulterous wives. Miss Letty makes an offer to adopt Boy, but her delicate entreaties are roughly repulsed. Removed from her good influence, corrupted by France, Boy goes to Sandhurst, but takes to the bottle and before very long is expelled. He gambles, is blackmailed, and tries to embezzle Miss Letty's money; finally he is slain in the Transvaal, gasping out appropriate penitence. As Miss Corelli implies, it is a pitiful story, but it is not without its moral. Boy was just one of a crowd of young people who owe their mistakes and miseries to the 'blind tyranny and selfishness' of their parents.

> From the earliest beginnings of childhood, all the seeds of his present misery had been sown,—by neglect, by carelessness, by bad example, by uncomfortable home surroundings, by domestic quarrellings,—by the want of all the grace, repose, freedom, courtesy, kindliness and sympathy, which should give every man's house the hall-mark of 'Home'.

This seems a fairly well-filled charge-sheet, but Miss Corelli is anxious not to make her message too straightforward, and so she introduces the suggestion that not only upbringing is to blame. Heredity, too, is a possible factor; the author is quick to pounce on bad breeding and she also believes strongly in the power of noble blood. For instance, Major Desmond has a niece who is jilted and who responds to this misfortune with a spirited tirade; the Major expresses his approval here by bellowing in her face: 'There spoke Jack Morrison's girl! . . . Blood will out!' (It probably will, we suspect, with the Major around.) The same adage crops up later in the book to explain Boy's drunkenness at Sand-hurst.

Parents, though, despite this complication, could hardly be expected to feel responsible for their own heredity, and indeed the main burden of the book's indictment falls on the shortcomings of their behaviour. What is remarkable is how heavily it falls, and with what a shrill, windy noise. By 1900, it seems, the country's best-selling novelist could count on a large and eager audience for a book which attributes a young man's misadventures almost entirely to the neglect of his parents, to their culpable laxity in bringing him up. The idea was trite and acceptable, was ripe for mass assimilation, was, in short, ready for Marie Corelli. And yet, as an article of popular faith, it was not an ancient idea. It depended on a notion of parental responsibility little more than a century old.

A hundred years previously the message of Marie Corelli's book would not have been generally accepted. For children were seen differently then and the task of parents differently conceived. The nineteenth century witnessed an enormous change in attitudes to parent-child relations. The concept of childhood took on a new shape; parental duties diminished in breadth but grew in intensity. Decade by decade parents were deprived of legal and material powers; but what was expected of them, although altered, remained demanding and taxing enough: a moral and emotional influence, a desire and ability to bring up their children with loving and scrupulous care. The significance of children, the role of their parents—these things were extensively revised, and the process, confused, distressing and comic, is reflected in the literature of the time. The purpose of this book is to examine certain documents—fiction, journalism, autobiography—in which this vast development is embodied or discussed.

But firstly the question must arise of how and why such tendencies originated—tendencies that had so great an effect on Victorian domesticity. Broadly speaking the causes seem to be of two kinds: on the one hand, socio-economic conditions; on the other, the confluence of ideas, both secular and religious. These causes were of course closely connected; in the following discussion they are separated for convenience of analysis.

(ii)

The study of attitudes to childhood in the past, together with research into the function of the family (the second a necessary context for the first), is only a recent development in historiography. A number of disciplines have converged on the subject: sociology and psychoanalysis, demography and anthropology. Moreover a good deal of the most ambitious work has been offered by writers with no previous reputation as professional historians. The result has been what one might expect: provocative theories, multi-disciplined mosaics, crazed over with confusion and conjecture. So far there has been little synthesis—even less any definite progress towards an agreed methodology: quite often convergence has meant collision. And some of the pioneering attempts, although undoubtedly stimulating, have yielded suspiciously patchy results, unreliable in many particulars. As a consequence any summary of recent findings is likely to hesitate and qualify, to slide off into the tentative. For the whole question of the relations, in history, between social and economic circumstances and the rearing and general treatment of children is still tangled with doubt and difficulty, despite being currently cultivated by a multitude of various researchers. The history of the family is still being written; at the moment the most one can hope to do, by way of a brief introductory survey, is sketch out a few major trends.

Throughout the last four hundred years, but especially since the eighteenth century, the position of children in Western society has altered in two basic ways. Children have gradually been segregated from the community at large; and—partly a cause of this, partly a consequence—their capacities and needs have been acknowledged as different from those of adults. Instead of working with or for their elders, children have been sent to study in schools. But, oddly, this has not cut them off from their parents. Their integration with their families has not diminished but grown; and the nature of the bond, once mainly economic, is now mainly emotional.

Until quite recently this change was often identified with the 'rise of the nuclear family'. It was alleged by historical sociologists that the extended family, with numerous relatives, had contracted to the nuclear or parent-child group; the cause was uncertain, but frequently connected with the growth of industrialism. This theory found favour with literary critics and also some social historians (for example, Ivy Pinchbeck and Margaret Hewitt, in their *Children in English Society*). But over the last decade, under pressure from historical demography, the theory has begun to break down. In his *Household and Family in Past Time* (first published in 1972) Peter Laslett has assembled an artillery of evidence for the case that in Europe, for at least four centuries, nuclear families have always been the norm. If Laslett and his fellow contributors are correct, the notion of the extended family is a sociological myth.

These conclusions, however, don't entail very much about family attitudes. It is true they deflate certain facile beliefs about pre-industrial life: the togetherness, the multitudes, the co-operative proximity of a colourful assortment of kin. But to ascertain the average size and structure of the family is not to discover its function: the fact that the family, as a kinship group, has not contracted physically doesn't mean that, as a concept and an ideal, it has not importantly changed. A number of historians would argue that it has; among the most persuasive is Philippe Ariès, whose *Centuries of Childhood*, concerned with the function of the family, has often been misinterpreted as making claims about its 'nucleation' (Gathorne-Hardy, 1972; Mazlish, 1975).

Ariès's book is an examination of the concepts of childhood and family life in the *ancien régime*. Its conclusions apply mainly to the history of France (it was first published in French in 1960), but Ariès also uses evidence from England. Ariès stresses, and perhaps exaggerates, the vast change of thought that took place. He believes that the concept of the close-knit family, as a refuge from society and a self-contained unit, advanced as the sociable community-life of the Middle Ages receded. The actual function of the family changed: from being in the first place a material arrangement, it came to specialise in sentiment, to be welded together by warmth of affection and devoted to the nurture of children. This change was connected with the 'discovery' of childhood as a special phase of existence. Bound up with the new interest in education, this discovery, though started earlier, became salient in the seventeenth century. In this period the iconography of the family became more profuse; some boys ceased to be dressed entirely like grown-ups; the idea of childhood innocence appeared; apprenticeship was being replaced by schooling; there was an insistence on supervision, early discipline and juvenile modesty. These trends continued in the eighteenth century. Primogeniture began to be questioned: '. . . it was repugnant to a new concept of equal rights to family affection.' But the most significant thing was that a new severity, a more continuous vigilance, were practised by those persuaded of the importance of upbringing. 'But this severity was the expression of a very different feeling from the old indifference: an obsessive love which was to dominate society from the eighteenth century on.'

Ariès believes that the process he describes was at first confined mainly to the middle classes. 'Between the eighteenth century and the present day, the concept of the family changed hardly at all', he says. 'On the other hand, it extended more and more to other social strata.'

The details of Ariès's thesis can be, and indeed have been, severely criticised (Stone, 1974). But for the purpose of the present exposition only two qualifications need be made. The first is that Ariès probably overestimates the rapidity with which ideas about the special nature of childhood achieved general recognition. The concept of the family may have been complete, except for class permeation, by the middle of the eighteenth century, but the doctrine of the child's special nature was only then receiving, in Rousseau's *Émile*, its first full articulation.

More important, Ariès's argument is unwarrantably nostalgic. He believes that children were less miserable before they were 'discovered': their discovery led to strict discipline, confinement and the birch. Efficiently schooled and domesticated, children were robbed of their independence; concern for their special nature resulted in repression. The weakness of this view has been exposed in a recent American symposium, *The History of Childhood*, edited by Lloyd de Mause. The evidence from this book reassures us that children have not been treated worse since the rise of school education: they had always been treated abominably. Indeed, de Mause contends that the treatment of children has steadily improved; the further back one goes in time, the more savage and uncomprehending the attitudes of adults are found to be. In antiquity it was common for unwanted babies to be thrown on dung-heaps or exposed on hills; children who were not so fortunate might grow up to be castrated or sexually abused. Infanticide was not classified as murder until A.D. 374; it was still a widespread practice in eighteenth-century London (hence Thomas

Coram's Foundling Hospital). Warming to his case with indignant zeal, de Mause has little difficulty in gathering evidence from every period of cruelty, exploitation and neglect. Babies have been tossed about in swaddling-clothes (occasionally being dropped and brained), kept quiet with stupefying drugs, and beaten as soon as weaned. The child's later nurture has taken the form of systematic terrorisation, improving visits to public hangings, and a hardening process composed of starvation, inadequate or punitive clothing, and immersion in icy water. This was the kindly side of upbringing—designed for the child's own good. But adults have also exploited children, employed them for personal ends. At various times they have been mutilated to provoke pity (or sometimes laughter), sold into slavery or prostitution, utilised as hostages, or solemnly awarded pride of place in sacrificial rites. At all times they have toiled for the adult world, not only in the potteries and factories and mines, but for centuries as servants and labourers; and at all times they have been beaten.

De Mause's contribution to *The History of Childhood* effectively refutes the nostalgic assumptions in Philippe Ariès's thesis. Unhappily it tries to accomplish far more: de Mause is anxious to advertise 'a new paradigm for history', the psychogenic theory, whereby the relations between parents and children develop independently of social change (or economic or political change), and evolve instead through the parents' ability, in one generation after another, to regress a little more 'empathically' to the psychic age of the child. There is no space here to discuss this theory, so excitedly promoted and so heavily loaded with scholarly testimonials. Suffice it to say that de Mause is more adept in amassing than in sifting or interpreting evidence—his quotations, for example, quite often fail to substantiate, and sometimes attenuate, his argument; and it appears that, to their credit, not a few of his co-authors have found it somewhat impracticable to support his general line. Even so his piece remains valuable: it offers a comprehensive bibliography, a welter of fascinating information, and even some reliable conclusions.

Among the latter is de Mause's finding that the eighteenth century was a crucial period for the better treatment of children; it was this century, according to him, which 'saw the biggest decrease' in beating. Other evidence for the importance of this period has been supplied by J. H. Plumb in an article in *Past and Present*, 'The New World of Children in Eighteenth-Century

England' (May 1975). Professor Plumb details the symptoms of an increasing concern with the young: the growing informality of family portraits after about 1730; the success and proliferation of small private academies (some of which, in their prospectuses, boasted of an absence of corporal punishment); the vastly increased expenditure on the amusements and pleasures of children. It was the eighteenth century that saw the emergence of a literature specifically designed for the young. From 1742 to 1800 the number of published children's books rose steadily each decade. Parents were more willing to spend money on their children—not only on books but on toys. In 1700, although toys were available, there was no shop, not even in London, which specialised in their sale. Throughout the century the situation changed; and eventually children were being regaled with circuses, puppet shows, exhibitions and educational games. Professor Plumb believes that discipline, too, became less brutal and rigorous—at least until the end of the century, when a certain amount of severity returned with the Evangelical revival. Like many historians of the period, he attributes this interlude of lenience partly to the influence of John Locke, whose *Some Thoughts Concerning Education*, first published in 1693, was reprinted no fewer than nineteen times before 1761. Yet this in itself would hardly account for so profound and far-reaching a change in parent-child relations. Professor Plumb's article, though prodigal with symptoms, is less forthcoming with causes.

The more liberal and solicitous attitude to children was caused by their closer association with their parents, and this in its turn was determined by a number of socio-economic developments, several of which originated well before the eighteenth century. Some of these developments have been touched on already; but five in particular deserve to be briefly stressed.

First, although the extended family was never the norm in England, there was an important difference between the pre-industrial family and the one we know today: this was the frequent presence of servants and apprentices. After the end of the seventeenth century, increasing wealth among sections of the middle class enabled them to provide separate living quarters for servants. Ivy Pinchbeck and Margaret Hewitt, in their *Children in English Society* (volume 1), contend that, as a result of this development, parents and children were left 'free to develop more intimate family relationships and a degree of family self-consciousness in a way hitherto impossible'. The emotional ties between them were strengthened.

A similar result sprang from the decline of apprenticeship. When children were sent into another household after the age of seven or eight, they would tend to lose contact with their parents. But from the sixteenth century onwards more and more parents were finding it necessary to procure an education for their children. The responsibility of parents therefore increased. They now provided food and clothes for their offspring and also saw them more often (even if the child was at boarding school, he would come home during the holidays). By the end of the eighteenth century the traditional system of apprenticeship had begun to break down altogether; technically it became inadequate for the needs of a changing economy. But even in the mid-seventeenth century, when apprenticeship was still flourishing, it seems that some parents were retaining their children until they were somewhat older (Macfarlane, 1970).

Moreover, the multiplication of schools, segregating children from the adult world, itself encouraged the conception of childhood as a separate phase of existence. Schools, once established, were material proof that children were not grown-ups; they sanctioned a preparatory period in life, a time when the child could be withheld from mature responsibilities. Parents alert to this implication were nudged into making a certain allowance for juvenile shortcomings. But the effects went further than this. Contrary to expectations, the growth of schools strengthened parental influence, instead of undermining it. At first, it is true, schools were seen as a threat to domestic socialisation; many wealthy parents distrusted them and thought them only fit for younger sons. Educational thinkers of the late eighteenth century regularly recoiled from them, viewing them as breeding-grounds of vice or dumps for the surly and delinquent. But schools survived and multiplied because they answered a need; the only alternative, instruction at home, proved largely unfeasible. And, as Frank Musgrove has demonstrated in *The Family, Education and Society* (1966), in the long run the expansion of schooling pressed children more closely to the family bosom, for it cut off their opportunities for independent earnings.

Indeed the economic function of children, changing over the centuries, affected the way they were treated. It would be a mistake to think that in pre-industrial England children were exploited callously as material investments. But when property was owned by households rather than by individuals, it was natural that the importance of the individual should be subordinated to that of the house. Personal feeling between parents and children, like love and private affection in marriage, came second to family ambition. But with the rise of individualism, children were no longer subordinate units, mere limbs of the body-domestic. Even so they remained, in the eighteenth and nineteenth centuries, quite rigidly articulated by parental and family demands. For as society became more open, the stigma and cachet of birth less distinct, parents of all classes had more urgent incentive for concern, ambition, control.

A final factor in parent-child relations was possibly the rate of mortality. When juvenile death was expected and frequent, affection may have been stifled: if their children were always likely to die, a degree of detachment, on the part of the parents, would be almost inevitable. The greater concern for children at the end of the eighteenth century has been linked with the falling incidence of child mortality (by, among others, Frank Musgrove, in *Youth and the Social Order*). This is an interesting hypothesis, though it cannot be securely accepted without further evidence. Ariès and others have exaggerated the indifference to child death in the past (one need only read Ben Jonson for doubts to arise, and such doubts are corroborated by the articles in de Mause). In any case, the relations between demography and the economy are exceedingly difficult to assess (Chambers, 1972): far more so the effects of demographic phenomena on attitudes and emotions. However, it remains quite possible (if not conclusively demonstrated) that as their chances of survival improved, children were valued more highly.

The cumulative effect of these five developments was to bring the family closer together, both physically and emotionally. Hence the new lenience in the eighteenth century, the signs of which are itemised in Professor Plumb's article. But hence, too, the broadening of this concern throughout the Victorian period, a time when, contrary to the usual assumption, children were treated better than ever before: more widely educated, more generally protected, more praised and appreciated. It was in this period that a regard for the young bit deeply into Western culture: when children figured frequently in articles and novels and, as the next chapter hopes to show, a swelling tide of attention rolled through every area of their lives. Why then the popular stereotype—the stern Victorian paterfamilias, booming from the Bible and flexing his cane, while his wife bites her knuckles and his children cringe? As G. M. Young says in *Portrait of an Age*: '. . . any one who supposes that there was such a thing as a "Victorian" family or "Victorian" father should meditate Norris of Bemerton's *Spiritual Counsel*, 1694.' Severity was no invention of Victorian times—it had been used far more often in the past. And yet the point made by Professor Young overlooks an important distinction. For if we do meditate *Spiritual Counsel*, or at least read it, we discover a rather curious fact about Norris's conception of childhood: he didn't conceive of it at all. John Norris (1657–1711) was an Anglican clergyman; his book, although it claims to be 'the father's advice to his children', is a block of conventional piety unadapted to the juvenile mind. Among his recommended reading, Norris offers the works of Descartes. At the time of writing his eldest child was not above four years old.

Few parents in the Victorian age, whatever their opinions on discipline, could have been so loftily unaware of the difference between children and adults. The Victorians paid keen attention to childhood; they were willing to acknowledge its limitations and yet to extol its strengths. But it was this—the greater awareness of what it meant to be a child—that gave to Victorian parental behaviour its peculiar and now notorious stamp. For when children are regarded mainly as miniature adults, no one can expect them to be cherished with particular care. But when they are studied and petted and admired, in some cases wept over and exalted as saints, the partial survival of brutality and disdain seems more indefensible. And this is the curious paradox, the chief distinguishing characteristic, of Victorian parent-child relations: that within one society—sometimes within one particular person—tenderness and even cloying affection could co-exist with fierce discipline and a brooding suspicion of sin. Harshness to children had always existed; but seldom, as in the Victorian period, combined with curiosity and love.

To explain this duality of attitude will require some contribution from the history of ideas. Victorian responses to children were the product of two quite different intellectual traditions. One was broadly the legacy of Rousseau; the other of John Wesley. Coiled together, these two traditions could create weird patterns of thought.

(iii)

There are two perennial pictures of children: one tends to stress their incapacity for evil, the other their incapacity for good. The second of these was incorporated in the Christian doctrine of original sin. The first survived in resistance to this as a version of primal innocence. Throughout the nineteenth century, with evangelical morality and romantic aspiration, both of these propensities were present in a sharpened form.

The doctrine of original sin had, of course, assumed a larger place in Calvinist theology. At the same time the general thrust of protestantism was to emphasise the necessity of a well-ordered family unit. Christopher Hill has argued that 'The Reformation, by reducing the authority of the priest in society, simultaneously elevated the authority of lay heads of households'. (Hill, 1964.) The complete subordination of the child was a powerful and pervasive ideal in seventeenth-century thought. The puritans believed that in both nature and society there was a strictly hierarchical order. In nature, man ruled over the animals, and God ruled over man; in society, kings and governors ruled over their subjects, husbands over wives, parents over children. To flout or confound this system of order was to violate God's decree (part of Adam's sin was to put Eve above God). It was evident, therefore, that a child's disobedience could count as not only a domestic offence, but also a species of tyranny and an affront to the laws of religion (these assumptions crop up in *King Lear*). This view was not, indeed, confined to the puritans: comparison between the household and the state was a commonplace of the age; and the conception of the father as God's deputy on earth, asserted even in patristic literature, was still quite often promulgated at the end of the nineteenth century.

But strict control of children was also necessary because of their innate depravity. The puritans did not readjust their theology to accommodate a fondness for the young. The child was conceived in wickedness and, in the words of Richard Baxter, 'there it lay in darkness, filth and blood'. After birth it was still 'polluted'; it could only be saved by the grace of God, conviction of sin, and conversion. Later Christians have balked at the doctrine that children are essentially depraved. But, as Leslie Stephen remarked apropos of Jonathan Edwards, it was a perfectly logical corollary of the belief in original sin: 'If human nature is corrupt and therefore hateful to God, Edwards is quite right in declaring that the bursting bud must be as hateful as the full-grown tree.' (Stephen, 1892.) Evil was evil, and even babies were not exempt.

A number of practical conclusions followed naturally from this contention. First, since childhood was the opposite of virtuous, it was seen as a phase that should be completed as quickly as possible. Richard Baxter's poem 'Man', from which the above quotation comes, continues with these remarks:

> How long by patient mother's care and love
> Doth feeble, useless, troubling age subsist?
> Should man continue such, we could not prove
> That he in kind is better than a beast.

Children needed indoctrination from the earliest possible age. The longer the period before conversion, the greater the danger of being damned (one must always keep in mind the much higher rates of infant mortality). Protestants would teach their children to read, for knowledge of the Bible was necessary in order to attain salvation. Conversely, the playfulness of children was regarded as a snare and a hazard. The toys, the games, the levity of children were deeply mistrusted by godly parents in the seventeenth century. Christian, in Bunyan's *Pilgrim's Progress*, explaining why his family are not progressing with him, complains that his children 'were given to the foolish delights of youth'. The task of parents was to bring up children who were sober, staid and devout.

The Pilgrim's Progress might help us to appreciate another pervasive belief: that family affection, though commendable in itself, should never usurp the love of God. When Christian's wife and children remain unpersuaded by his warnings of the wrath to come, he deserts them, although they are dear to him, and seeks his salvation alone. He acts at this point with perfect propriety according to Bunyan's belief: he is 'clear of their blood if they perish'. The ultimate duty of both parents and children was not to one another but to God (the religious responsibility of the individual was, after all, the cornerstone of protestant theology in general). Consequently, parents were often warned that a love for their children should not be allowed to supersede their religion; affection for one's family could mean clannishness—as

it did, in the seventeenth century, among the New England puritans (Morgan, 1966). On the other hand this theory conceded to
children a powerful liberty: they were free to reproach or even
defy their parents for the sake of fidelity to God. Among the
Calvinists precocious conversion was encouraged and publicised;
the sanctified products were sometimes depicted as more scrupulous than their elders. But this pattern did not become popular
until the evangelical magazines of the late eighteenth century.
In these, as in numerous Victorian tracts, adults would even be
guided to God by virtue of their youngers and betters.

Innate depravity, precocious conversion, infant saints who
spurned all frivolities—these were characteristic features of the
Calvinist ideal of nurture: how far the reality conformed with
this is still largely conjectural. But that the *ideal* was widely
accepted we may see from the contents of a children's book
which was lastingly popular. Written by James Janeway, a non-
conformist divine, and appearing in two parts in 1671–2, the
book was entitled *A Token For Children: being an Exact Account
of the Conversion, Holy and Exemplary Lives, and Joyful Deaths
of several young Children*. This work became something of a
juvenile classic and in the eighteenth century 'it was regarded as
the standard reading for children of evangelical parents'. (Sangster,
1963.) It survived even into the nineteenth century, being 'read
with appreciation as late as 1847'. (Darton, 1958.)

Janeway begins by reminding parents that their children 'are
not too little to die, they are not too little to go to Hell'. The
best prophylactic against such a fate is first for parents to 'pray,
pray, pray' and then for them to supply their children with large
doses of his own writing. Janeway predicts that if children are
made to 'read this Book over an hundred times', one may 'observe
how they are affected'. He then addresses the 'dear lambs' themselves, asking them, with considerable urgency, where they think
they are likely to go if they persist in disobedience. 'Hell is a
terrible place', he says, 'that's worse a thousand times than
whipping; God's anger is worse than your father's anger.' However, these children may be reassured that a religiously receptive
state can quite easily be self-induced: 'Get by thyself into the
chamber or garret, and fall upon thy knees, and weep and mourn,
and tell Christ thou art afraid that he doth not love thee. . . .'

Then comes the major attraction of the book, the history of
all those holy youngsters who have heeded such strenuous advice.

All of them have died young, but, according to Janeway, they have not been consigned to hell. The details of their cases are extremely repetitious and the first may be taken as typical. The late Sarah Howley was converted 'between eight and nine years old'; she then sobbed and prayed in her room. After a little while, 'she was not contented at this, but she got her little brother and sister into a chamber with her', and did the same with them. Her humble devotion, says Janeway, was everywhere apparent: 'She was very much in secret prayer, as might easily be perceived by those who listened at the chamber door.' Sarah's filial emotions became more intense—'. . . she was exceedingly dutiful to her Parents, very loath to grieve them in the least.' She immersed herself in godly books which taught her to 'make religion her business'. So it continued for several years: she kept weeping, praying and calling out on God's name until 'when she was about fourteen years old, she brake a vein in her lungs'. The girl then went into a protracted decline, spitting blood and babbling prayers, devout despite her afflictions. Miss Howley's howlings, when she died, were not only for her physical collapse, but also for her spiritual state: 'O the piteous moan that she would make! O the agonies that her soul was in!'

Janeway is anxious to emphasise that a similar type of life and death is within reach of the youngest child. One of his stories is about a youngster between two and three years old who, out of piety rather than playfulness, 'would be oft upon his knees, by himself, in one corner or other'. But apparently even some contemporary readers jibbed at the juvenility in this case, for in the preface to the second part of his book Janeway laboriously rebuts accusations that his prize example is 'scarce credible'.

A Token For Children was always highly regarded, but it was rediscovered with fresh enthusiasm during the period of Wesleyan propaganda. After that its child saints became commonplace: philanthropic as well as moribund, they throng evangelical tracts (Avery, 1975). The religious revival set in motion by Wesley had a slow but pervasive influence on the country's morality and thought. It is possible to argue that, from one point of view, this Methodist revival was a liberal movement, a theological counterpart of certain democratic ideas (Semmel, 1974). Nevertheless, as regards the treatment of children, it marked a return to the past: it encouraged a resurgence of that strictness and intensity which, under latitudinarian influence, had at least partially lapsed.

Wesley, like his mother, was convinced of the necessity of breaking the child's will. He believed emphatically in original sin and the consequent need for the earliest possible religious indoctrination (Body, 1936). But these ideas did not remain specific to Methodism. They were also warmly accepted by the later Evangelical movement—and this, as many historians since Elie Halévy have insisted, was a primary influence on 'Victorianism', the assumptions and practices characteristic of the whole Victorian age (Quinlan, 1941; Jaeger, 1956). To illustrate the Evangelical outlook one might take William Wilberforce's *A Practical View of the Prevailing Religious System*, published in 1797 and probably the most celebrated single work in the course of the Christian revival. The book opens with the charge that contemporary religion is mostly 'cursory and superficial', and adduces the scandalous negligence of the great majority of parents. Instead of conscientiously instructing their children in the principles of the faith they profess, they follow a lazy policy of well-meaning muddling through. For Wilberforce this is deplorable because, as he goes on to argue later, the way we bring up our children is surely a reliable index of our true regard for religion. Despite their professions, most Christian parents injuriously forget that they hold in trust the care of an immortal soul. Nor should the effects of original sin be blithely brushed out of sight: for Wilberforce they are manifest in 'the perverse and froward dispositions perceivable in children'. Wilberforce believes it a spineless error to condone the peccadilloes of youth. 'Innocent young people—term much abused', declares a sour marginal heading. The phrase might well be regarded as appropriately symbolic: in one sense it sums up a whole tradition in Christian thought about childhood; but it also reveals how frequently, by the end of the eighteenth century, this tradition had come to be challenged.

(iv)

If the Evangelical movement (and the Christian beliefs it revitalised) was the first major influence on Victorian attitudes to children, the second was in most ways its diametrical opposite—the cult of childhood innocence. Yet this too could trace its origins back to ideas in the Christian religion. In antiquity, it is probably safe to say, there was no exaltation of the child. Aristotle habitually likens children to animals; in the *Nicomachean Ethics* he states it as self-evident that 'no one would choose to retain the mind of a child throughout his life, even though he continued to enjoy the pleasures of childhood with undiminished zest' (Book x). Richard B. Lyman Jr., writing on 'Barbarism and Religion' in de Mause's *The History of Childhood*, concludes that the ancients could only express tenderness when children were conveniently inert: a sleeping baby was considered good, but the best child was a dead child. However, for children the arrival of Christianity, with its stress on the importance of the individual soul, 'may well have meant the beginning of a slightly less grim outlook'. As well as the doctrine of original sin, the Christian religion contained the seeds of child-idealisation.

Lloyd de Mause himself, predictably, is very far from satisfied with the Bible's allusions to children. He complains that when, with the aid of a concordance, he inspected its two thousand references, he failed to find a single one that was genuinely empathic; even the familiar 'Suffer little children . . .' turned out to be a description of Near Eastern exorcism (de Mause here carefully omits the clause 'for of such is the Kingdom of Heaven'). But whether we ourselves approve of a text is not, historically, the important question: what matters is how, at particular times, it has in fact been received. One could almost write the history of attitudes to childhood by charting the changing exegesis of a text like Matthew 18:3, 'Except ye be converted, and become as little children, ye shall not enter into the Kingdom of Heaven.' (Now often understood as an exhortation to innocence, but formerly as a spur to obedience.) The Bible has always proved usefully pliant. It is true that, until the last century, the majority of those who pored over its pages in order to find helpful advice for parents tended to settle with greatest enjoyment on the more disenchanted texts (a favourite, used even by the genial Dr Watts, was the prediction of Proverbs 30:17 that undutiful children would have their eyes picked out by ravens of the valley). But writers revering the innocence of childhood have likewise seldom had difficulty in deriving a scriptural sanction.

Even in the Middle Ages some Christians were exploring the doctrine of innocence, especially as to sexual feelings (Lloyd de Mause, though, implies that this 'medieval fiction' may have been a cover for child-molesters, keen to pretend that their catamites were not essentially harmed). But the idea that children may be wiser than adults has only been seriously advocated since the early modern period. From the sixteenth century onwards writers have increasingly turned with praise to the pristine responses of youth. A possible explanation for this has been put forward by George Boas in his book *The Cult of Childhood* (1966). Boas identifies this cult as a species of primitivism; the Child—just like, at different times, Woman, the Folk, the Noble Savage, the Neurotic and the Collective Unconscious—has been regarded as a repository of the primitive, intuitive virtues. But primitivism, Boas believes, is largely a hostile reaction to the claims of science and reason. The cult of juvenile wisdom and virtue is part of an anti-intellectualism which, in the last few hundred years, has developed almost step by step with the progress of natural science.

Boas's argument, worked out in some detail, is undoubtedly persuasive and clearly relates to strong currents in Romantic thought. And factually it appears to be the case that most of the writers who have eulogised childhood have been, in other de-monstrable ways, quite consciously hostile to reason. But Boas's book is most useful in explaining why particular biblical texts— those recommending the qualities of childhood—were not for many centuries exploited or emphasised. At any rate, by the seventeenth century the idea of childhood innocence was no longer something egregious. It emerges quite often in Shakespeare's plays, together with the notion that filial duty is part of the natural order. But interestingly its keenest exponents are the seventeenth-century mystics. Both Henry Vaughan and Thomas Traherne return to childhood as a period of spiritual illumination. It is a critical commonplace that Vaughan's 'The Retreate' antici-pates to some extent Wordsworth's Immortality Ode. One would not wish to build up from this a general comparison between adapted Platonic doctrine and later Romantic nostalgia: Vaughan's 'angel-infancy' was not the same as Little Nell's. (Vaughan com-bines belief in the innocence of children with the doctrine of a sinless pre-existent state—Martin, 1938.) Nevertheless, in his poem 'Childe-hood', Vaughan does fleetingly touch on the theme of innocence versus experience. Likewise Traherne, in his *Centuries of Meditations*, celebrates the child's divine intuition, a faculty for truth less laborious than the grown-up's 'highest reason'. For Traherne the two phases of spiritual knowledge, in infancy and maturity, are radically disconnected; unlike Wordsworth he doesn't postulate a continuous inner development. All the same, quite a few of his sentences foreshadow ideas which in the following century became influential. He blames the social environment instead of original sin:

> Our misery proceedeth ten thousand times more from the outward bondage of opinion and custom, than from any inward corruption or depravation of Nature. . . . It is not our parents' loins so much as our parents' lives, that enthrals and blinds us.

A similar supposition, remarkably explicit for the period, emerges from the portrait of the untainted child in John Earle's *Microcosmography* (1628). In this the child, although still introduced as essentially a grown-up cut down ('a Man in a small letter'), is also the closest approximation to prelapsarian innocence ('the best copy of Adam before he tasted of Eve or the apple'). Earle continues:

> He is nature's fresh picture newly drawn in oil, which time and much handling dims and defaces. His soul is yet a white paper unscribbled with observations of the world, wherewith at length it becomes a blurred note-book. He is purely happy, because he knows no evil, nor hath made means by sin to be acquainted with misery. . . . The older he grows, he is a stair lower from God; and like his first father much worse in his breeches.

Earle's child is certainly a *tabula rasa*, but in Earle, unlike Locke, the impressions of experience deface the soul's simplicity and generate moral confusion ('blurred note-book'). For the child any contact with the world is likely to spell corruption.

In the early seventeenth century ideas like this were exceptional even as theoretical propositions; much less were they allowed to influence the practical treatment of children. But in the eighteenth century, in response to far-reaching social change, the doctrine of childhood innocence was gradually amplified: it came to form part of a whole philosophy of the virtues of unspoilt nature. What is more, its domestic implications began at last to be faced. The figure at the centre of this revolution was, of course, Jean-Jacques Rousseau: magnetically rhetorical, his prose could attract the most scattered ideas and arrange them in shining new shapes. But Rousseau was serious in desiring change; if children really were innocent, the traditional methods of bringing them up would have to be swept away.

Émile, first published in 1762, describes the education from birth to maturity of an individual boy by an individual tutor, and Rousseau insists that in ideal conditions the father himself should bring up his child: in either case the context of education is domestic rather than institutional. This fact deserves to be emphasised, for nowadays the book is frequently read by those in search of principles that might be applied in a school. Not that Rousseau would object to this—elsewhere he advocates state education—but when schools were by no means ubiquitous, it was just as reasonable to regard the work as primarily a domestic treatise, a programme for parents rather than teachers, a smouldering source of subversion which could revolutionise the home. Certainly Rousseau affected schools, though less in his own day than later: adapted and enlarged by Pestalozzi and Froebel, his ideas underpin a good deal of today's 'child-centred' education (Evans, 1955). But he also influenced the treatment of children by parents, and it was to this subject that many of his earliest readers assumed his proposals to be addressed.

These proposals all derive ultimately from two major propositions. The first is that childhood develops by stages, each with its own abilities and limitations, and that every one of these stages is different from every other; moreover, all of them are quite distinct from the final, mature stage: children are different in kind from adults. 'Childhood', says Rousseau, 'has its own ways of seeing, thinking, and feeling; nothing is more foolish than to try and substitute our ways.' It was this attempted substitution that irritated Rousseau most. The job of parents and tutors was to study children realistically, not to try and make them conform to some preconceived adult ideals (the majority of which, in any case, Rousseau happened to despise). He says at the very beginning of *Émile*:

> We know nothing of childhood. . . . The wisest writers devote themselves to what a man ought to know, without asking what a child is capable of learning. They are always looking for the man in the child, without considering what he is before he becomes a man.

Rousseau does consider what a child is, and outlines four different phases of growth. Set against the findings of modern child-analysis, these may appear crude and conjectural, but the general principle of development (later confirmed by Piaget and others) was a valuable notion at the time.

Rousseau's second proposition is the natural purity of children, their innate propensity to turn out well unless besmirched by grown-ups:

> Let us lay it down as an incontrovertible rule that the first impulses of nature are always right; there is no original sin in the human heart, the how and the why of the entrance of every vice can be traced.

From this follows Rousseau's advocacy of a 'negative' education: nature should be allowed to pursue its own course, and not be artificially speeded up; children should be taught only what they are old enough to understand. The chief rule of education, he says, with a paradox aimed at the Christian tradition, is not to save time but to waste it. Here Rousseau, for modern educational tastes, is clearly on the side of the juvenile angels, but his argument, despite this, rests rather unstably on the cloudiness of its central term. Even if we accepted the benignity of nature, we might disagree in defining its scope. Rousseau's own definition is a generous one: it is part of 'nature's law' that half the children born should die before they are eight. The term 'nature' is also elastic enough to be especially binding on women. Females are naturally passive and weak and incapable of brilliant thought. While male roles are subject to social change, theirs are unalterable. For example, Rousseau warns at one point against the futility of preparing boys for any exclusive trade: the accepted social order is on the edge of collapse, the great monarchies of Europe will not endure. 'You can neither foresee nor provide against the revolution which may affect your children.' It turns out that this should be amended to 'your boys', for the flames of revolution will not, it appears, consume the traditional status of girls, who will still be brought up for pleasing men and tidying things in the house (a decently accurate historical prediction, but a rather anomalous ideal).

It was not this aspect of 'nature', however, that gave most offence to contemporary readers. In Paris and Geneva the book was burnt for its recommendation of a 'natural religion' which was free from sectarian bias: Christians of all denominations united in protest. Repugnant, too, to Christian sensibility was Rousseau's insistence that abstract moral perception was quite unnatural to the small child. Sermons and precepts were therefore useless; the child should first come into conflict with *things*, and learn the limitations of selfish behaviour by having to suffer its results: for example, if he broke a window, he should be made to sleep in its draught. Punishment should not involve a clash of wills, but as far as possible be represented simply as a matter of cause and effect. With a young child, said Rousseau:

> The very words *obey* and *command* will be excluded from his vocabulary, still more those of *duty* and *obligation*; but the words strength, necessity, weakness, and constraint must have a large place in it.

This, of course, hit at the whole tradition that wilfulness in children must be suppressed, that overt moral indoctrination could never begin too young. The Christian reaction to Rousseau's book was appropriately outraged. John Wesley described it contemptuously as 'the most empty, silly, injudicious thing that a self-conceited infidel wrote'. Mrs Trimmer condemned it bitterly in *The Guardian of Education*. And yet, before the end of the century, over two hundred treatises had been published in England which were influenced by *Émile* (Roddier, 1950). On existing schools Rousseau had little effect, but numerous individuals were stirred by his call for a 'natural' treatment of children. The radical deist, David Williams, who actually founded a school in Chelsea inspired with Rousseau's ideas, confirmed, in his *Lectures on Education*, that after the publication of *Émile* there were many experiments in bringing up children as noble savages (Stewart and McCann, 1967). The influence of Rousseau was often bizarre, for since his philosophy was so flexible, even his most literal-minded admirers were liable to bend and adapt its doctrines to suit their personal needs. There were a number of thinkers (and feelers) who professed the principles of Rousseau, but failed with any degree of thoroughness to translate them into practice. The first of these was Rousseau himself, who sent all his five children to a foundlings' home: wonderful ammunition for his enemies. The later disciples and victims of Rousseau were a strange assortment of people. Robert Southey related how his little sister was dipped every morning in a tub of cold water as part of the toughening-up process that Rousseau recommends. Mrs Gaskell, in her *Life of Charlotte Brontë*, conjectured that the Rev. Patrick Brontë had 'formed some of his opinions on the management of children' from a reading of Rousseau's works. Clearly the doctrine, judiciously selected, could be reconciled with Christianity. Anna

Sewell was brought up on its principles, although her mother was a Quaker (Chitty, 1971). This mother, Mary Sewell, was affected by Rousseau through the *Practical Education* of Richard Lovell Edgeworth and his famous daughter Maria. In his early life Edgeworth, admiring *Émile*, had reared his own son on its theories; later he presented the results to Rousseau, but the philosopher found the boy 'prejudiced' (Edgeworth, 1821). Edgeworth's friend, Thomas Day, was prominent among those who combined adulation of Rousseau with a quite undaunted disregard for what he actually said. In his celebrated children's book, *Sandford and Merton* (discussed at length in chapter III), he attempted to reduce Rousseau's rhetoric to a course of moral lessons which the young could enjoy, but only succeeded in boiling it down to a plate of pedantic gristle. But other writers rose to the challenge of Day, with the result that, in Georgian children's books, Rousseau became associated with lengthy lectures and kindly beggars and soporific catalogues of Fact.

But Rousseau was also associated with something more potent and lasting—with the whole Romantic conception of children as creatures of deeper wisdom, finer aesthetic sensitivity, and a more profound awareness of enduring moral truths. Not that Rousseau himself alleged that children possessed these strengths; for him original innocence was chiefly a negative virtue. But Wordsworth and Blake and Dickens, and the multitude who shared or inherited their concerns, were offering far more than a rejection of original sin. The viewpoint they promoted was that children were spiritually wiser than adults, better equipped by nature as seers, prophets and guides.

The effects of Rousseau and Romanticism on the imaginative literary treatment of childhood can hardly be exaggerated. It was only after the late eighteenth century that children became prominent in literature—a fact which has long been acknowledged (Scudder, 1894). One might mention, in support of this proposition, the evidence furnished in 1924 by an American scholar, F. Lamar Janney, who, after much reading and extensive research, attempted a detailed, painstaking survey of *Childhood in English Non-Dramatic Literature from 1557–1798*: only to discover again and again, that the treatment of childhood in the writing of his period was peripheral and superficial. In the nineteenth century, on the other hand, childhood won enormous popularity as a literary symbol and theme. It was valued as a period of heightened perception, a reservoir of imagination to be drawn on in later life; it could also be used less affirmatively as a focus for neurotic retrogression, a sump for unhealthy regrets. An intriguing discussion of both of these trends can be found in Peter Coveney's *The Image of Childhood*, in which he argues that the literary treatment of children underwent a sentimental degeneration, collapsing from the peaks of Wordsworth and Blake into sickly and evasive nostalgia. Coveney charts the various debasements of the Romantic image of childhood, including, as well as regretful nostalgia, the feeling of many Victorian authors that if maturity must lead to corruption, it might be a kindness to kill children off—at least in the context of fiction. The doctrine of innocence collected fungus; a species unmentioned by Coveney, but dear to those who dealt with domestic drama, was the concept of the 'old-fashioned' child. Popularised by Dickens's Paul Dombey, the term came to designate all those children endowed with even more than the average share of mystical penetration. Quaint, broody, closer to God, sedate and usually ailing, such children disturbed their benighted elders with the clarity of their vision. The emergence of these creatures was significant, for it marked a stage in the evolution of responses to precocity. In the sixteenth century and before, when childhood was almost universally seen as an inferior mode of existence, precocity in children was highly esteemed, and examples of child prodigies were amassed. But in the eighteenth century, with the growing recognition of the child's special nature, precocity began to come under suspicion as not only unusual but unnatural. In the last two decades of this century it was censured by certain educationalists (Musgrove, 1964), and censure has continued ever since. Nevertheless, there was still a chance for octogenarian children. For as Romantic ideas extended, and, as well as the child's separate nature, his innate wisdom was emphasised, a kind of precocity came back into favour, since children could utter intuitively the maturest thoughts of the learned. The nineteenth-century 'old-fashioned' child was an offspring of this persuasion.

The enjoyment supplied by 'old-fashioned' children—including Marie Corelli's Boy—was no doubt a make-believe. Providing easy pathos and oddity value, they obviously offered no genuine threat to customary parent-child relations. Indeed a suspicion of condescension hangs about the whole notion of childhood innocence as treated in Victorian fiction. The doctrine was only rarely invoked by writers with practical matters in view; more often it was safely symbolic. But where Rousseauism and Romantic thought did effect a profound shift of attitude was over the question, long debated, of filial and parental dues. Previously, the emphasis had always been on the bounden duties of children. In the numerous domestic conduct books of the sixteenth and seventeenth centuries the Bible was cited continually to enforce the child's subjection. The reciprocal duty of parents to children was standardised and straightforward: it was simply, in the words of one historian, 'to bring them up in godly wise, to settle them in an occupation and in marriage' (Powell, 1917). But whether parents did this or not, their children still had to obey. The puritans in particular stressed the absolute nature of each individual's duty. As Levin L. Schücking expressed it in his book *The Puritan Family*: 'The sets of duties incumbent upon one party are quite independent of those incumbent upon the other. Children whose parents do not fulfil their duties towards them are thus in no sense relieved of duties towards their parents.'

By the middle of the nineteenth century all this had been grievously undermined. In the first place the emphasis had been transposed from the duties of children to those of parents; the sharpest censure was now reserved for cruel or negligent fathers. Children might still be severely punished for ignoring the fifth commandment; but—among novelists at any rate—it was now parental delinquency that seemed the more damaging sin. The reasons for this are not far to seek. Belief in the potency of early impressions, and the power of society to blight and deform, depleted the moral autonomy of the individual child. A man was not only what he made of himself, but also what others had made him.

Secondly, the very concept of parental duty had acquired a different complexion. The traditional requirements lingered on: parents were to teach at least the rudiments of religion, to guide and advise in choosing a job, in some cases (but less frequently) to nominate a possible spouse. But they also had subtler obligations, rarefied psychological tasks which had never been known in the past. They were told to have tact and empathy, to observe and respect the child's character, to guard against any temptation to bully or interfere. Certainly they were not to be sadists or thugs, but gradually the attention of novelists moved from the crasser abuses to more finespun crimes (a process exemplified in the work of Dickens). Parenthood was seen as a sensitive art, with its own skilled methods and its own mystique; incompetence, even though well-meaning, could maim a developing mind. This line of thought, not surprisingly, was to worry and fluster mothers and fathers, though it was not until the twentieth century, with the teachings of J. B. Watson and Freud, that parental anxiety was to reach its height (Storr, 1972).

Thirdly, by the end of the nineteenth century the idea that children should always be obedient, even if their parents were grossly remiss, had begun to be seriously questioned. This scepticism was connected with the restriction of parental rights. In factories, in education, and finally in cases of domestic cruelty, the father's discretion was limited by the intervention of the state (Goodsell, 1934). It was legally acknowledged that certain parents were unfit to have charge of their children. But this made it indisputable that the moral authority of some parents was greater than that of others. It was possible, therefore, that some were less worthy of obedience and respect.

No doubt these latter developments were only tenuously associated with the Romantic image of childhood. Nevertheless the cult of juvenile innocence—embryonic in Christianity, maintained as a version of primitivism, full-grown in the writings of Rousseau—exerted a powerful influence on Victorian sensibility. Lent force as a feature of Romantic thought, it introduced children into literature, encouraged the growth of concern for their rights, and, unhampered by Freudianism, created a widespread mood of nostalgia for sexless simplicity. Most important of all, it offered an alternative to evangelical strictness.

(v)

We should now be able to bring together the factors in Victorian parent-child relations. Firstly, over several centuries, as a result of social developments, relations within the family had become more intimate. Even before the industrial revolution, economics had ceased to minimise the role of the individual child. Parents had more reason to care for their children—and, in a growing number of cases, more money to spend on the task. The whole idea of upbringing was beginning to seem important. What is more, its importance was emphasised both by those who detected evil in children and by those who glimpsed innocence—and, as we have seen, by the nineteenth century both of these contrary impulses had evolved an ideology.

One strong tradition in Victorian thought, nourished by the Wesleyan and Evangelical movements, believed devoutly in original sin and the need to break the child's will; distrusting specifically juvenile ways, it preached the importance of weeding them out and replacing them as quickly as possible with the sober habits of age. This tradition might be termed, for convenience' sake, the Puritan attitude to children.

The other tradition, which we might term Romantic, believed in the natural goodness of children, suggested they might well be wiser than adults, and surrounded their actions and feelings with pathos and sentiment. Writers imbued with Romantic ideas were more likely to recommend friendship and kindness—partly since, being more secular, they were less convinced that strict upbringing was a passport for the world to come. Also they would tend to reject the need for unceasing supervision. Contending that corruption came from without—from society rather than original sin—they would warn of the dangers of meddlesomeness and display the value of freedom.

In Victorian literature concerned with children these two traditions were inevitably in frequent opposition. Curiously, though, in one respect the direction they took was the same: both of them set their subjects on the path to the cemetery. Deathbed scenes were favoured by both, but though the destination was identical the reasons for approaching it differed. In Puritan writing the primary motives were cautionary and triumphal: child death was either a warning or an exhibition of faith. Numberless examples might be given, but to illustrate how much some Christian writers could dwell on calamity and death, and how much this habit was riveted to teaching and discipline, we might examine the typical contents of a periodical like *The Children's Friend*, edited by the Rev. Carus Wilson (Mr Brocklehurst in *Jane Eyre*). In the issue for January 1826 (an issue selected entirely at random) the contents were as follows: first, an account of a Moravian mission, their fears, prayers and penitence; then a description of the loss of the *Kent*, sailing from England to Bengal: lurid scenes of horror—a judgement, we learn, for 'broken sabbaths and profane lives'; then 'A Brief Memoir of Samuel Bastow', the protracted deathbed of a Sunday-school boy; finally,

the breathtaking piety of a young man who died of consumption;
and, to round off, a poem called 'New Year', offering, of course,
not hope or renewal, but infants who reflect that before the year
is out 'we may chance be laid upon our bier'. The next volume
begins with an African mission and offers for its readers' entertainment the 'History of the Plague in London'. Following this is
the story of a girl who grumbled about having to be thrashed,
but was enlightened by her six-year-old friend: 'Why, it is because they love us.' Then, after a brief attack on the Jews, a
section on the cruelty of children to parents: heathens, who aban-
don their progenitors to expire in a mud hut. 'Ah! what reader,
who loves his dear parents, will not bless God for giving him
birth in England.'

Corpses had always played a large part in the Puritan tradition
of upbringing, but it seems somewhat harder to understand why
the Romantic view of children should also entail an obsession
with their death. However, this was certainly the case—indeed,
with many authors, the greater their sympathy, the less the child's
chance of survival. One lethal sympathiser was Florence Montgomery, whose enormously popular *Misunderstood*, first published
in 1869, sold twelve thousand copies in four years. The book was
a lachrymose defence of a child called Humphrey who, ignored
by his father, accidentally crippled himself in a pond: his deathbed, embroidered with flowery pathos, soaked up the last third
of the book. Or one might take *The Mother's Book of Poetry*, an
anthology of poems on children and childhood (including some
famous ones, some minor, and some both) selected by Mrs Alfred
Gatty, the editor of *Aunt Judy's Magazine*. No one could accuse
Mrs Gatty of lacking a lively appreciation of children, yet of the
111 poems in her volume (first published in 1872) no fewer than
fifty-nine are devoted to the subject of death. Nevertheless in her
preface she apologises for the paucity of such themes: 'We are
conscious of having omitted from this collection many verses
(often on infants and the early death of children), which would
have been very acceptable to some of our readers, and to the
young ones especially.'

The spectacle of a child dying, it seems, was so relished by
those who were fond of children that enjoyment of it was even
assumed in the potential participants. The reasons for such an
attitude varied. No doubt to a large extent it was due to that
current of maudlin escapism which Peter Coveney detects: it

turns out with Humphrey the Misunderstood that departure is really for the best, for natures like his 'are not fit for this rough world'. But part of the motive was undoubtedly to stimulate compassion. Winning sympathy for children was easier when, instead of admitting their independence, you depicted them as mortally injured, or starving, or writhing with fever; and if, in addition, their death was the outcome of some kind of social injustice, so much the better for the potency of the effect: pity grows rankly in an atmosphere of righteous indignation. Sentimental deathbeds also borrowed some trappings from evangelical magazines. Faith vindication had long been a feature of Christian reports on a mortal's last hours, and in puritan tracts and periodicals the vindication was often dramatic. The death of children was especially favoured, and their passing-over was usually the occasion of some positive religious manifestation—a vision of heaven, the gift of tongues, an indefeasible message from the other side. As evangelical attitudes pervaded Victorian fiction, these wonders, so crushing to doubters and scoffers, were to become increasingly commonplace, till eventually almost any respectable death was attended with the obligatory miracles, chords of celestial music or strangely prophetic last words (Houghton, 1957). But the function of these scenes became less doctrinal than pathetic and decorative. So it was that the two leading attitudes to children converged on the coffin and grave. It was hardly surprising that the youngsters in fiction, exploited by both of these literary conventions, were unlikely to survive very long.

It seems fitting to speak here of 'literary conventions', even though it is still very frequently claimed that the great number of child deaths in Victorian fiction was simply a reflection of social fact. Certainly, throughout the nineteenth century, early death was more common than it is today; but it would be rather naive to assume from this that the incidence of death in fiction is anything like a reliable index of its incidence in real life. It can hardly be doubted, for instance, that more children died in the literature of the nineteenth century than in that of the century before; yet in real life the opposite was true. Writing in *The Lancet* in 1836, T. R. Edmonds pointed out that 'The very great diminution of the mortality of infants in England is one of the most remarkable phenomena of modern times.' The London Bills of Mortality showed that in the period 1730–79 the percentage of children who died before they were five was 66·2; but from

1780–1829 it was 37·8. (Outside London the mortality rates were lower; but the question here is the relative percentage over a period of time.) By the beginning of Victoria's reign childhood death was rarer than it had ever been before; in imaginative literature, however, it was gravely on the increase. The recurrence in fiction was not simply a result of the prevalence in fact. The obsessive return to juvenile death was due to the *significance* attached to it—a significance determined by enormous changes in attitudes to children and childhood.

But if 'Puritan' and 'Romantic' approaches both led to a concentration on death, they differed deeply in their recommendations while the child was still alive. The Puritan school gave more power to parents, warned against softness and laxity, and strove to make children fit into the world of pious, responsible adults. The Romantics granted more freedom to children, protested against severity, and argued that the ways and ideas of the young were as good as or possibly better than the rigidities of grown-ups. The Victorian family is usually supposed to have been dominated by the first of these codes. But in literature it was definitely the Romantic approach which was steadily gaining ground. One sign of this was the number of books which attacked not children but parents. Apart from forgettable religious tracts and threadbare cautionary tales, there wasn't much space in Victorian fiction for filial exhortation. A distaste for children, admittedly, was often evident in children's books; but even here, as we shall see, the trend was towards a defence of juvenile ways. On family conflict the finest books were those which criticised parents: Dickens's *Hard Times* and *Dombey and Son*, Meredith's *The Ordeal of Richard Feverel*, Butler's *The Way of All Flesh*. Works like these had never appeared in any previous age.

This is not to deny the obvious fact that their authors were building from established themes: gruff and overbearing fathers, insipid and scatter-brained mothers, were the standard characters, the expected props, in a good deal of fiction and drama. But what was new to the Victorian books was the thoroughness of their indictment: not only was it detailed, tenacious, sustained, it insisted that the business of upbringing was a matter of the highest importance. And so we come round to Marie Corelli, who in 1900 could take it for granted that the faults of children were certainly caused by the failings of their parents.

Marie Corelli's serene convictions, and the manner in which

she treated her theme, were an ultimate vulgarised presentation of thoughts and feelings which had gained in acceptance throughout the century. Deriving from ideas and social developments that had crystallised in previous periods, these thoughts and feelings added up to a shift in human sensibility: a profound, far-reaching and powerful movement in favour of the Child. In the following chapters this movement will be traced in nineteenth-century literature: the theme of these chapters is the partial displacement of 'Puritan' by 'Romantic' beliefs. The process is conspicuous in children's books and aspects of it can be illustrated by contrasting the novels of Jane Austen and Dickens, major writers from early- and mid-century who focus on upbringing. Likewise in two books that are frequently cited as criticisms of the 'Victorian father' we may measure a similar movement. In Samuel Butler's *The Way of All Flesh*, a work suffused with Romantic assumptions, 'a long course of Puritanism' is bitterly blamed for estranging parents and children. And in Edmund Gosse's *Father and Son* (written at the beginning of the twentieth century) the Puritan methods of treatment and training are criticised with sorrowful astringency from a more or less Rousseauist position.

It is, unquestionably, in imaginative literature that the themes and conflicts outlined above are most vividly embodied. But a full appreciation of this literature depends on a knowledge of certain ideas—ideas on the role and duties of parents, on the management of children. In this chapter we have offered an aerial view of the changing pattern of such ideas, their growth and interrelation. But clearly the discussion must also include the Victorian period itself. Before we can fruitfully turn to the fiction we need to possess a more detailed map of the particular treatment of these beliefs in the nineteenth century. The question, though, is which sources to use in order to make this map.

Chapter II
PERIODICAL ARTICLES

'The nineteenth century regards childhood far more
intently than any previous age.'
    HORACE E. SCUDDER, *Childhood in Literature and
    Art* (1894)

(i)

It is possible to study the history of the family without consulting
literature at all. Indeed some historians recommend the practice:
Edward Shorter, for example, in *The Making of the Modern
Family* (1976). It depends, of course, what you want to know. In
the 1950s French historians showed what could usefully be inferred from hitherto fairly neglected sources: frescoes and
portraits, title deeds of property, educational manuals. The growth
of historical demography, concentrating on contraception, infant
mortality and family structure, stimulated a feverish interest in all
kinds of catalogues: parish registers were collated and analysed,
so were probate inventories, so too was every kind of listing of
household inhabitants. Undoubtedly the results of this research
are pioneeringly exact; conclusions based on quantitative data
make a good deal of previous pronouncement on the family seem
rhetorical and impressionistic. But the results are also narrow in
scope. What they lack is illuminating discussion of domestic
thoughts and sentiments, for these cannot adequately be deduced
from external circumstances. Again and again the leap from
statistics to generalisation about family feelings has collapsed into
sheer conjecture.

If your primary interest is in *attitudes* (in this case, attitudes to
parents and children), it is necessary to move to different sources
—vaguer, certainly, than statistical ones, but wider in application.
One possibility is legislation, which in older histories of marriage
and the family was usually much exploited. Naturally it has its
value: if, say, we find ferocious laws relating to wives and
children, we cannot help but learn something about the society
in which they were framed. In eighteenth-century England, for
example, as Rosamund Bayne-Powell has pointed out, 'children

were imprisoned and even hanged for offences which the proba-
tion officer would now deal with' (Bayne-Powell, 1939). But
legislation is only of moderate use for the historian of attitudes.
Quite apart from the question of how far it was enforced, or
whether it was in advance of public opinion or trailing decades
behind, its usefulness is mainly confined to the extremes of social
conduct. Legislation fixes the borderline of what society will
permit: about the large, shifting hinterland of customs, opinions
and moral ideas it has very little to say.

Perhaps we should turn, then, to novels and plays, possibly
even to poems. It has long been recognised that imaginative
literature can be used to infer contemporary assumptions and
accepted social values. In the later chapters of the present book
this will to some extent be attempted, with evidence taken from
minor writers and three or four major ones. But the dangers of
this enterprise are manifest, the objections manifold. Most literature isn't naively mimetic—even the dullest naturalistic novel
will depend on invention and artistry, on frequent selection and
interpretation, on a personal vision of social fact. Indeed it could
be said that the better the book, the less serviceable it is likely
to be as a sociological source. Only minor works, after all, are
slavishly 'representative', exemplars of a particular philosophy,
true records of the commonplace. Great novels have to be appreciated as works of art in their own right; to scour them for
straightforward factual data is usually to misunderstand their
purpose and to overlook their techniques. The result is either
crass literary criticism or unreliable history.

A further objection is that attitudes in novels need to be checked
against non-fictional sources: we need some larger general framework in which they may be placed. There is certainly no shortage
of relevant material: essays, sermons, letters, diaries may all deal
with parent-child relations and throw light on the development of
standard beliefs about family rights and duties. But for tracing
the development of such ideas throughout the nineteenth century
there is probably a superior source: articles in periodicals are not,
unlike diaries and correspondence, necessarily personal, nor, unlike
sermons, necessarily religious—they may not even be didactic.
Many of them appeared in magazines which enjoyed enormous
circulations and altogether they certainly catered for a wide
spread of middle-class thought. Of course these articles, too, have
their drawbacks. They may be purely singular expressions of

opinion, with no representative value at all (in this case, broad reading is the only corrective: two hundred seems a reasonable sample). They may be based on ignorance and prejudice—or on years of observation and thought. They may well sacrifice truth to amusement, realistic assessment to a pious wish. But whether or not this invalidates them depends largely on the uses to which they are put. In particular their fallibility matters much less if they are used not for what they describe but for what they embody, not for the statements they make *about* the climate of opinion but what in themselves they show it to be.

The following is an attempt to use periodical articles in this way: to trace the development of ideas about parents and children throughout the nineteenth century by seeing what people wrote on the subject—what arguments they employed, what estimations they made, what aspects they considered important. The resulting account hopes to do justice to the diversity of the opinions expressed and, at the same time, to extract from it a coherent overall pattern. It may be objected that such a pattern must mislead by implying that the development of thought on this subject proceeded in a single, continuous line: in fact the various periodicals represented various groups. But although this is true, it can still be maintained that a general tendency of thought can be seen; and, where they are adjudged to be significant, party interests will be pointed out.

(ii)

The first feature of this 'general tendency' is obvious enough: as the nineteenth century progressed more notice was taken of children. This is evident simply from the number of articles on 'children', 'childhood', 'the family' and 'parents' (compiled from the subject indexes for periodical literature). At the beginning of the century there are hardly any; after 1850 the volume swells; by 1900 there are dozens of them, surging over every creek and crevice of childhood feeling and childhood life (except, of course, infant sexuality, which was not fully studied until after Freud). And together with this broadening of interest there was usually an increase in sympathy, a respect (and sometimes nostalgia) for the pristine responses of youth. Almost everything to do with young people and children was submitted to eager analysis—their toys, their emotional anxieties, their characters, their sayings and their clothes.

This revolution was commented on by a writer in *Chambers's Journal* in 1887. 'Like all humane sympathies,' he said, 'this sympathy with the concerns of childhood has increased of late years.' For proof, he added, one need only look at the importance which 'Childish Things' had assumed. 'All the surroundings of child life', he declared, 'receive increased attention.' Modern nurseries, for instance, were bright and comfy, very unlike the 'Spartan' attic where *he* used to lie awake. Children's literature had changed too: 'Mrs Ewing's genial teachings have superseded Mrs Sherwood's grim severities.' And, most notably, the discipline of children had been softened and humanised: the 'rod of castigation' had been transformed into a 'fairy wand'. 'Oh, little children of fifty years ago,' he exclaimed, 'how you were goaded to righteousness! How narrow and strait was the way made for your feet!'

Actually this statement is an exaggeration: it underestimates how early in the century new approaches to children had begun to take shape. It may be doubted whether children of the thirties and forties were really groaning before the goads. It was not mentioned, at any rate, by most of those who pondered the subject at the time. 'Childhood is the laughing month of May', announced a writer in *Fraser's Magazine* for November 1842, reinforcing the remark with five more metaphors of similar frantic gaiety. The article, called 'Children' and written in a style of ejaculatory glee, began:

> What a charming word is the one we have written—'Children!' It speaks of joy, of hope, of filial gratitude and love, of happy homes, of cheerful fire-sides, of family banquets, of festive holidays . . . of healthful games and mirthful sports, of fun and frolic, and of the poetry and sunshine of life, without either its tempests or its clouds.

This hardly bristles with critical objectivity, but it does suggest that the Romantic apprehension of children was even by the forties fairly well advanced. As for the religious strait and narrow, there is evidence that this, too, by the thirties and forties, was threatened by schemes for expansion. As early as 1832 the *Christian Observer* was grumbling that:

There is not, perhaps, much general danger of overstrictness in these matters in the present day; the tendency is usually to a lax rather than a rigid system of family religious discipline.

Traditionally, the upbringing of children had been regarded chiefly as a religious matter, but throughout the first decades of the nineteenth century secular proposals were being made. Gradually those in favour of a godly rigour were forced to adopt a defensive stance. In 1844, for instance, we can find the *Christian Remembrancer* indignant at the suggestion that attending a daily service proves wearisome to children: 'In truth, such a thought is an injustice to them; in this cold, earthy, business-like age they are dealt with unfairly.'

Nevertheless, it must be admitted that in the early part of the century good training was largely identified with the inculcation of religion. Romantic liberation was a minority movement and so was a secular treatment of children. The philosophy of training to be met with most often was that of the Evangelicals; indeed they were one of the very few groups who took a detailed interest in the subject. Quite a few of the earliest articles that deal with the relations between parents and children are to be found in their magazines.

We can study the philosophy of the Evangelicals in the pages of the *Christian Observer*. This magazine was the organ of the Clapham Sect and was edited from 1802 to 1816 by Zachary Macaulay, father of the historian, friend of Wilberforce and tireless campaigner against the slave trade. In the *Christian Observer* in 1806 a correspondent signing himself 'Pater' divided a Christian education into discipline, instruction and example. The first was more important than parents generally thought, for 'as a parent is to his child in God's stead, he ought to require from the child an intire submission to his authority'. But though discipline should be steady, not capricious, it should also be 'gentle'. And it was necessary simply because of the child's fallen nature. Pater had noticed that 'children are perpetually endeavouring to break through the absolute authority of their parents'. They would attempt this with 'amazing sagacity'. His remarks on instruction told the same tale:

> Children should be taught, as soon as they become capable of reflection, to attend to the workings of their own minds; that they may discover the deceitfulness of their hearts, and become thoroughly acquainted with their inbred corruption.

Pater's main stress is on the child's depravity and potential wili-
ness in wriggling out of right and duty. He lays no stress on harshness of discipline.

An article signed 'B.T.' in the same periodical for 1811 clarifies
the position further. B.T.'s complaint is that 'the period of infancy
is generally suffered to slide away with little or no attention to
the work of education'. Children are petted and indulged and
this 'unquestionably fosters those seeds of evil which abound in
our nature'. B.T. wants moral culture to start young. But the
methods he recommends are far from Draconian. Parents need
tact and ingenuity; they should appeal to the child's emotions,
as well as its reason. It is absurd for the Catechism to be taught
like the lessons in a spelling-book. Above all, parents themselves
should set a good example. B.T. is against a mechanical system
of rules and discipline: 'In correcting a fault, look to the heart
rather than to the outward act.' He is against a Sundays Only
morality. He insists that the course taken by parents 'must be
carefully adapted to the age and character and attainments of
the child' (but neglects to supply details). Mid-century conflicts
of opinion about child-rearing may tend to confuse what is at
issue here. The contrast is not between a 'hard' system of sternness and discipline, and a 'soft' system of indulgence and freedom. It is between a system, *some* system, of moral guidance and
no system at all: casual neglect.

Parents should shoulder their responsibilities, adopt an organised
approach to child-training: this was the message of the early
articles. In 1819 the *Christian Instructor* set a stern face against
the idea that childhood should be spent in a thoughtless, playful
state. Pressure of daily business must not be made an excuse for
neglecting parental duty. Religious instruction should begin early
and be taken seriously. But 'a *tender age* peculiarly requires a
tender treatment': parents need not be 'harsh and rugged' or
'rigidly solemn'. Harshness and solemnity were not the main
dangers, though. The writer's dread was of parents so prone to
laugh and play with their children as to forget about guidance
and instruction. A parent 'is sunk into a pitiable degeneracy', he
warned, 'if his children are accustomed to receive him only in
the capacity of a playmate'.

Calls to order of this kind attest to the growing interest in
childhood. Upbringing began to be acknowledged as a delicate
procedure. The child's nature was unique, and important in itself

(later parental villains, like Dombey, were to regard their offspring as miniature adults). Notions of innocence were culled
from Blake and Rousseau; Original Sin began to recede. Stereotyped attitudes were formed, as the air thickened with Words-
worthian clouds of glory. A contributor to *Blackwood's Magazine*
in 1822 offered six closely-printed pages of lachrymose nostalgia
for the joys of childhood, explaining how he liked to forget
himself 'in the little happy being whose heart and fancy luxuriated
in a world of beauty and happiness'. But the new concern for
children did not automatically entail liberal tendencies: it was
overlaid with the older tradition of religious vigilance. In 1829
the *Quarterly Review* was heavily advocating that the law should
not only protect a child's physical rights but should also safe-
guard his moral and religious interests. The article identified
parental cruelty or negligence with an irreligious upbringing.
Atheists were bracketed with drunkards and adulterers, and
Shelley came in for some harsh words. The idea that a religious
upbringing could itself be cruel was not ripe for full-length treatment in fiction till Butler's *The Way of All Flesh*.

Gradually the child cult made parents conscious of their duties,
and opposite extremes of opinion emerged. Both severity and
lenience became systematic. The result was a coexistence of
attitude peculiar to the nineteenth century: writers like the one
in *Fraser's Magazine* for November 1842 penned their besotted
eulogies on the charms of childhood, and meanwhile discipline
tightened. That the merry words could conceal some severity
perhaps needs no demonstration. But the *Methodist Magazine* for
1836 helps to show what later writers meant when they remembered the strait and narrow of their youth.

In an article called 'On the Training of Children' a father of
seven described, in tones of solemn self-congratulation, the success
that could be achieved by 'an inflexible behaviour towards children, in establishing submission and good order'. His children have
turned out to be exemplary—that is, Stewards and Leaders in
Methodist Societies. For this, he says, God should greatly be
praised, and after reading an account of their upbringing we are
unlikely to disagree. As soon as his first child could walk, a few
threats of punishment had 'self-will nipped in the bud'. 'All
Childish contentions were prohibited', says the proud father, and
so were all toys. Books were shrewdly restricted so as to exhibit
'the advantage of that which is good'. The value of cash was

soon inculcated by giving the children pocket money and 'calling on them constantly to account how they laid it out'. Watch-
fulness and 'constant control' worked wonders, the results being
supplemented by some 'ceaseless agonizing with God in private'.
To the father's gratified surprise, God responded with alacrity and
readily supplied the children with 'preventing grace'. Nevertheless,
even when they were equipped in this way, the father was
convinced that:

> There must not be the smallest relaxation, at any time, or
> under any circumstances, nor must there be the least devia-
> tion from any fixed rule laid down for the government of
> children.

Among his fixed rules was that 'children were never suffered to
be noisy in a room'. There was also an absolute prohibition on
crying. ('The common disposition of children to cry', he explains,
'has often been very unpleasant to me, in visiting other families.')
The programme did not cease with infancy: at the age of nine or
ten the children were sent to school and 'my correspondence
with them while at school always tended to bring their minds
towards God, and keep alive those principles of uprightness which
they had received'. On leaving school they had the benefit of
continual discourse with Methodist preachers. And so hard did
the father pray that eventually the Lord

> blessed me with the opportunity of employing my four sons
> in my own business, instead of other clerks, so that my eye
> was upon them, as it were, every hour.

The whole enterprise, the father emphasises, was a huge success—
'Discord . . . never manifested itself for a moment; satisfaction
was seated on every countenance'—and we may rest assured
that his children, in addition to their spiritual pre-eminence, are
'respected in any polite circle'. So great, indeed, was his success
that he began to try his methods on other people's children. He
describes how, being anxious about his friend's daughter, who
was 'indulged to excess' and always crying, he invited the 'little
vixen' to spend a few months at his house. He collected her and,
'as soon as we got on the turnpike-road', threatened her with a
portentous harangue, which he reproduces for us *in toto*. After
this, he reflects, the child was 'exceedingly particular in noticing
my countenance' and behaved beautifully, but unfortunately the

girl's grandmother called and was lenient towards her, and so it was not long before she relapsed and was steeped in sin. But his own children he could completely control and they will, he is sure, 'look back with gratitude' on their early influences, 'the peace and happiness', as he puts it, 'which always surrounded my fireside'.

A heartwarming conclusion. Edmund Gosse, born thirteen years after this article was published, later showed, in *Father and Son*, what it felt like to be on the receiving end of the non-conformist conscience. He too had his reading matter expurgated. He too was honoured with an uplifting correspondence (from his end it looked like a 'postal inquisition'). Elevated ideas about the importance of childhood could undoubtedly accompany crushing severity. But it would be wrong to suggest that the growing regard for children in the first half of the century was all sheer rant. Theory steadily filtered through into action. The year after the last-mentioned article, for instance, nine children's homes and twenty-two schools for older children were sponsored by Wesleyan-Methodists. It was shortly after this that the ragged school movement began. Another sign of the new concern was the growth of children's periodicals. At the end of the eighteenth century two attempts had been made to cater for children, with John Marshall's *The Juvenile Magazine* (1788) and *The Children's Magazine* (1799): neither survived long. But in the 1820s two successful cheap periodicals were established: *The Child's Companion* (1824), published by the Religious Tract Society, and *The Children's Friend* (1825), edited by the Rev. Carus Wilson, whose friendship for children, as we have seen, revealed itself most frequently in instructing them how to die. Both periodicals were, of course, undeviatingly scriptural, but the former sometimes sweetened its edification with a few funny anecdotes. Religious journals continued to flourish, but after about 1850 there was much competition from lighter productions. *The Boy's Own Magazine*, begun in 1855, gave away prizes and featured well-known contributors. In 1866 Mrs Margaret Gatty, already a noted novelist for children (and later the compiler of *The Mother's Book of Poetry*), founded *Aunt Judy's Magazine*, which won contributions from Lewis Carroll and Hans Andersen, as well as from Mrs Gatty's daughter Juliana, who became, in fact, the genial Mrs Ewing commended by *Chambers's Journal*. By the end of the nineteenth century there were almost a hundred periodicals for children (Thwaite, 1972), varying enormously in quality and content: a whole new country of popular readership exploited in seventy years.

Whatever the motives of the publishers (who ranged from educational missionaries to casual entrepreneurs), the effect on children was certainly immense: so too was the change in the adult conception of what children expected and deserved. Of course this means mainly middle-class children, but comparable conclusions might be inferred from the history of nineteenth-century factory legislation, which affected the working-class young. The first governmental regulation of conditions of employment in factories was established in 1802: an act promoted by Sir Robert Peel the elder limited the work of poor-law apprentices to twelve hours a day. A further act of 1819 forbade the employment of children under nine and fixed a twelve-hour limit for children under sixteen. But it applied only to cotton mills and was powerless in any case, for it failed to provide for inspection. Nevertheless, the act was important for laying down parliament's right to interfere with the freedom of employers—and also with the discretion of parents. It is important to remember that these textile factories would often contain almost independent family units, who were disciplined by the father. Hence the objection of Lord Stanley, speaking in the Commons on 27 April 1818: 'One consequence of this Bill would be to create disunion between parents and children.' (Documents, 1959.) The first partially effective act was passed in 1833, providing inspectors to enforce its regulations. A committee of enquiry the year before had stirred public opinion. Richard Oastler reported that in Yorkshire he had seen a boy of ten whose face had been 'cut open by the thong' and back 'covered with black stripes' merely for stretching three pieces of woollen yarn (Documents, 1956). The act of 1833 excluded children under nine from textile factories and limited the working week of children under thirteen to forty-eight hours, of children under eighteen to sixty-nine hours. Again the result was to limit the power of parents as well as that of employers. Numerous other child-labour acts followed, some effective, some circumvented, but serving on the whole to remove children from their fathers, to establish precedents and mobilise opinion. The course of this legislation was complex, but the propaganda on behalf of children, its use as a spearhead in the attack on current conditions, was a fairly recurrent feature of the process, and highly significant as an index of public feeling. The Victorian period was distinguished from its predecessors not by its notable cruelty to children, but rather by its novel attempts to offer them protection.

By mid-century it had become difficult to ignore the plight of suffering children. In the thirties and forties, of course, there was Dickens. A huge audience responded to the deaths of Smike and Little Nell and Paul Dombey. Dickens inspired imitation. Early death became quite popular, as the market filled with writers who liked a good cry and a big readership. If the old villainy had been to make children grow up too soon (stuffing them, for instance, into grown-ups' garb), the new fashion took drastic measures to keep them eternally young. The fictional infant-mortality rate soared alarmingly. Meanwhile more genuine concern protested against real-life infant mortality. Harriet Martineau claimed in *Once a Week* in 1859 that over forty per cent of the country's children died before they were five. She exaggerated a little, but the more reliable estimate of twenty-six per cent, supplied by W. Farr in the *Journal of the Statistical Society* in 1866, was itself high enough to warrant much reform. And reform came, though slowly.

'Hard' and 'soft' schools of child management opposed each other in the middle of the century, and the 'soft' school was winning. Its exponents often employed the same style of automatic assertion as their antagonists. Thus in 1852 we find a writer in *Hogg's Instructor* taking up cudgels against 'the champions of the rod and rule'. Love and respect should be substituted for scolding and whipping. Talk of 'natural depravity' is wrong. It is parents who are responsible for a child's behaviour.

> Think of it as you will, and censure nature as you please for the moral defects of your child, its little heart is a mirror that faithfully images your own character and disposition.

Others argued the liberal case more thoughtfully. The *British Quarterly Review* in 1858 printed a closely-reasoned, thirty-page article that advocated lenience but doubted whether a perfect system of education could produce forthwith an ideal humanity. Even if a perfect system existed,

> It is forgotten that the carrying out of any such system presupposes, on the part of adults, a degree of intelligence, of goodness, of self-control, possessed by no one. The great

error made by those who discuss questions of juvenile discipline, is in ascribing all the faults and difficulties to the
children and none to the parents.

In fact both children and parents are at fault. The writer outlines
his own scheme in detail. His principle is simple enough: the
penalty for misconduct should be experience of its natural consequences. A child who loses something should replace it from
his own pocket money. A child who is unpunctual for walks
should not be taken out. This echoes Rousseau, but the tone and
tendency of the article are closer to Locke, whom the writer
quotes with approval. Coercion should be a last resort, he argues,
for the parents' aim should be to produce a *self-governing* being;
not to produce a being to be *governed by others*. A plausible
psychology of child management is proposed. The writer's point
is that lenience works: if affection exists between parent and
child, the parent will not have to inflict harsh punishments; disapproval will be sufficient, the mere withdrawal of caresses. The
premise is that when one person offends another, 'the amount of
genuine regret he feels . . . varies with the degree of sympathy
he has for that person'. Rational and earnest, the article puts the
liberal case well, the argument plodding steadily to its firm conclusions.

The year after this article Meredith's *Ordeal of Richard Feverel*
appeared. Many critics received it as a tract on education. *The
Times* and the *Saturday Review* took the bogey to be Sir Austin
Feverel's 'System'—Meredith was proving certain policies wrong.
The misreading, though more pardonable than has been thought
(Meredith's conception is less than clear), shows that the treatment
of children was an important popular issue by this time. 'Is not
our own time distinguished from all that have preceded it by the
intensity of its interest in and regard for children?' asked
Chambers's Journal in 1863. It certainly looked like it. In the
sixties children's literature flourished and the voices of child-
defenders throbbed with emphatic emotion. James Payn, editor
of *Chambers's Journal*, and friend of Dickens and Harriet Martineau, concluded an article in 1868 with this counsel to parents:

> No severity should ever be used; for if the necessity arises
> for it, the fault is ours: something in the past has been
> suffered to go unreproved. It is ourselves, not they, who do
> in reality deserve to be smitten. Some folks have an idea that
> children should be taught to 'put up' with everything, where-

as their sense of justice is most accurately delicate, and a wrong inflicted may warp the whole future character.

Payn's resentment had a personal basis: after being bullied at prep school and choked with Latin and Greek at Eton, he had wilted under the rigid discipline of the Woolwich Academy. A similar warning to parents concluded an article in *Fraser's Magazine* for March 1862: 'You may sour the human spirit for ever', said A. K. H. Boyd, 'by cruelty and injustice in youth.' Boyd's article, 'Concerning the Sorrows of Childhood', remarkably anticipates *The Way of All Flesh*. Eleven years before Butler began to chronicle his grievances Boyd had them docketed in detail. After some words on 'the cruelty, injustice, and incompetence of many schoolmasters', illustrated with tales of a 'malignant blockhead' who ministered to him in youth, Boyd thumps out his major accusation:

> But, doubtless, the greatest cause of the sorrows of childhood is the mismanagement and cruelty of parents. . . . There are two classes of parents who are the most inexorably cruel and malignant. . . . One is the utterly blackguard: the parents about whom there is no good nor pretence of good. The other is the wrong-headedly conscientious and religious; probably, after all, there is greater rancour and malice about these last than about any other. These act upon a system of unnatural repression, and systematized weeding out of all enjoyment from life. These are the people whose very crowning act of hatred and malice towards any one, is to pray for him, or to threaten to pray for him. These are the people who, if their children complain of their bare and joyless life, say that such complaints indicate a wicked heart, or Satanic possession; and have recourse to further persecution to bring about a happier frame of mind.

Boyd, who wrote a column for *Fraser's* called 'Recreations of a Country Parson', adds that such parents of course 'caricature . . . the pure and kindly religion of the Blessed Redeemer'.

Boyd gives short shrift to the grumble that parents are going soft:

> You hear a great deal about parents who spoil their children by excessive kindness; but I venture to think that a greater number of children are spoiled by stupidity and cruelty on the part of their parents.

Stupidity and cruelty—these were the cornerstones of Ernest Pontifex's upbringing. Ernest had teachers who believed that 'pleasure had in it something more or less sinful in its very essence'. Boyd too assails the 'wicked principle that all enjoyment is sinful'. He is well acquainted with this line of thought:

> The great doctrine, underlying all other doctrines, in the creed of a few unfortunate beings, is that God is spitefully angry to see his creatures happy; and of course the practical lesson follows, that they are following the best example when they are spitefully angry to see their children happy.

Curiosity about parental spite is swiftly satisfied. Boyd spills over with samples of the ingenious methods open to middle-class parents who wish to torment their children without exposing themselves to charges of gross physical cruelty. He goes into all the subtle refinements of humiliation, anxiety and discomfort. Again many of his cases coincide with *The Way of All Flesh*: 'shutting them up in a dark place', for example (Ernest was 'shut . . . up in a cupboard'), or instilling guilt feelings (Ernest 'believed in his own depravity'). Terrorism tactics outlined by Boyd, like suggesting to a child that he 'may very probably have to become a wandering beggar', point forward to old George Pontifex's harangues. Admitting that he has 'been writing in a style which, to say the least, is snappish', Boyd finally breaks off overpowered with distress.

Another piece bearing on Butler's grudges appeared in Dickens's *All the Year Round* in 1864. Entitled 'To Parents', the article began by mentioning cases of cruelty that attract the public's attention. But, it continued,

> there are innumerable other instances, not the 'cruel fathers' or 'heartless mothers' of fiction, but everyday, well-meaning respectable people, who are nevertheless domestic Molochs, before whom every successive child must pass through the fire.

The writer discusses various family tensions and speaks of the case when 'the elder generation is, in mental and moral calibre, decidedly inferior to the younger. Not bad people, but only narrow'. Butler's situation appears to have been this, and the writer's further comments corroborate *The Way of All Flesh*:

> If nature has made one of their children in any way different from themselves, of larger mould and wider capacities, the extent to which that child is martyrised, even with the very best intentions, is sometimes incredible. Yet outside, everybody says what excellent parents they are, and what a happy

home their children must have! a fact of which they themselves are most thoroughly convinced.

Theobald Pontifex, we recall,

> considered himself, and was generally considered to be . . .
> an exceptionally truthful person, indeed he was generally
> looked upon as the embodiment of all those virtues which
> made the poor respectable, and the rich respected.

However, in certain other ways the author of this article is
very different from Butler. He is sympathetic, and perceptive,
about young people's problems, but in the last resort a staunch
upholder of the fifth commandment. Parenthood is a bond which
'came by the ordination of Providence'. And:

> It may be a great burden, even a great misfortune, but there
> it is: and nothing but death can end it. No shortcomings on
> the parental side can abrogate one atom of the plain duty
> of the child—submission so long as submission is possible,
> reverence while one fragment of respect remains; and, after
> that, endurance. To this generation of Young England, which
> is apt to think so much of itself, and so little of its elders and
> superiors, we cannot too strongly uphold the somewhat out
> of date doctrine, 'Honour thy father and thy mother'.

The defensive tone tells us that a stand is being taken against
current tendencies. Sympathy is fine, but it can go too far. Others
were coming to share the revulsion from 'Young England'. Childhood—if not always children—had been saturated with sympathy
and importance, and inevitably a reaction began to take shape.
In 1868 *Temple Bar* carried an article called 'About Goody Children' by Francis Jacox. Mr Jacox quoted from books, essays and
articles that made merry with the contemporary fondness for
premature piety. Children will become unhealthily priggish and
self-conscious, he suggests, if they are bred up on stories idealising
infant saints, voluble in scripture, who go about converting their
fathers and mothers. Nor has he any time for tales of poignant
martyrdom:

> It has been said that if anybody can get a pretty little girl
> to die prattling to her brothers and sisters, and quoting texts
> of Scripture with appropriate gasps, dashes, and broken sen-
> tences, he may send half the women in London, with tears
> in their eyes, to Mr Mudie's or Mr Booth's.

In his opinion nothing but harm can come from these 'early
surfeits of pathological piety'.

As the century moved into the seventies such mockery began to be heard more often. It proved insufficient, however, to deter those who worked within the childhood-rhapsody genre, which continued to thrive despite the bilious rumbles. A standard offering appeared in *Once a Week* in 1874. In an article called 'Scented With Lavender' a lady heartily adverting to herself as an 'old maid' confessed to feeling that 'there is something so cheerful and inspiriting in the presence of children', and communicated her enthusiasm with phrases like 'And then the intense spring and vitality in these little people!' Advocacies of liberalism, though just as plentiful, were usually less depressing. 6 January 1877 found *Chambers's Journal* making bold to declare that ' "Little people should be seen and not heard" is a stupid saying', but conceding, significantly, that:

> We must, however, thankfully acknowledge that people are beginning more and more to conform their education to children's opinion; that is, generally speaking, to the promptings of Nature. It is found that those turn out worse who during youth have been subjected to most restrictions.

This conclusion (here unsubstantiated) is what Locke had maintained. The article went on to place the responsibility for children's behaviour squarely on the parents, to recommend gentleness, and to plead for sympathy with the toddler's queries, the adolescent's 'trials and sorrows', and the young man's anxiety about choosing a job. In an editorial note in the same issue *Chambers's* congratulated itself on being 'to all appearance more acceptable as a Family Magazine than ever'. Times were changing.

It was also in the seventies that secularism came to a head. Two decades of militant scepticism had frayed the traditional tie-up between child-training and religion. In 1875 the *Westminster Review* summoned up its agnostic indignation and scholarly scorn for a trenchant attack on the 'strongly conservative bias' governing the religious education of children. Christianity was not becoming more moral, less doctrinal, said the writer: dogmas were instilled as much as ever. Probably it was the 'cold and severe garb' in which religion was presented that made it the case that 'the almost insuperable dislike children evince towards religion is a fact to which universal experience testifies' (needless to say, this 'universal experience' was not experienced universally —not, for example, by the *Congregationalist*, discussing 'The Religious Education of Children' only the year before). Looking at 'various little volumes destined for the spiritual guidance of the young', the *Westminster Review* discovered three different methods. The first was 'the Doctrinal System'. The writer took as typical of this 'A Manual of Catechetical Instruction' by the Rev. E. B. Ramsey, and showed with a few quotations how it skipped blithely over abtruse theological issues almost certainly beyond a child's reach. Illustrating 'the Terroristic System' he offered some doses of country-rectory brimstone from the Rev. Dr Wilson's 'Sermons for the Very Young', and pointed out their appeal to panic-stricken expediency. Thirdly there was 'the Hysterical System'. 'The literature employed in this method of religious culture evinces a great deal of unreal sentiment, and a sublime indifference to anything so grovelling as fact', the writer began. He then drew attention to the 'mere puling senti-ment' displayed in a couple of hortatory tales about infant martyrs.

This ruthless diagnosis exposes its victims with ease. It seems largely, though, like many secularist polemics in the nineteenth century, an attack on conditions already superseded : less a diag-nosis than a post-mortem. It neglects to mention, for instance, that Ramsey's Catechism, though once widely used, had been published forty years before. Not that sermonising at children had ceased to be popular. In the last quarter of the century it still bulked large, but it differed in kind from its antecedents. Inheriting the same assumptions, but hesitating to assert them, it would veer uncertainly between truculence and cajolement. A new tone was evolved to cope with the crumbling certainties, a more defensive tone, sometimes chummy, sometimes cranky and fractious. Rationalisations sprouted up. Certainly many children would be justified in suspecting that their mentors, though pro-lific of good counsel, were thin on common sense. In *Good Words* in 1873 an article claiming to be 'by the author of *Lilliput Lectures*' (who was in fact William Brighty Rands, creator of the lyric 'Beautiful World') set out to explain why parents should be honoured. The answer was that children would never be here at all if the parents had not first shown certain noble qualities. 'To begin with, there must have been love between the father and mother.'

But the quintessential flavour of the later moralising can best be savoured in an article by the Rev. R. F. Horton that appeared in the *Sunday Magazine* as late as 1894. Horton is worth quoting at length, since he crams into one article attitudes and opinions scattered over dozens of others. The tone, too, is very typical.

Horton takes two texts 'Children, obey your parents in the Lord' and 'Fathers, provoke not your children to wrath' (Ephesians 6:1 and 4) as props for a two-part sermon. The first part is for children only, the second for parents only. For the first part Horton adopts a style of childlike simplicity, but in the second he is weightier and brings in historical references and foreign words. He begins by saying that his texts would be difficult to handle in a public sermon, with children and parents present together. But it is 'easier to preach a sermon in a magazine', since the preacher can then 'safely reckon on nine-tenths of his readers, and all the children, skipping his pages'. Apparently pleased with this bizarre advantage, Horton begins his sermon to children:

> Now, children, I will give you four reasons why you should obey your parents, and we will hang one reason on each of the letters in the word *obey*. Of course there are fifty reasons, but we do not want more than four.

The mnemonic works as follows. 'O' stands for 'perfection, the faultless circle', and part of the perfect harmony of the universe is juvenile obedience. To obey is 'the most happy and the most complete condition of mind'. In fact the *happiness* is more important than the completeness, for '. . . to do what we ought is most pleasant. Fools always want to give orders. Wise men want to take them.' Warming to his subject, Horton explains to his non-existent child readers that the great advantage, the great happiness, of childhood—'a happiness which can never come again'—is that children have no choice: 'Grown-up people have the burden of choosing whom they are to obey. That is chosen for *you* by Nature, by God. You have to obey your parents.' Miserable adults, Horton points out, yearn to obey someone without question, 'and they will', he adds, with a startling uprush of sectarian fervour, 'thrust their foolish heads under the Pope's heel because they are tired of not knowing'. But children, by being blindly obedient to their parents, have a useful way of avoiding such excesses.

'B' stands for 'Better'. 'Another reason for obedience is that your parents know *Better* what is good for you than you do yourselves.' This is because 'God has given them the knowledge of what is best for you', Horton explains, but he generously supplies an alternative suggestion: 'It is their business to find out this knowledge.' A child who asked his parents why he had to do a thing would be 'foolish and weak'.

Thirdly, children are 'Embraced' in the love of their parents, who 'give all and ask nothing'. Horton reminds children that their parents 'brood over you, they bend faces of unspeakable affection over your cot when you are asleep'. Such love should obviously be requited.

The last reason for obedience and the 'strongest of all' is:

> the *Yoke* of Jesus, 'Learn of me, for I am meek and lowly of heart.' Even when He was a big boy of twelve, we are told that He went down to Nazareth with His parents, and was 'subject unto them'; which means that He not only did what they told Him, but was all the time at their beck and bidding, and never dreamed of asserting His own will against theirs.

To accept this account of Christ's visit to the Temple would surely require powers of unquestioning credulity beyond even Horton's model children. Scripture, though, is not this preacher's strong point, as he shows in his next paragraph with a description of Christ's childhood:

> For if you go back into the childhood of Jesus, you will see that it is just like your own; it has the same troubles and the same joys. Mary wants Him to do something for her when He would rather be on the hills playing. Joseph is stern and hard, forgetting that he was himself a child. He says sharp things which bring the blood into the boy's delicate cheek. He even strikes Him in moments of anger, and says that boys are always in the way or always in mischief.

These heartening fictions conclude the first part of the sermon. Horton next tackles the precept for parents. He finds himself unable to apply this with such gusto, for he is dubious about its relevance in the licentious atmosphere of the nineteenth century:

> If St Paul were writing to English and American Christians, however, I doubt if he would not utter a warning on the other side before he proceeded to deprecate the wrath of fathers. Would he not have something to say about maintaining the paternal authority and exercising the right of government?

Perhaps so, perhaps not; Horton, anyway, decides to act as St Paul's ventriloquist:

'Parents, control your children in the Lord', I can easily imagine him saying, with the facts of modern life before his eyes. We have lighted on an age of petty anarchies. And amongst the rest is the dethronement or voluntary abdication of the parent. Count Tolstoi's ideal is realised in our homes; there is no government, except that of the last born child. Each child does its best to assume the reins of power. Undeterred by the failure of their parents, they seek to bend the household to their *regime*.

St Paul, of course, was writing before things had come to such a pass, speaking 'in that fine ancient world where the dethronement of the parent was as yet only a nightmare of prophecy'. *That* was why it was apt for him to give a warning to fathers. So, at least, Horton feels; though he is still not quite happy about Paul's peculiar dictum. He suspects in fact:

> that we have here one of the most difficult precepts in the Bible to carry out consistently. For on the one hand you are bound to correct your child, to repress natural instincts, to educe reluctant powers, to thwart his will, and to work out of his system certain follies which will hardly come out by any process short of braying in a mortar; while, on the other hand, you have to carry out this irritating process without causing irritation, without arousing the wrathful element in the child at all.

Horton clearly feels exasperated by the whole business. Anyway it is St Paul's affair, not his, and as for anyone who does not know what to make of it, 'let him settle his account with St Paul and the Spirit of God'. Horton feels he must mention, though, that 'men not ill-meaning often provoke their children to wrath'. It is the children's fault because they misjudge intentions: they are sometimes irritated less by an 'insult of forethought' than by 'a well-meant banality'. This sounds plausible enough, but Horton ends less querulously by recommending that parents should pray for tact and control of anger.

An interesting sidelight on the Hortonian attitude to children appeared in the same magazine a couple of years later. Horton this time had four articles under the rather unfortunate title 'On the Art of Living Together', which art he considered more important than playing the piano or violin and 'would even venture to say that it is of more vital value than the indispensable art of arithmetic'. One of these articles dealt with living in the family. Here Horton divulged to parents that 'Sir Moody, or my lady of that ilk, may suffer admonition' and that 'punishment, which may be necessary, should be calm, self-restrained, and, if one may say so, *polite*'. But his most telling comment was that, though we should 'make some allowances' for the period of youth,

> youth . . . would do well to remember that for others it is almost as disagreeable as measles, and it is wise therefore to keep out of the way and to avoid provocation.

What oft was thought, but ne'er so bluntly expressed.

Still, at least it *was* expressed, at least children were thought to be worth a good deal of discussion. In the eighties and nineties the interest in childhood boomed. References to the subject, both frivolous and solemn, could command a wide audience. Writers found they could make up an article by scraping together examples of children's funny sayings ('the comical element among youngsters'). In 1893 the editor of the Catholic magazine *The Month* spent fourteen large pages sorting out papal pronouncements and patristic writings on 'The Condition of Unbaptized Children After Death' (conclusion: they would be happy, and probably have visits from the Virgin Mary, but would be excluded from the Beatific Vision). Children's books and magazines abounded, their obligatory didacticism long since shaken off. The magazine pages were full of pets and jingling poetry, of puzzles and serialised stories, copiously and often beautifully illustrated. At the beginning of the century children had largely made do with fiction originally intended for adults; in the eighties adults began to enjoy fiction designed for children (*Treasure Island, King Solomon's Mines*). And juvenile readership itself was widening as the education acts took effect.

Child-study became scientific, pioneered by Darwin and the German physiologist, Preyer. But private theories about upbringing and family life were also in plentiful supply. Charlotte M. Mason, writing on 'Character in Children' in *Murray's Magazine* in 1888, announced that:

> It is the age of child-worship; and very lovely are the well-brought-up children of Christian and cultured parents. But, alas, how many of us degrade the thing we love! Think of the multitude of innocents to be launched on the world, already mutilated, spiritually and morally, at the hands of doting parents!

Miss Mason did not, though, desiderate old-fashioned punishments, but modern, 'scientific' principles of upbringing. In *Murray's*

Magazine the following year she wrote some stories to explain how these principles worked. One, 'Home Rule in the Nursery', instructs parents how to cope with infant tantrums. Father cures his passionate tot by diverting his attention or getting him to run round the garden. The cure is shown to be scientific by having it issue from a twinkling-eyed doctor. Everyone to his theory. A writer in the *Spectator* in 1886, discussing 'The Instincts of Family', concluded that:

> It is almost always likeness which causes aversion. . . . You fear or dread or shrink from that in your family which you feel has a tendency to expose your weak points.

This applied well, the writer believed, to a topical murder case; some French children had sprinkled their mad mother with holy water, then burnt her to death. It also applied to Hamlet and Gertrude.

But the big child-parent issue of the eighties was institutionalised prevention of cruelty. Prime mover of the N.S.P.C.C. was the Rev. Benjamin Waugh, philanthropist editor of the *Sunday Magazine*. In 1884 he established a London Society for the Prevention of Cruelty to Children, and it shifted to a national basis in 1888. The issue at stake was the delimitation of parental freedom. Factory and Education acts had lopped the father's discretion in the public sphere; the child-cruelty Societies sought to tamper with his rights in his own home. Dozens of articles debated the law's right to intervene in cases of ill-usage, starvation or neglect. Many, like Waugh, thought something should be done about a father who clubbed his son's head in with a hammer handle, or a mother who locked her little boy in an orange-box every day for three months (cases cited in 1886 by Waugh and Cardinal Manning in the *Contemporary Review*). Others, however, defended the individual's right to beat up his children. *Patria potestas* still survived. As time went on, it became harder to deny the achievements of the child-cruelty campaigners. Till 1891 Waugh was hampered by lack of funds, but after that he prospered. The early response to his aims was commonly grudging agreement. In 1884 the *Spectator*, strident for individual rights, welcomed the proposed Society but warned against unnecessary meddling. A father who flogs an offending child should not be summonsed, it said, adding sagely: 'There are many things which a father ought not to do, and yet ought not to be restrained from doing.' It explained that, unless the borderline between hardship and cruelty had been passed, 'interference can only do harm', Cruelty, one assumes, to satisfy the *Spectator*, would have to be defined fairly rigorously. The *Saturday Review* had a different objection. In 1883 it doubted how much a recently-founded Society in Liverpool could accomplish. Surely, vast social issues were involved: bad treatment occurred mainly among the hard-drinking Irish poor. Cruelty was connected with squalid living conditions. Waugh denied it. Writing with Cardinal Manning in the *Contemporary Review*, he said the London Society had found that:

> Against the poor, the terribly poor, it can bring hardly a complaint. As a class they seem full of a rough kindness which costs them much sacrifice. . . . The true English savage is often quiet, and is generally the earner of good wages.

Of course, this suited the Society's outlook: it believed in individual philanthropy, not wholesale social reform. Still, Waugh and Manning's opinion must be respected. Waugh had devoted his life to the cause, and knew the facts better than most. The 'Children's Charter' of 1889 (by which a child could be taken from cruel parents and committed to care) was, although sponsored by A. J. Mundella, largely due to Waugh's efforts.

The child-cruelty furore assisted the advocates of lenience. It promoted sympathy for children's sufferings, and preventionists tended to deprecate not only cruelty but strictness. In 1893 Mary Bolton, assistant secretary of the N.S.P.C.C., writing in the *Sunday Magazine* about 'The Discipline of Children', admonished 'stern disciplinarians' of the Bible-and-birch persuasion. In the Society's own treatment of children, she said, 'deprivation of pudding has been the severest discipline used'. Tiresome slop, this, perhaps, to tough-minded traditionalists, but undoubtedly preferable to a red-hot poker in the mouth, which is how one of Miss Bolton's clients chastised her little girl, the child standing by while the instrument was warmed. Justly or not, some of the odium stuck to the 'sternness' school.

By the end of the century everyone seemed convinced that things had got softer for children. As James Sully said in the *Fortnightly Review* in 1897:

> Although the present fancy for children's ways is by no means so new as it is sometimes said to be, it has undoubtedly begun for the first time to show signs of gathering the volume and the energy of a new interest.

A 'new interest', but not so new as people said. Others were similarly anxious to equip the phenomenon with precedents: vast change induced a need for reassurance. Talking about 'The Love of Childhood' in the *Sunday Magazine* in 1890, A. L. Salmon admitted that 'its attainment to the dignity and importance of a social and religious factor is a comparatively modern event'. But, he said, 'This so-called spoiling of children is by no means a new feature in society.' It could be traced back at least to the Greeks, as readers of Plutarch would realise. Ancients had anticipated the Moderns.

Interestingly, as active concern for children reached its height, the gushing appreciation of them began to peter out. Its practitioners naturally lamented the loss of their audience. In *Macmillan's Magazine* Frederic Adye declared that his love for little Paul Dombey remained unshaken, despite 'the onslaughts of a certain school of modern criticism ever on the alert to detect false pathos and predisposed to disparage even genuine enthusiasm'. Mr Adye's embarrassment is, however, all too understandable. His glowingly 'poetic' appreciations of childhood have a dated air for 1893. He slides easily into archaisms and hackneyed metaphors and draws heavily on the reverent-diction reservoir hollowed out for childhood descriptions earlier in the century: 'a nature so intrinsically sweet and noble . . . the heaven-born spirit . . . the loving clasp of little warm white arms about our neck . . . the smile of a seraph, and a voice like a lute'—the phrases wash over the reader, thinned down by years of repetition. More typical of the times was a piece in the *Idler* the same year. 'The Idlers' Club', a light-hearted symposium on various subjects of popular discussion, addressed itself to the question 'Is childhood the happiest or the most miserable period of one's existence?' Most of the contributors were far from intoxicated with nostalgia for juvenile joys. Several mentioned the influence of parents. Florence Marryat, a daughter of Captain Marryat, said:

> If I am to choose one, or the other, extreme, I should say decidedly the most miserable, and made so by the folly, ignorance, or neglect of parents. Not one hundredth part of the men and women who marry are fit to become fathers and mothers.

Mrs Panton thought that 'childhood is the happiest time we can possibly have', but only 'if the child is in proper hands' and not among 'tyrants'. Robert Barr, joint-editor of the magazine, believed that:

> the small boy, poor little chap, lives under the most galling despotism that exists on the face of the earth. There is no court of appeal for him. His father is at once his judge, his opposing counsel, his public prosecutor, as it were, his jailer, and his executioner . . . the kingdom of which the small boy is a subject remains what it always was.

Vehemently put, and not everyone in the nineties could stomach such talk. Trying to stomach it, in fact, was liable to bring forth from the *Spectator* a violent discharge of exasperation. Middle-class children 'are liberated for all the earlier years of their lives from care', it stated in 1892, and 'have ceased altogether to fear their parents, for whom they invent pet-names usually tinged with a comic irreverence'. Pet names for the executioner: the view was hardly reconcilable with Robert Barr's. Strangely, though, the *Spectator*'s article was ostensibly applauding the 'healthy advance made in general opinion' as regards the treatment of children. Sympathy for them had been growing for forty years, it said, and offered its approval in these terms:

> The whole treatment of children has changed within that time, and the idea of severity towards them, especially while they are little, has become, even with people of harsh character, utterly abhorrent. 'Whipping', which even in the 'forties' was the regular and proper method of discipline, is considered an almost diabolical cruelty; 'sending to bed', which was really a method of inflicting solitary confinement, is entirely disused; and 'standing in the corner' is condemned as inflicting 'humiliation'. There is, in truth, in a majority of comfortable households, no way left of punishing a child beyond a reproving look, a lecture which must not be too protracted, and, in extreme cases, a deprivation of some promised and greatly desired indulgence.

Even poor people, the writer continued, were treating their children well. Was it all to the good? His cheerfully affirmative answer trailed a baleful qualification:

> We hope the change will go yet deeper, for upon the whole it produces only good. There is no doubt a little too much unrestrainedness in the children of the well-to-do . . . They have far too little patience, and are defective—as also are becoming the children of the poor—in the fine old virtue of obedience which we believe modern teaching is accustoming men to scorn.

With characteristic ambivalence the article concluded that the progress of good treatment

> will certainly be accelerated, not hindered, by the new feeling for children, we almost call it the new affection; and if that produces evils of its own, and is sometimes displayed in dangerous projects like free dinners for all at school, why, this is not the age of miracles. . . .

The tone of this was quite common at the end of the century among writers discussing the childhood revolution. It was an advance, of course, and a creditable thing, but surely all this molly-coddling was going too far. 'It is a commonplace of the day', said the *Quarterly Review* in 1896,

> to congratulate our children on their singular good fortune in having been born some sixty years later than their grandparents. If comparative luxury with far greater indulgences be an unmixed good, there is no denying the proposition. Whether they are better or even happier, are questions less easily answered.

The writer himself, it soon transpires, rather resents some of the changes. Like the writer in the *Spectator* one thing he begrudges the modern child is his dinner. 'Probably the young people of the olden time', he speculates, 'owed their immunity from serious illness to the rough but wholesome fare, which hardened robust constitutions.' Children received 'unsavoury rations', he admits, but they seldom caught cold, whereas 'now . . . the children are always catching cold'. Clothes too: the healthy youngsters of the past were scantily clad, while their sickly counterparts in the present trot around in 'silks and brocades'. At the same time they 'are taught to look forward to rounds of dissipation at the high festivals of Christmas and Easter-tide'. Still, they could be worse, they could be like American children—gorged on candy and precociously overdressed. Whether children are better than they were, it seems, is not so hard to answer after all.

This reaction had been gathering for some years. It had first found its voice in banter against fashionable infant piety. Later, the resentment extended in scope and became rather shriller in tone. Many adults, despite official approval, felt gravely alarmed by the consequence, the attention as well as the greater indulgence, increasingly granted to children. There began to develop a certain nostalgia for the less tender practices of the past, the bracing adversities. Such feelings are evident, for example, in Sarah Tytler's *Childhood a Hundred Years Ago* (1877), a book which opens with a sombre account of 'What Childhood Had Not a Hundred Years Ago'. Here we learn how children had to be satisfied with confinement and physical hardship, spelling-books with passages from Demosthenes, a dearth of agreeable literature and only the simplest toys. But in the second chapter the note is changed; the author now cheerfully specifies 'What Children Had a Hundred Years Ago':

> Why, children had their young bodies, fresh minds, and trustful hearts. They had God's blue sky and his sunshine above them, even when daylight in-doors was most grudged. . . . Children had the faithful protection and love of parents and kindred, though boys and girls had to say 'sir' and 'madam' to father and mother, and bow and curtsey when they said 'good morning' to their nearest relations. . . . It is true that the formality and reserve which were one side of the times—with their strict discipline where discipline existed at all—sometimes pressed heavily, and robbed parent and child of the mutual confidence which is their best safeguard and sweetest joy. But love which has its roots in awe is the noblest, most influential, and most enduring form of love. . . . Following without fail in the train of unhesitating compliance and submission, came serene content and buoyant cheerfulness.

Clearly the past was really quite fine, and even the 'strong meat' given to children—the rote-learning of Pope or Demosthenes—was likely to produce, the author now feels, 'early vigour and solidity of understanding and character'. Only 'little dolts and dunces', she suggests, 'or the incorrigibly volatile and trifling', were worse off a century before. Starting with approval of the new concern for childhood, the book ends with a plea for subordination, a return to the view that submissiveness is the best part of juvenile virtue.

Towards the end of the century, then, there was a widespread feeling that the doting on children was altogether excessive. Parents as well as young people began to find their champions. People wearied of being told that they were responsible for their offspring's conduct. Writing in the *Sunday Magazine* in 1896 John Watson condoled with parents who had 'Vexatious Children'. 'One would like to get the ear of children', he said, 'and suggest to them how much their parents' life . . . depends on their conduct.' Children, too, had duties; even those brought up devotedly could easily go astray. Anyway, he reassured his readers, 'prodi-galism in children has often produced saintship in parents'. It seems a rather desperate consolation.

A writer in *All the Year Round* in 1894 was more pugnacious. Determined to strip the tinsel from all the talk about upbringing, he contended that children caused parents much trouble, had a great deal of freedom, and 'are not so teachable as certain of the moral-mongers would wish us to believe'. In his youth, he says, he decided that when he had children, 'They should be free as the air, unshackled as the wind.' Now his ideas about upbringing are not so sure; now he can see the parents' side. French parents, he believes, 'exercise more self-denial' for their children, but have more control over them : can choose their marriage partners, for instance. But :

> In England it is all the other way. The tendency of our legislation is towards, not only the freedom, but it would really seem also the license of the child.

Why should parents sacrifice themselves by saving up for their children's marriage, when the children are likely to go off and marry whoever they like? Girls do this and boys are even worse :

> They merely mention in the home circle the fact that they are going to marry in a casual sort of way—not infrequently they forget to mention it at all till the thing is done.

Exaggerated? Perhaps. But clearly because the writer believes that 'The influence of the parent over the child has been, and still is, exaggerated.' His article simply hits back. 'In good, sober truth', he says, 'the more strenuously you may endeavour to train a child to walk in any given direction, the more likely it is to move in a diametrically opposite one.' His conclusion shrugs off the vast literature of earnest advice to parents :

> No, go easy with children. . . . Do not, if we can help it, let us regard them as subjects for experiments. Above all do not let us cram down their throats our crotchets, our theories.

These sentiments were shared by Stephen Gwynn, reflecting on 'Modern Parents' for *Cornhill Magazine* in 1900. After a century of unprecedented concern for the young, Gwynn's article con-stitutes a wry postscript. He begins on a note of guarded approval ('I am sure that the sense of parental responsibility has developed to an extraordinary degree within the century that is just closing'), but is soon talking about 'that physical and moral coddling which is the deadly vice of the modern parent'. Not that he fails to understand the historical factors that have changed the complexion of parent-child relations. He connects the new attitudes with the rise of the individual, 'who sought his own good and his own completion irrespective of his family connections', and he identifies the uncertainty characteristic of contemporary parents:

> Nowadays we are in a lamentable transition period. We still think our children a nuisance—for the modern parent is at heart deplorably unregenerate—but we do not think ourselves entitled to think so.

He unravels the Rousseauist presuppositions of fashionable education and defines what he sees as the fundamental premise on which a good deal of it rests: 'The modern theory is, I imagine, that children should not be preached to or exhorted, but that they should be unconsciously guided in a desirable direction.' But, he argues, this will either diminish the child's individuality or make him 'develop character by an instinctive rebellion against the directing influence'. He concludes, therefore:

> I believe that both character and health are best promoted by judicious letting alone. There is often worse mischief done by parental interference than by parental neglect: I appeal to Mr George Meredith and the example of Richard Feverel.

(iii)

Approval of 'judicious letting alone' seems a strange ending to a story that began with bugle calls to parental duty. Strange, too, that an author who mirrored the new concern for children should be enlisted as an apostle of neglect. But the paradox is more apparent than real: Gwynn's article was a reaction against tendencies still in the ascendant. By the end of the century neglect and cruelty were still most often stigmatised as the gravest parental sins; a minority, however, was becoming aware of the dangers of interference.

But although the increased attention to the lives of children was applauded by some late Victorian commentators and frowned upon by others, what no one denied was that it had happened: a vast change of attitude had taken place. In public life the effects of this change were palpably apparent. In 1900 children no longer pulled tubs along the tunnels of mines or slaved for a pittance in fetid kilns. Laws protected them at school, work and home. More of them could read and more were surviving to do so. Specialist studies had begun to be made of their capabilities and their needs. In private life, too, it would appear that their status had changed, even though the evidence here is more abstract and impressionistic. Certainly parents were encouraged throughout the century to take more account of their children. A debate on childhood was inaugurated which fell into three different phases. The first was the demand for greater domesticity and more order and consistency in training. The second was the outcome of this demand, the growth of concern and attention: either a religious insistence on continual supervision or a Romantic celebration of the innocence of children's ways. The third was a reaction against the second phase—a distaste both for all kinds of meddlesomeness and for excessive idealisation. Parental duty was first established as a worthy objective, secondly propagated in various ways, and finally—among certain writers—resented. But the total effect of all these phases was an unprecedented expansion of interest in the young.

It seems, then, that the article in *Chambers's Journal* in 1887 with which this survey began was accurate enough in its general conclusion: it was indeed a massive understatement that 'this sympathy with the concerns of childhood has increased of late years'. It might be remembered that the author of this article went on to adduce, as part of his evidence, the change in children's literature: 'Mrs Ewing's genial teachings have superseded Mrs Sherwood's grim severities.' This remark, though apparently casual, opens up a new and curious field for the study of family relations; but the development of thought within children's books deserves a chapter on its own.

Chapter III
CHILDREN'S BOOKS

' "This is a child!" Haigha replied eagerly . . . "We only
found it today. . . ."
"I always thought they were fabulous monsters!" said
the Unicorn. "Is it alive?" '
    LEWIS CARROLL, *Through the Looking-Glass* (1872)

(i)

Children's books are written by adults; they depict the child as
his elders imagine him. They chart not so much the changing
ways of childhood as the development of the adult imagination.

It is easy to see that this is so with the early, didactic juvenile
books. Contrived, stilted, they obviously throw less light on
their child heroes—or villains—than on their authors. Paralysing
children in moral tableaux, they inflate their misdeeds and de-
press their high spirits for the sake of taboo and exhortation: what
emerges is the author's philosophy, not the features of any con-
ceivable child. But, it may be objected, what of the later, non-
didactic books—may not they tell us more about children's real
behaviour? Certainly we may get more of the truth from an
author who is intent on observation rather than moral improvement; memory, too, may take him closer to what childhood feels
like from the inside. But the fact is that non-didactic books can
contain their own distortions. At the end of the nineteenth century a genre emerged in which children were portrayed as winsome pixies, or else as apple-cheeked rollicking scamps lost always
in innocent fun. These books simply replaced didacticism with
gaseous wish-fulfilment; like their predecessors what they revealed
was less the true fabric of children's lives than their authors'
obsessions and needs.

It would be useless, therefore, to examine nineteenth-century
children's books in the hope of discovering how children really
conducted themselves, and how their conduct changed; how, for
example, the majority of children behaved towards their parents
at different periods. At best the books can only yield clues—not
full and reliable fact. Nor, by discovering which children's books

sold well, can we map out with accuracy the shifts in juvenile preference. For one thing, the area of choice widened enormously after about 1850; the earlier big-sellers had comparatively little competition. Then again, we do not know how many children chose their own books; the sales of some maudlin evergreens seem to have been bolstered by Sunday schools and well-meaning aunts. A third reason is that, for much of the century, children's reading remained the same: they read books originally meant for adults. Amy Cruse, in *The Victorians and Their Books*, claims that the stories most widely read by young people were *The Pilgrim's Progress*, *Robinson Crusoe* and *The Arabian Nights*. In 1884 a questionnaire for children from eleven to nineteen, sent to all types of school and eliciting answers from 790 boys and over a thousand girls, found that the two most popular authors were Dickens and Scott (Salmon, 1888).

What, then, can we discover from nineteenth-century children's books? Not the behaviour or tastes of children but the minds of adults. We discover the authors and their changing ideas about childhood—their conception of its role, its rights and obligations, its permissible range of thought and activity. And, if we confine ourselves to best sellers, we unearth some of the influences on other Victorian writers, provide a context for themes in Dickens and Jane Austen and the revulsion of feeling in Butler and Gosse.

The following is not a comprehensive survey of adult attitudes in nineteenth-century children's fiction. It is a comparison of 'popular' juvenile books read by early Victorian children with a selection of those available later in the century. Its aim is to illustrate changes in the conception of parent-child relations: old and new ideas about parental power and privilege and about children's rightful demeanour towards their elders. It is hoped that this will enlarge the frame of reference for the study of later authors.

The fundamental change in nineteenth-century children's books is clear enough: the move from instruction to entertainment. The early books instilled facts and morals in a hastily assembled fictional setting; the emphasis was on adult wisdom. Later, as the discovery of childhood progressed, the emphasis shifted to children themselves; their childish ways were not to be plucked out but rather to be cultivated. They were allowed not only to learn from their elders but also—occasionally—to laugh at them. Interest in childhood eventually blunted the edge of adult authority.

Eventually; its first effects were quite the opposite; it spurred parents into oppressive concern for their children. The emergence of special books for juvenile readers at the end of the eighteenth century was certainly an indication that childhood was no longer being ignored, but, as we have seen, the new interest in children didn't always entail any power or wish to enter into their minds. Lectures and sermons of every sort were the staple fare in fiction for adults and a similar diet of wholesome gruel was assumed to be healthy for children. Moreover most of those who wrote for the young were conservative in their approach; even the crusading champions of Rousseau fell back very often on worldly prudence and traditional common sense. As for Evangelical writers, it was natural that their interest in the training of children should be tinctured by their doctrines of sin.

(ii)

In the first decades of the nineteenth century a handful of Georgian children's books dominated juvenile literature. They were: Thomas Day's Sandford and Merton (published in 3 volumes, 1783–9); Mrs Barbauld's Hymns in Prose (1781) and Evenings at Home (6 volumes, 1792–6); Mrs Trimmer's Fabulous Histories (1786); the various tales of Maria Edgeworth; and Mrs Sherwood's The History of the Fairchild Family (1818). All these works were best sellers. All were reprinted continually till the end of the century (though with alterations, as we shall see). Amy Cruse believes that the juvenile reading list in 'almost every early Victorian family where the children's education and general reading were carefully supervised' would include The Fairchild Family, Sandford and Merton and Maria Edgeworth's tales. Mrs Molesworth, born in 1839, recorded how children of her generation always had this same group of books to read (Molesworth, 1891). The books aged ungracefully, but many late Victorians looked back on them with affection (one might see, for example, Mrs E. M. Field, The Child and His Book).

It is important to remember that these Georgian books were among the very first children's stories by personal authors. The market for children's literature had been opened up in the mid-eighteenth century by two publishers, Thomas Boreman and John Newbery, who specialised in anonymous tales to amuse and instruct the young. Prior to that children could read fables, chap-book stories, adapted novels and a few nursery rhymes, as well as hosts of stolid school-works—ABCs, primers, spelling-books. They could sample the seventeenth- and eighteenth-century puritans—Bunyan, Watts and James Janeway. Or they might be given moral tracts and manuals of etiquette. These, preoccupied with Christian homily and heroic exempla, rarely condescended to consider real children. Inspection of some late eighteenth-century tracts shows how far at that time the discovery of childhood had yet to go.

It was from such flinty soil, fertilised by more generous theories of childhood's importance, that the early, didactic children's books sprang. Their didacticism is of two kinds: the Rationalist, repre-sented by Day, Mrs Barbauld and Maria Edgeworth; and the Evangelical, represented by Mrs Sherwood. Mrs Trimmer embodies the first tipping over into the second.

Rationalist parents and guardians are usually portrayed as cool, self-possessed creatures, always ready with a superior smile and a wealth of antithetical advice. Their principles are benign but immovably austere, their monologues sound like extracts from an encyclopaedia, and sometimes are. The children, on the other hand, are rumbustious, unthinking pleasure-hounds who, however, respond immediately to Socratic dialogues. Grown-ups can soon damp their reasonless elation. Obedience is expected, but not wearisomely harped upon. Children *must* obey after rational explanations.

Doyen of the Rationalists was Thomas Day, who wrote *Sandford and Merton*, so he said in its preface, to rectify 'the total want of proper books' for children. Day venerated Rousseau, and even read his books, though apparently without much attention. He said that *Émile* was 'a most extraordinary work—the more I read, the more I admire. . . . Every page is big with important truth' (Edgeworth, 1821). Rousseau, however, believed that adults should not reason with young children, for reason is a mature faculty: 'If children understood reason they would not need education.' Day ignored this. Likewise the first task of *Sandford and Merton*'s six-year-old educational guinea-pig is to learn to read, whereas Rousseau had said: 'Reading is the curse of child-hood. . . . *Émile*, at twelve years old, will hardly know what a book is.' Day picked up Rousseau's fondness for the natural, and seems to have lifted certain details directly from *Émile*, but many of his master's most basic principles he simply left untouched.

Sandford and Merton is the story of a good boy and a bad one. Sturdy, animal-loving Harry Sandford, the son of a bluff, honest farmer, has been trained according to Nature under the worthy clergyman Mr Barlow. Lazy, priggish Tommy Merton, son of a prosperous merchant, is also placed under Barlow's care when his father fears for his character. At the end of three volumes Tommy has been redeemed by Barlow's lectures and Harry's good example.

This central story line is brightened up by various tales that Barlow gets the boys to read. Frequently these are glutted with factual information, on geography, astronomy, history or whatever. In the first volume alone Tommy learns about building, gardening, crocodiles and the manufacture of cider. Or else the tales introduce protagonists corresponding to Harry and Tommy, pitting hard work, charity, and thrift against indolence, meanness and improvidence. Sometimes the tales are animal fables, but here again the moral contrast is maintained: all animals are sheep or goats in the end. Tommy keeps backsliding, Harry radiates goodness, and Barlow preaches Simplicity in convoluted syntax.

Real parents are relegated to the bottom of the cast-list, for Barlow is, with grim zeal, *in loco parentis.* Harry's mother and father, seen rarely, have all the nobility one would expect from such natural, earthy folk. With Tommy's parents Day ran up against a problem. Tommy was supposed to be spoilt, so someone had to spoil him; but to make both parents imperfect could be hazardous, subversive. Accordingly, all Tommy's faults are backdated to his mother: her witless snobbery has made him what he is. Mr Merton escapes with his dignity unimpaired. Even he, however, cannot compete with Barlow in militant rectitude. Parents too, it seems, must meekly accept lectures when virtue like Barlow's is on the offensive. Child readers no doubt relished the episode in which Mr Merton gets a taste of the medicine he has prescribed for his son: consoling him about Tommy's conduct Barlow smoothly enquires:

> You have, I doubt not, read the story of Polemo, who, from a debauched young man, became a celebrated philosopher, and a model of virtue, only by attending a single moral lecture. Indeed, said Mr Merton, I am ashamed to confess

that the various employments and amusements in which I
have passed the greater part of my life, have not afforded
me as much leisure for reading as I could wish. You will
therefore oblige me very much by repeating the story you
allude to.

And Barlow does oblige the sheepish father, for the space of
seven pages. The passage, incidentally, presents a fair sample of
the book's style. Day noted proudly in his preface that 'as to the
language, I have endeavoured to throw into it a greater degree of
elegance and ornament than is usually met with in such com-
positions'. Maria Edgeworth said Day always spoke like a book—
'and I do believe he always thought in the same full-dress style'.

Sandford and Merton, which Gosse's father 'admired extremely',
is awe-inspiringly didactic. Its two heroes first meet when Harry
obligingly frees Tommy from a snake that has wrapped round
his leg. The whiff of unreality—for surely it's not symbolic?—is
typical, and derives from the book's need to keep a moral crisis
continually on the boil. Day heaves a literally-meant moral into
any setting he can find, and ends up with yarns like the one about
the Russian sailors in East Spitsbergen : this story shows Tommy
how much better it is to be a worker than a gentleman if you
find yourself stranded on an arctic island. Similarly, Barlow's parish
seems to consist almost entirely of brigands and cripples, snares
to be avoided and material for charity.

What is the morality that the children must imbibe? On moral
matters Day had two main tenets. The first was that poverty
makes for virtue. Again and again we see the ennobling effects
of discomfort and a meagre diet. 'The rich do nothing and produce nothing, and the poor every thing that is really useful', says
Barlow. He concludes, though, not that the poor are exploited,
but that they are morally superior. They must be, since they are
closer to Nature. Luxury corrupts; Day expends much energy
denouncing the fripperies of fashion, the rotten effete vanity of
the expensively dressed, their gowns and powders and—worst of
all—shoe-buckles (on the subject of shoe-buckles Day once had
an argument with a French fencing master that led to his friend
Edgeworth's violent intervention). All the hollow pomps of the
rich—playing cards or listening to opera—the poor have honesty
enough to disdain.

Day's second moral tenet was that virtue pays. This comes out
most clearly in the story called 'The Good-Natured Little Boy'.

Out for the day to perform an errand, the boy helps a half-starved dog, a horse about ready for the knacker's yard, a blind man stuck in a pond, and a legless sailor. He even manages to fit in his errand, but his philanthropy makes him so late that he loses his way in the dark. The moment, however, he is menaced by robbers, his decrepit beneficiaries come speedily to his service (the ruffians are repulsed by the legless sailor on the blind man's shoulders). 'I see by this', declares the boy, 'that a good turn is never lost.' In real life Day was not so sanguine. He eventually came to believe that 'generosity is more frequently injurious than beneficial' (Edgeworth, 1821). But in the book the consequences of generosity are seductively dramatised. When Tommy saves a poor woman from the bailiffs by discharging her debt, she throws herself before him 'embracing his knees and kissing his feet'. The process is almost mechanistic: volume three, page 99— Tommy gives a hard-up stranger a shilling; volume three, page 101—the stranger saves Tommy from a savage dog. When Tommy goes to stay with Harry's parents, Farmer Sandford turns down Mr Merton's grateful offer of cash on the ground that it would make his family lose their simple pleasures; nevertheless Mr Merton buys him a fine new team of horses. Virtue is its own (material) reward.

It is obvious that Day's two tenets engender an absurdity. If poverty makes for virtue, and virtue prospers, then poverty makes for prosperity. The virtue of Day's characters dismantles itself.

Day was at one with the Evangelicals in an aversion from wealth and worldly pleasure. He differed about Original Sin. Rousseau had said there was no such thing and Day apparently thought the same in private. He vacillates somewhat in *Sandford and Merton*. Barlow says he is 'convinced that human nature is infinitely more weak than wicked; and that the greater part of all bad conduct springs rather from want of firmness than from any settled propensity to evil'. In its context 'firmness' seems to mean not parental severity but self-discipline and perseverance in good habits. Disbelief in Original Sin weakened the rationale for an early and astringent supervision of children. No wonder Mrs Sherwood was to talk with contempt about the covert infidelities of 'Mr Day, Mr Edgeworth, and all that party' (Sherwood, 1854). But Day could not quite embrace Natural Innocence. About Tommy's character he cannot make up his mind. Tommy, we are told at the outset, 'had naturally very good dispositions, although he had been suffered to acquire many bad habits'. But when he is corrupted by the wastrel sons of the gentry, we discover he 'had . . . resumed his natural character'. Likewise Barlow records his admiration for 'the savage grandeur of man in his most simple state', but immediately condemns the savage's 'passion for revenge'. The conflict betrays itself most sharply in Day's remarks about animals. When a cat kills Tommy's pet robin, Barlow tells him that instead of being angry he should 'endeavour to teach the cat that she must no longer prey upon little birds'. Two pages later he informs the children that the 'natural food' of cats consists of 'birds, and such small animals as they can seize by violence'. Nature, then, does not always know best; animals are not innately benign. Elsewhere, though, Barlow takes trust in natural decency so far as to commend the wisdom of expostulating with an enraged elephant. Day's uncertainty on this issue eventually proved of consequence, for in 1789 he was riding an unbroken colt, in the belief that benevolence could tame any animal, when it threw him to the ground and killed him.

Maria Edgeworth thought *Sandford and Merton* 'a delightful book' and Mrs Barbauld honoured Day as 'distinguished . . . for courage and presence of mind'. Their own works are similar in tenor and intention. In *Evenings at Home* Mrs Barbauld arranges parents and children in teacher-pupil postures, then wheels out the usual mass of information on leguminous plants and why the earth goes round the sun. She urges stoicism, religious tolerance and the importance of 'taking pains'. Like Day she scorns the adulation of rank, but she is far less willing to canonise the poor: the best she can do is approve of them for being 'content with their lot, and free from anxious cares and repinings'. Also like Day is her easy acceptance of the family hierarchy. It can be seen in her *Hymns in Prose for Children*, a blend of theology and idyll which supplied most Victorian youngsters, including Butler's Ernest Pontifex, with their earliest moral ideas:

> The father, the mother, and the children, make a family; the father is the master thereof. . . . They kneel down together and praise God every night and every morning with one voice; they are very closely united, and are dearer to each other than any strangers.

It is a simple statement, balanced, reliable, gnomically assured; it has no need to insist testily on obedience and submission.

Maria Edgeworth shared Day's rationalist approach but her didacticism was more discreet. She produced genuine stories, with suspense and lively dialogue, not just vehicles for instruction. In *The Parent's Assistant* (1796) the moral emerges from the stories without being doggedly hammered out at the end, though the children do sometimes depart with a rueful resolve to behave better next time. Her most famous children's tale, 'The Purple Jar' (in *Early Lessons*, 1801), reveals at its grittiest the unyielding practicality of the Rationalist parent. For a present a little girl prefers a chemist's purple jar to what her mother recommends, a pair of shoes. She discovers her mistake at leisure. She is sorry to have chosen some useless coloured water when her shoes gradually wear out and at last make her miss an outing she had longed for. Her mother looks on with quiet satisfaction.

The writings of Sarah Trimmer, the first woman involved in the Sunday school movement (Balfour, 1854), provide a bridge between the Rationalist and the Evangelical attitudes to children. Her famous *The History of the Robins* (first called *Fabulous Histories*) is predominantly Rationalist. But her private journal and her propagandist periodicals disclose a temperament more fervently religious than anything in Day, Mrs Barbauld or Miss Edgeworth.

The History of the Robins tells how two children, Frederick and Harriet Benson, learn to be kind to a nest of robins. Sections dealing with the Benson family alternate with those about the redbreasts. The baby robins are called Robin, Dicky, Flapsy and Pecksy, but the whimsicality we might expect from such names (the last two borrowed from a Newbery publication) could never live within the lumbering rhythms of Mrs Trimmer's prose. Mrs Trimmer was solemn. She explained in her introduction that the bird-conversations in her book were not authentic—'for that it is impossible we should ever understand'.

The book employs all the Rationalist methods but scrupulously shuns any 'levelling' sentiments. It clings fast to respectable values. The children learn to be kind to animals, but the receptive, middle-class nestlings learn more: they must avoid 'bad company' and comments on personal appearance, maintain moderation and politely hand round the spiders. Other objects of attack include laziness, hasty judgement and the evils of backbiting, both figurative and literal. But what ornithology enforces most is the necessity of obeying one's parents. Mrs Trimmer reverts continually to this theme, underscores it with singular vehemence. She introduces two children, Lucy and Edward, whose thoughtless cruelty is caused by absence of parental control. She provides her good robin, Pecksy, with sentiments of treacly compliance:

> Pecksy had no outward charms to recommend her to notice; but these defects were amply supplied by the sweetness of her disposition, which was amiable to the greatest degree. Her temper was constantly serene, she was ever attentive to the happiness of her parents, and would not have grieved them for the world.

For her parents, Pecksy, the paragon of all feathered virtue, can sing out paragraphs-full of flattery and gratitude. Her deference can outdo their strictest commands: 'Pecksy answered, that she knew the value of parental instruction so well, that she should certainly treasure up in her heart every maxim of it.'

The book's parents are so keen on being obeyed that they even begin to give reasons. Mrs Benson says: 'Children can do nothing towards their own support; therefore it is particularly requisite, that they should be dutiful and respectful to those, whose tenderness and care are constantly exerted for their benefit.' Father Redbreast puts it more bluntly: 'If you persist in obstinacy, I will certainly turn you out of the nest before you can fly.'

Such explicit insistence on obedience was unusual among the Rationalists, but Mrs Trimmer was an authoritarian. She liked an accepted hierarchy of power, in society as well as in the family. This comes out faintly in *The History of the Robins*. Pondering a beehive, Mrs Benson declares: 'There is something very wonderful . . . in the strong attachment these little creatures have to their sovereign, and very instructive too.' But for Mrs Trimmer's mature views on civil and filial government we must turn to *The Guardian of Education*.

This periodical, which Mrs Trimmer conducted from 1802 to 1806, supplies invaluable evidence about attitudes to children at the beginning of the nineteenth century. Mrs Trimmer had already stated unequivocally in an earlier periodical, *The Family Magazine*, that children should always submit to their parents—for two reasons: because the Bible said so and because parents paid for the child's upbringing (Trimmer, 1789). But it was after the French Revolution had threatened both altar and throne that she saw fit to affirm her opinions at length; both religious and civil authority, she feared, stood in need of desperate defence.

The Guardian of Education was set up to combat 'a conspiracy against Christianity' in educational and children's books. It inspected hundreds of stories for any taint of infidelity. It opened its columns to embittered emigré priests. It poured out hysterical abuse of Rousseau, Voltaire, Hume—even Pope. It advised parents how to oppose the 'nefarious designs' : with strictness, severity, unrelaxed supervision. Its importance is twofold: it reveals the impact of the Revolution on domestic life; and it casts an interesting sidelight on the works of those like Day.

Fear of the Revolution keyed up religious zeal and thereby harmonised with the Evangelical temper of the times. Mrs Trimmer belonged to the Established Church and was anxious to disown 'the Enthusiasts'. But she shared their perfervid advocacy of the earliest possible religious training. Like them she linked parental and religious authority. Where she differed, and showed her Anglicanism, was in connecting these with the social power structure. Her religious and familial fears have a political inspiration. Children must be dealt with severely to uphold not only religion but also the very concept of authority and rank. She quotes with approval from an author (Dr Barrow) who maintained that a revolutionary temperament was the outcome of an indulged childhood: 'Parental authority is universally relaxed, and in many instances nearly relinquished'; allowed to disobey parents, the child grows up to disobey teachers and then aspires to 'transgress the laws of his country, and eventually to overthrow them'.

Hence the fierce calls for the child's suppression. Mrs Trimmer talks of the 'good purpose of keeping him in subjection'. She recommends firm handling, solitary confinement and the use of the rod. When and how these persuasions are to be administered she does not fully lay down, but we can get some idea by glancing briefly at a book by a close friend of hers, Dorothy Kilner's *The Village School*. This was a collection of crudely punitive tales to deter seven-year-olds from telling fibs or missing their lessons. Its parents' methods are unsentimental, to say the least. When a boy annoys the local schoolmistress, his father breezes into the classroom declaring he will 'soon give him what he deserves, and take the skin off his back', and proceeds to horsewhip him all the way home; he then locks him in a 'dark closet' all night, 'for such a naughty child did not deserve to go to bed'. A little girl who should have conned her lessons earlier pores over them on the way to school; consequently, she trips up and smashes her face. Wailing and pouring blood, she runs home to Mama, who draws the benevolent conclusion: 'Though I am sorry you are hurt, still I do really think you deserve to be so for your own indolence and folly.' The book's knockabout conventions show that its deterrents are to some extent exaggerated. What remains significant is that writers like Miss Kilner and Mrs Trimmer considered such warnings appropriate, and that at the turn of the century there was a frightened clamour to make the warnings a reality.

The Guardian of Education also reminds us what Day and Mrs Barbauld looked like to an Evangelically-inclined Anglican of the upper-middle class. Mrs Trimmer was not satisfied with Day's murmurs of homage to the Gospel. She scented the Rousseauist in him and condemned *Sandford and Merton* as fraught with 'great danger of sowing the seeds of democracy and republicanism in the youthful breast'. She had many faults to find with *Evenings at Home*. It failed to imply a literal interpretation of Scripture. It could impress children 'with a prejudice against the higher orders of society'. And one of its animal stories, which had a dying cat declare, 'Adieu, my dear children. . . . perhaps we shall meet again', provoked her to comment: 'There is nothing revealed in Scripture concerning *a future state for brutes*.' She praised *Hymns in Prose*, but took exception to a line about skipping lambs that said, 'We will not offer you in sacrifice.' We realise how mild and secular were Day and Mrs Barbauld compared with the Establishment of their age.

But it was in Mrs Trimmer's mould that the future was cast. She laced the earnest pedantry of the Rationalists with Evangelical ardour, and Evangelicalism was to be the biggest influence on later didactic books for children. Part of her programme—strictness prompted by political fear—did not survive, but Evangelical strictness did: it was something more possessive, more pious and heartfelt. It spread throughout society and its proposals inform most early nineteenth-century articles on the family. In theory, at least, it did not demand severity, merely firmness: religious concern and systematic control. How it worked out in practice we can find from Mrs Sherwood.

The History of the Fairchild Family must rank as a major document of nineteenth-century puritanism. It moved beyond Evangelical circles into Sunday schools and middle-class homes everywhere. Harvey Darton, the chief historian of juvenile literature, believes it 'was known to almost all English children up to about 1887' (Darton, 1958). First published in 1818, with parts added in 1842 and 1847, the book was reprinted, with abridgements, well into the present century.

Late in life Mrs Sherwood described the nature of her own upbringing. She was a happy child, she said. During the day, from the age of six to thirteen, she had to wear an iron collar round her neck and a backboard strapped over her shoulders. Thus attired, she did all her lessons standing in stocks. She was fed on dry bread and cold milk. She never sat on a chair in her mother's presence. All this she looked back on without bitterness—indeed she spoke wistfully of her 'beloved father', and praised her mother's 'undeviating strictness'. Against her parents she brought but one reproach: neither of them, she said, 'had any distinct ideas of human depravity' (Sherwood, 1854).

The same deficiency could not be remarked in Mr and Mrs Fairchild, who spend most of their time defining depravity for their three children, Lucy, Emily and Henry (who spend most of *theirs* exemplifying it). Lucy is 'about eight', Emily 'next in age', and Henry 'between five and six' (thus the first three editions; subsequently each age was raised by a year). The Fairchild children are peculiar. They combine thieving, lying and mutual spite with an unstoppable propensity for pious utterance. The peculiarity derives from the book's double intention: while exposing 'the exceeding vileness of our hearts', it also wishes to demonstrate, in the words of the subtitle, 'the importance and effects of a religious education'. As a result, its triumphant moral comes out somewhat askew. We see that the parents who have trained their children to perfection have only to put a foot out of the front door for their little ones' innate depravity to erupt in glorious force. One day when the parents are out, for instance, the well-trained trio devote the morning to missing prayers, dismembering breakfast, chasing a pig and getting drunk on cider. (At least they get 'drunk' in the earliest editions. Later they got 'tipsy' and by 1902, 'giddy'. Mrs Sherwood was indeed watered down.) During the evening frolics, Henry has his coat torn and Emily gets her teeth knocked out. It all goes to prove that their hearts are full of sin.

At the same time, however, their mouths are full of religion. To call the Fairchild children religiously precocious would be an understatement: each one is a Bible concordance on legs. They

volunteer lengthy but word-perfect renditions of Scripture, excitedly averring, for example, that they 'know what the children
of Noah did in the Plain of Shinar'. The enthusiasm is all-per-
vasive. When Mr Fairchild brings home a globe, Emily at once
asks to be shown where the Garden of Eden was. During another
cosy chat Mr Fairchild, with a hefty quotation from Hebrews 11,
extols the fortitude of the faithful, remarking how they were
stoned, sawn asunder, tempted, and slain with the sword. ' "Oh
Papa," said Lucy, "what pretty verses!" ' We are unsurprised to
learn that 'of all the days in the week, Sunday was the day the
children loved best'. And if we query the announcement that
Henry is going to be a clergyman, it is only because we feel he
could rout most theologians already. Accusations of Scriptural
forced-feeding, however, Mrs Sherwood adroitly insures against:
she carefully writes in a miscreant who dubs premature piety
'laughable'.

The book draws up a complete religious agenda for Evangelical
children to work through. Heading it, of course, is conviction of
sin. Each chapter ends with a prayer that provides the children
with lines like, 'My heart is altogether filthy and evil', 'our hearts
are so exceeding wicked, so vile . . . When I speak, I sin; when I
am silent, I sin.' Coupled with this is the terror of hell. 'Had I my
deserts, I should now be living with the devil in hell', the children intone. Lucy and Henry warn a pert playmate that she
might end up in everlasting fire; their worries are well-founded—
she does. The desire to save children from eternal torment was
what made temporary torment so righteous and benign. No doubt
infant readers (or listeners) duly shuddered at the episode in
which Mr Fairchild, having caned his children for squabbling,
shows them how naughty they have been by taking them out to
a dark wood to look at the gibbeted and decomposing corpse of
a man who murdered his brother (Cain and Abel is the text for
the day). The book's savage parts can sometimes slice open dark
fears. But Mr Fairchild's motive is soul-salvation: for the ill-fated
brothers, he points out, 'when they first began to quarrel in their
play, as you did this morning, did not think that death and hell
would be the end of their quarrels'.

Physical death itself is on the list of subjects to be studied. Its
terrors, so the theory goes, will bounce children into Faith. It
will also act as a vivid reminder that judgement can overtake
them at any time. Coffins and funerals are never far away

in this book, which, all tolled, lays at least ten of its characters to rest: the volume is a pocket mortuary. Mr Fairchild's preaching powers are always improved by the proximity of a corpse. When Roberts the gardener dies, his widow invites Mr Fairchild to come over and look at the body. Mr Fairchild accepts and considerately enquires whether the children would care to come too: 'You never saw a corpse, I think?' They say they have not (they apparently forget the man on the gibbet, but perhaps he was too crumbly to count), but add that they 'would like to see one'. They all walk to the house of death, quoting texts on the subject, and then Mrs Sherwood describes Roberts' body in detail: the smell of its putrefaction, its 'ghastly and horrible' appearance. So it is that Mr Fairchild, closeted in a small room with a two-days'-dead body, three small children and the body's ex-wife, begins to hold forth, declaring that, though he has high hopes for the man's soul, the 'taint and corruption of the flesh' just go to show the 'horrible nature' of sin and how the sinful body must fall to dust in the grave. ' "Oh, sir!" said Mrs Roberts, "it comforts me to hear you talk!" '

After Bible-reading and corpse-visiting the next stimulus to conversion is meticulous self-scrutiny. Mrs Fairchild gives Lucy a diary in which to write down her naughty deeds. Lucy scribbles away in this sin-ledger ('When Papa gave Henry the strawberry I was angry again' etc.), then runs and shows it her mother, saying: 'Oh, Mamma, Mamma! . . . you cannot think what a wicked heart I have got! Here is my journal; I am ashamed to shew it to you.' The most virtuous boy in the book is little Charles Trueman, because he can always find vice in himself: 'He was never heard to speak of himself but as a sinner.'

By the book's theology, the smallest misdeed can entail damnation. Sin is sin, a violation of God's will. At one point Mrs Fairchild confesses the wicked ways of her own childhood. She tells how, as a little girl, she once broke a plate and cunningly pinned the crime on her aunts' tabby—'and . . . I was glad that puss was beaten instead of me'. Then, on a Sunday, she shinned up a cherry tree and picked forbidden fruit. These surprisingly spirited escapades she calls 'those great sins which I had been guilty of . . . lying, stealing, and deceiving my aunts'. Details of an offence are unimportant; what matters is the sin-category it comes under.

Moreover an offence cannot be judged in isolation; it is weighted with the burden of malice aforethought, it is the climax of cumulative wickedness. To us it may seem hard that young Henry, after stealing an apple and failing to own up, should be locked in a little room at the top of the house all day, denied food and left in darkness, crying in fear lest he 'should die, and go to hell'. But Mrs Fairchild explains: 'The great sin you committed this morning was growing in your evil heart some days before it came out.' Henry first looked at the apple, then fancied it, then desired it; thus swelling, his thoughts at last gave horrible birth: he ate it.

God, the children are told, is always watching such sins. And it is graphically proved true when Emily takes to pilfering preserved damsons (fruit-filching again—the Fairchilds are biblical even in their vices). Emily is afflicted with terrifying dreams 'that a dreadful Eye was looking upon her from above. Wherever she went, she thought this Eye followed her with angry looks'. The dreams are 'so horrible . . . that at length she awoke, screaming violently'. She falls into a fever, nearly dies, but survives to repent. She praises God: 'How good, how very good it was of Him not to send me to hell for my wickedness!'

Usually, though, the parents do not need the help of God's Eye in keeping a look-out on their children's mischief. They are tiptoeingly attentive themselves. Mr Fairchild stands still on the stairs to 'hearken' to trouble in the nursery. Mrs Fairchild enters the girls' bedroom unseen to overhear pride and sedition. Similarly, a good old lady called Mrs Howard listens in on whole dramas of childhood malice. Of course, the adults are not depicted as snoopers; the motif is meant to discourage children from thinking they can get away with misconduct.

Obedience to parents features as one of the primary virtues, no doubt because it is a prerequisite of the whole Evangelical programme. Mrs Sherwood devotes several chapters to proofs of its necessity. Her first argument is starkly terroristic; she thrusts home the Fifth Commandment in a chapter entitled, literally enough, 'Fatal Effects of Disobedience to Parents'. The exciting tale is roughly sketched with a few didactic lines: Godless Lady Noble had told her Godless daughter, Augusta, not to carry candles about the house; but the child disobeyed, was dreadfully burnt, and 'died in agonies last night—a warning to all children how they presume to disobey their parents!' (This cheerful news, incidentally, is brought by Mrs Roberts, while her husband is still decaying in her upstairs room.)

Next Mrs Sherwood tries pathos. Mary Bush, an ageing morsel of holy poverty, tells the children how blessed they are in their parents. They should be dutiful to them, for the time will come when they will be taken away and the children will be sorry to have been disobedient. 'Disobedience to parents', she says, '. . . is one of those sins to which man's vile heart is naturally inclined; just as it is inclined to murder, adultery, covetousness, and hatred to God' (she is probably taking the sentiments from Romans 1:28-31). Mary Bush then recites the touching story of how she herself lived to regret the way she hoodwinked her doddering old mother, whose lengthy deathbed pieties stabbed her to the heart. Lucy and Emily have a weep, and the chapter concludes with a child's prayer that he may behave well to his parents and avoid, as it interestingly adds, 'shunning their company, as my sinful heart would have me to do'.

Finally, Mrs Sherwood lays out a full exposition of the rationale and methods of parental power, in a chapter called 'Story of the Absence of God', which is about the absence of Mr Fairchild. Master Henry mulishly refuses to learn his first Latin lesson, even after being stimulated by a diet of bread and water. 'Mr Fairchild then took a small horsewhip, and, making John hold him, he flogged him well, and sent him to bed, telling him he must say the lesson before breakfast.' But Henry does not say it, for he knows that if he learns this first lesson he will have to learn all the subsequent ones, and he fears he is unequal to the task. Mr Fairchild therefore declares: 'Henry, listen to me: when wicked men obstinately defy and oppose the power of God, he gives them up to their own bad hearts.' An amazing disclosure seems imminent, but the claim tapers off into analogy: 'I stand in the place of God to you, whilst you are a child'. And so Henry is debarred and excommunicated from the presence of his father. Family and servants all shun him too, though Lucy lets the side down by spiriting him a note. Left in snuffling solitude, he luckily chances upon little Charles Trueman, who, with some discourses on God's wrath that would be the envy of Jonathan Edwards, eventually pulps him into piety.

The Evangelicals revitalised patriarchy by their explicit insistence that parents were surrogates for God. It was an attractive notion. As late as 1890 one can find a 'modernist' educator calling parents 'the immediate and personally appointed deputies of the Almighty King' (Mason, 1890).

Mrs Sherwood considers parental authority so important that she is willing to suspend other doctrines in its favour. She believes strongly in hard work and universal depravity, yet Mr Fairchild, as F. Anstey remarked, appears to have no occupation apart from being oppressively good, and we never see Mrs Fairchild struggling against 'the wicked inclinations of this vile body' which she claims are always causing her trouble. The parents are exempted so as to be ever-present and ever-esteemed: they toil not, neither do they sin.

The Fairchild regimen is one of benevolent severity, and it should be remembered that the parents, when they are not laying on the horsewhip or a visit to the gallows, are very loving to their children, taking them on picnics and kissing them while they sleep. Furthermore the book's second and third volumes, written many years afterwards, are much milder, and startle us by impugning severe punishment and making Mr Fairchild speak 'jestingly'. In fact Mrs Sherwood changed her theology; she so frightened herself with reflections on hell-fire that she decided to believe in final salvation for all, a doctrine that offended the orthodox and, in 1856, incited the *Christian Observer* to protest against 'the morbid cravings of her . . . benevolence'. Her books were also expurgated over the years, as we can see from the edition of 1902, introduced by Mary E. Palgrave. The introduction lets us know what 'an interesting and attractive person' Mrs Sherwood was and hopes she will win more 'lovers and admirers' through 'this new edition of a dear old book'. But this new edition, tricked out with sugary illustrations, strips the dear old book of all its hymns and all its self-flagellating prayers, all the corrupting corpses, and canings, and spasms of guilt-filled terror; gone are the gloating funeral descriptions, the gibbet, and the macabre evocations of hell: Mrs Sherwood is dexterously gutted.

Yet despite this kind of softening and expurgation, Evangelical attitudes survived for many years. It is time to turn to books that question many of these attitudes, but it must not be inferred from these that didactic juvenile literature ever died out in the nineteenth century. Tracts and manuals for children persisted in as great abundance as in the eighteenth century; the difference was that they no longer comprised the bulk of children's reading matter, merely a fragment of it. Didactic fiction survived too. Quite late in the century some publishers for the young were still busying themselves with the plodding inculcation of platitudes. William Nimmo's of Edinburgh, for example, turned out many a tale of the 'And so Frank perished, a victim to his disobedience' type (*Do Your Duty*, 1871). What is more, didactic fiction remained popular, as is evident from the sales of Dean Farrar's notorious *Eric, or Little by Little*, a work which, as Charlotte Yonge felicitously put it, 'enforces by numerous telling examples that the sure reward of virtue is a fatal accident' (Yonge, 1869). Like *The Fairchild Family* this book, arguing that sinfulness piles up in the heart by degrees, encourages children to brood on the significance of their slightest transgressions. Or so at least it seems from the text: Farrar wished to warn against sexual malpractices and no doubt felt he had plenty to go on. When he wrote *Eric* he was working at Harrow, where, the year after its publication, the headmaster was secretly forced to resign because of an affair with a boy. But the frantic obliquity of Farrar's warnings creates only bathos and puzzlement. As far as outsiders are concerned, action and moral comment fail to tally; there is always a ludicrous disparity between what we are seeing and the noises coming over on the theological soundtrack (the metaphor is not exaggerated: parts of *Eric* are pure Hollywood). Eric, the hero, has a dark night of the soul for not rebuking a new boy who swears: his failure to speak up endows him with a 'canker' and 'crimson stains', it entails 'irreparable harm'. Another boy's bad language is stigmatised as a 'deep, intolerable, unfathomable flood of moral turpitude and iniquity'. A local publican figures improbably as a demon bent on corrupting young souls. Naturally the book sanctifies filial attachments. An early pointer to Eric's moral decline is 'the blunting of his home affections'. Eric squirms in anguished shame whenever he thinks of his worthy parents, and his ravingly spectacular death is prompted by the news that his dishonour has dealt his mother a fatal blow. 'Oh, I have killed her, I have killed my mother!' he sobs.

The huge sales of *Eric* may have been partly due to its popularity as a gift-book, but it cannot be doubted that many children really liked didactic works, or at least thought them more respectable. Take the reasons children put forward for their preferences in the previously-mentioned survey of 1884. One boy liked *The Boy's Own Paper* because it had 'no slang' and another said: 'I hail the monthly numbers of it with pleasure knowing that, as well as simply reading, I shall also be instructed.' A girl remarked approvingly of *Westward Ho!*: 'It abounds in truly *noble* characters, men who are marked by their loyalty and love for the English Church.' The moralists continued to command an audience.

Evangelical works proved particularly viable, remaining vigorous and healthy (or vigorous and morbid) until the end of the century. Dozens of S.P.C.K. stories enjoined piety and contentment on cottagers and artisans and later circulated among the higher orders as well. After *The Fairchild Family* the most popular Evangelical children's book was probably Maria Charlesworth's *Ministering Children* (1854), the heroes of which are comfortably-off youngsters who use their time and money helping a phenomenon invariably referred to as The Poor. They do this by dispensing soup and Bible quotations. The Poor prostrates itself in gratitude for the soup (though quite often expires shortly afterwards), but its appetite for the Bible quotations is even bigger, well-nigh insatiable. Kindly-stern parents regulate the philanthropic flow whenever it seems in danger of becoming imprudent, or effective. There are also boozy parents whose exemplary offspring tick them off for impious language. Hot-gospelling children were common in this kind of fiction. Often they converted their parents: in *The Fairchild Family* Lucy reads a story called 'The History of the Good Child, who was made an instrument of turning his Father and Mother to the Ways of Holiness'. It is a curious fact that power-over-parents first crept into children's books through the Chapel door.

(iii)

Didacticism survived, but it did not maintain its pre-eminence. It was subverted by notions of democracy, by the deliquescence of Christian dogma, and by a boom in publishing that extended the range of commercially attractive alternative modes. By 1844 an early review of children's literature was complaining that 'the one broad and general impression left with us is that of the excessive ardour for *teaching* which prevails throughout' (Rigby, 1844). The same reviewer stressed the uniqueness of children's requirements: 'A genuine child's book is as little like a book for grown people cut down, as the child himself is like a little old man.'

The first children's book to snap some didactic fetters was
Catherine Sinclair's *Holiday House*, published in 1839. Harvey
Darton believes it was 'the best original children's book written
up to that time', and calls it 'the first example of real laughter
and a free conscience'. Its laughter and freedom are certainly
surprising, but so is the way it mixes them with incongruous
elements of conservatism.

The book is mainly about a youngish brother and sister, Harry
and Laura, who are 'heedless lively romps'. They have an elder
brother, Frank, who is almost grown up, and they are under the
tutelage of their uncle, Major David Graham, and their grandmother, Lady Harriet. Their function is to illustrate Catherine
Sinclair's belief that children can be naughty without being
wicked—but 'naughty' is hardly the word. Harry, like Mrs Sherwood's Augusta Noble, plays with prohibited candles, but instead
of lighting the fire he must live in for all eternity, he merely
burns half the house down. Uncle David comes home and Laura
confesses that, while her brother was about this inadvertent
arson, she herself was cutting off all her hair. The response?

> 'Did any mortal ever hear of two such little torments!'
> exclaimed Major Graham, hardly able to help laughing. I
> wonder if anybody else in the world has such mischievous
> children!'

If this seems rather remote from Mrs Sherwood, it also seems a
long way from verisimilitude. Miss Sinclair over-compensates. The
book's moral atmosphere is refreshingly relaxed, but one boggles
at the children's powerhouse mischief and the adults' inability
to keep a straight face.

The idea is that if the children are truthful, generous and cheerful, they can be forgiven unintentional misconduct. Uncle David,
we are told, 'was determined to shut his eyes and say nothing, unless they did something purposely wrong'. While the children 'continue merely thoughtless and forgetful,' he says, 'I mean to have
patience a little longer before turning into a cross old uncle with
a pair of tawse'. Miss Sinclair drops out blithely heterodox
opinions on punishment. She explains that the children's dour
governess, Mrs Crabtree, whipped them every morning because
'in those days it had not been discovered that whipping is all a
mistake, and that children can be made good without it'. And in
due course she contrives Mrs Crabtree's dismissal. Harry goes in

for gambling, but instead of being flogged he is made to wear his coat inside out. At the same time, though, Miss Sinclair feels obliged to make perfunctory obeisance to convention. When Laura is caught breaking bounds, her grandmother declares:

> 'My dear girl! you must of course be severely punished for this act of disobedience. . . . Parents are appointed by God to govern their children as he governs us, not carelessly indulging their faults, but wisely correcting them. . . . I have suffered many sorrows in this world, but they always made me better in the end. . . .'

What this wigging amounts to is that Laura must memorise 'The Burial of Sir John Moore'.

Adults in *Holiday House* are often flippant and mirthful, and sometimes even the targets of flippancy and mirth. They are not always fitted out with armour-plated authority. Laura and Harry go to stay with Lord Rockville, who acts for a time as their father-figure. Bloated, impatient, unpredictably irate, he pooh-poohs the children's claim to have been pursued by a mad bull, but later he is chased by it himself, and undergoes the indignity of having to haul his corpulence into a tree. It was unusual in children's books to show adults in an ignominious situation or to represent elderly grumpiness getting its deserts. Once he has made his wheezy escape, Lord Rockville tries to deport himself with gravity in front of the children, but he soon bursts into the inevitable 'loud peals of laughter'.

Holiday House contained something else that was new and that made it historically important: one of the first literary fairy-tales in English, 'Uncle David's Nonsensical Story About Giants and Fairies'. Fairy-tales were frowned upon at the time and Miss Sinclair's wafted in some welcome fantasy. Morally, however, it is not 'nonsensical', but firmly, even gruesomely, didactic. Though in some ways a pioneer, Miss Sinclair shared the predilections of her age.

This becomes increasingly evident in the second part of the book. *Holiday House* changes in mood and structure. Until the fairy-story it is frolicsome and episodic, a cascade of juvenile mishaps and scrapes. After that it becomes more solemn and sequential, one event being shown to lead to another. We follow the career of elder brother Frank, who goes grandly to sea and comes back five years later weak with wounds and fever. Uncle David intimates to Harry and Laura that their brother may not survive the night, but in fact he remains edifyingly moribund for another twenty-seven pages. His sickbed sets the ultimate test for the children's growing self-control: any disturbance will kill him, so they have to stay perfectly composed. His death ushers in their maturity. Laura muses that it is a 'heavy stroke' from God to bring them to their right minds. The book ends in a piously improving mood far removed from that of the earlier chapters.

Two other conventional strokes pare down the book's pioneering quality. The first is the homage paid to family life. Individual adults may be fallible or ridiculous, but the concept of the family itself is sacrosanct. Before he goes away Frank sobs as 'the whole family kneeled in solemn prayer together'. Uncle David attacks boarding-schools for breaking up the intimacy of home. 'Families were intended to be like a little world in themselves', he says, and concludes: 'Nothing can be called peace on earth, which does not consist in family affection, built on a strong foundation of religion and morality.'

Secondly, Miss Sinclair's remarkable lenience shines only on the children of the respectable classes. There are keener punishments for the classes below. When Frank and Harry help to catch a boy pickpocket, a constable sums up: 'A few weeks on the treadmill now, may save him from the gallows in future.' Harry wants to give money to an urchin begging outside the window. Kind old Uncle David, however, points out that the boy would probably spend the money on drink and that one should help only those members of the poor 'who worked as long as they could'. Laura pleads that the lad looks 'almost respectable', but Lady Harriet counters: '. . . street beggars, who are young and able to work, like that boy, it is cruelty to encourage.' Uncle David then flings open the window and barks abuse at the supposed malingerer. As it happens, the boy turns out to be a representative of the respectable poor, come to tout the moral platitudes his betters believe he should have, but this twist hardly redeems the episode. Everywhere the book's benignity divides down the lines of class. A tipsy coachman deserts Harry and Laura while they are travelling with Lady Rockville and makes off to a drinking booth. A friend of Lady Rockville's rides up and lays into the offender with a riding crop. This chapter is called 'The Amusing Drive'.

The innovations of *Holiday House* are prudently diluted. Even towards the end of the century, however, few children's books risk unqualified defiance of old attitudes. Some attempt a radical treatment of parent-child relations, but even these are dutifully ballasted with tradition. The authors fear for their impressionable audience. And the later, more radical books, unlike their didactic predecessors, have little collective impact: quirky and uncorrelated, they refuse to fall easily into groups.

This is not to deny that several new species of juvenile literature evolved. They did, and they usually tore free from some aspects of didacticism. The boy's adventure story, for instance, approved of mettlesome exploits unhampered by qualms of conscience; its heroes were upright and God-fearing, but would only turn to their Bibles when they were not busy with their guns. Parents were simply pushed off-stage; not only were the exotic settings unsuitable, but, for some reason, the young heroes were often orphans, brought up by quavering, white-haired aunts or pince-nez-peering grandmothers. Fairy tales and nonsense stories also loosened the didactic grip. The publication of *Alice's Adventures in Wonderland* in 1865 is often taken to mark the real beginning of pure entertainment for children. Part of the appeal of the Alice books is the way they inflate to distortion the infant's-eye-view of grown-ups; governess huffiness and classroom instruction blur into a surrealistic jumble.

Didacticism held on more tenaciously in the domestic story for girls. Mrs Gatty and Charlotte Yonge preached submission and anxious introspection, and made their heroines timidly dutiful. The inequality of restraint imposed on girls and boys increased in Victorian children's books. There had always been a tendency, of course, for girls to be more stringently curbed. Rousseau believed that 'Woman is made to submit to man and endure even injustice at his hands', and the education he proposed for his Sophie was a crampingly domestic preparation for subservience. But although in real life Thomas Day obviously agreed with Rousseau about woman's place, in *Sandford and Merton* he goes against his master, or beyond him, by maintaining that girls, too, should be brought up according to Nature: Sophie was hyper-sensitive to dirt, but Day introduces a young lady called Miss Simmons who has 'acquired an excellent character' by plunging in cold baths and not disdaining to walk in puddles. In *The Fair-child Family* also girls are treated about the same as boys, though their equal rights often amount to no more than the privilege of sharing a whipping. But as the age and sex of children began to

D

be more carefully distinguished, the differences in upbringing considered appropriate were more insistently defined.

Only one writer for girls, Mrs Ewing, broached the subject of discord between parent and child, and then it was in a book she wrote for boys. *We and the World* (first published in *Aunt Judy's Magazine*, 1877–8) is partly a domestic and partly an adventure story. Its first half deals with the boyhood of the narrator, Jack, at home in Yorkshire. Later, after family trouble, Jack runs away to sea, pals up with a castaway (merry and Irish) and a fellow stowaway (prickly and Scottish), and off they go to see the world, encountering storms and funny Chinamen. The interesting family analysis occurs in the first part. Jack's father favours his other son, Jem. He considers Jack too bookish, Jem more practical and straightforward, more like himself. Wrongheadedly he sends the boys to a private school whose headmaster, Crayshaw, is a charlatan and a bully. The decision and its motives are probed with a sharpness unusual in the children's literature of the time. The father emerges as gullible and obstinate, defending a mistake so as not to lose face. He makes sententious appeals to the hoary wisdom of former generations, grows eloquent on what was good enough for *his* old father. The boys go to the school, endure its terrors for a time, but eventually run home. Their father's response is rapid and invidious. He sends Jem to an 'expensive school in the south', but Jack has to return to Crayshaw's. Jack spends two more years at the school before its corruption and incompetence are exposed. Even then the father does not repent. Aware that he was duped, he transfers his annoyance to Jack, complaining that the boy 'kept him in the dark' about the nature of the place.

'Ill-educated' and at a social disadvantage, Jack wishes to join the merchant navy and satisfy his long-standing, book-inspired craving for travel. Instead he is placed as an office-boy in his uncle's business. He finally makes off when he fears that the premium his father must pay to have him articled may jeopardise Jem's expensive education.

Favouritism, self-deception, inflexibility—these, in such a book, were strange qualities to ascribe to the family head. It is to Mrs Ewing's credit that she ventured a serious excursion into territory previously under taboo. It would be quite wrong, however, to regard *We and the World* as anything like a juvenile *Way of All Flesh*. The book's criticisms are cautiously tempered: vestiges of the taboo survive. In any case, moderation and restraint are Mrs Ewing's way. She avails herself of sentiment and homily, for example, but never allows them to gush forth unchecked; she keeps emotion to a manageable medium. Likewise Jack's complaints are never embittered; his tone always modulates to a shoulder-shrugging stoicism. Mrs Ewing is anxious not to damage parental and adult authority as such. Jack carefully exempts the majority of schoolmasters from his strictures on Mr Crayshaw. When he tells how his father opposed his wish to go to sea by accusing him of 'flying in the face of Providence as well as of the Fifth Commandment', he quickly adds that he means no disrespect to the 'pure and God-fearing atmosphere' in which he was lucky enough to have been brought up. These instant-stick pieties are often irritating. Occasionally, though, Jack's vacillations can increase the tension by implying unspoken pressures of resentment:

> I was selfishly absorbed in my own dreams, and I think my dear father made a mistake which is a too common bit of tyranny between people who love each other and live together. He was not satisfied with my *doing* what he liked, he expected me to *be* what he liked, that is, to be another person instead of myself.

The first fourteen words bump a little startlingly against 'made a mistake', then harder and more deliberately against 'too common' and 'tyranny'; but 'tyranny' is insulated before and after by 'bit of' and 'people who love each other'—though this last phrase tapers off in its turn to the cooler, more neutral 'live together'. The next sentence speeds up to a plain accusation that takes us a good way from the first words of the passage. Powerful grievance as well as filial respect seem evident from this stop-start method of complaint.

But though the conflict is conscientiously drawn, there is never any real doubt about Mrs Ewing's allegiance to the virtues of Home. At the end she reconciles Jack and his father—though brusquely and without any wallowing pathos—and she suggests throughout that, though 'Home' may be hard, 'the world' will probably be harder. Even on the eve of his flight Jack is made to reflect that family miseries carry a special kind of compensation:

> I began to feel what one is apt to learn too late . . . that parental blunders and injustices are the mistakes and tyrannies of a special love that one may go many a mile on one's own

> wilful way and not meet a second time. . . . Would other
> men care so much for my fate as to insist on guiding
> it by lines of their own ruling?

This thoughtfully opens up new vistas on the conflict, but
Jack's tone is too tepidly resigned. By making his reflections so
measured, Mrs Ewing must forgo any scrutiny of the more distressing emotions that might issue from such a love-hate imbroglio.
What we encounter here is one of the differences between books
for children and books for adults: the former nearly always
move over a more limited emotional and intellectual terrain,
surrender earlier to the threat of incomprehension. It is a rare
book that can satisfy on both levels.

Parent-child discord is a particularly difficult subject for a
children's writer to treat with any penetration or profundity.
Most Victorian juvenile books ignore it altogether. Mrs Ewing
broaches it, but dare not depart too far from the involved adult's
viewpoint. Nowadays, of course, it is perfectly possible for an
author to take the opposite tack, and adopt the indignant child's
view of adults as pointlessly malicious buffoons. Only one Victorian juvenile book anticipates such an approach.

Helen Mathers' *Comin' Thro' the Rye* (1875) is perhaps not even
a juvenile book—adolescent rather. Its author was under twenty
when she began it (Obituary, 1920), and it patently caters for
teenage turbulence. It sold well immediately, and Gillian Avery
says she has 'first-hand evidence that it was dearly loved by girls
at the end of the century' (Avery, 1965). Sweeping forward in a
breathless first-person narrative borrowed from Rhoda Broughton,
it sets out to polish off paternal tyranny with gawky nature
worship and amorous intrigue.

The narrator, Helen Adair, is one of twelve children. In the
first volume, 'Seed Time', she is a thirteen-year-old schoolgirl. Her
racily disdainful comments, unique for the period, initially provoke
some astonishment. She introduces her father with the words:
'We all look upon the governor as a kind of bombshell, or
volcano, or loaded gun, that may blow up at any moment.' Of the
local clergyman she remarks that he 'has a smile that would butter
the whole neighbourhood; a smile that Jack and I *hate*, and
would wipe off his face with a duster if we could'. One cannot
imagine Charlotte Yonge's heroines cherishing such an ambition.
Helen has a kind word for Amberley the governess, though: she
looks upon her 'as a sedate and amiable old cow'.

Most of the mutinous feeling concentrates itself on 'the governor', all of whose children or 'white slaves', we are told, 'have no feeling for him save that of fear'. His character and appearance are generously summed up in Helen's statement that 'his face seems to be made of india-rubber, and takes every inflection and shade of ill-temper and uncharitableness'. He addresses Helen as 'you object', boxes her ears and imposes solitary confinement. He lords it over his wife and entertains his family by organising sadistic walking tours. While he is 'steaming on in front all alone', they are 'puffing, blowing, groaning, gasping' behind him. 'From time to time papa turns and surveys our scarlet and distressed countenances with a grim smile.' Not surprisingly, the news that papa is going away for a day or two brings 'shouts of delight'. At breakfast with him the children agree to make one remark each 'and thus divide the labour of conversation'.

Quite how this monster has come to be sharing the breakfast-room Helen does not divulge. She is niggardly with motives and circumstances. She is not overliberal with facts. We gather that her father is or was a colonel and is vaguely connected with some 'business'. His business activities consist chiefly of storming out of the house and 'swearing over the weekly bills'. The governor is a blustering effigy and no more. Helen apparently takes him to be a type-figure, standing for all fathers—'I can't think what fathers were invented for', she says—but his presentment is too tenuous for that: he stands only for all blustering effigies.

As well as abolishing paternity, Helen wishes to deflate the precious concept of the family a little. She enjoys going to the fair, she says, for 'when one has looked upon nothing but the face of one's own family for twelve months, anything is agreeable to the eye'. She also disparages family prayers, regarding them as an engine of paternal tyranny. 'The governor', she explains, 'goes through chapter, prayer and benediction as hard as he can pelt.' Curiously, her iconoclasm lapses when her mother is around: 'Whoever or whatever we love we always place them "after mother".'

Maybe it is not so curious, for *Comin' Thro' the Rye* resolves itself into a less original book than it promises. The domestic situation is psychologically vacuous because the book's real thematic core is True Romance. For the writers of True Romance contumelious fathers are a useful prop; so are downtrodden, secretly sympathetic mothers. In the first volume Helen's romantic feelings subsist mainly on goggling at her big sister's amours, but in the second volume she is eighteen and ripe for the sultry hero, Paul Vasher. Cliché and bathos then smother all novelty. Sharp-tongued Helen can be heard simpering about how beautiful is the 'spectacle of connubial bliss' and Mr Vasher denounces the movement for women's rights. The book does not even try to reconcile these sentiments with the marital situation it showed us at the outset. Helen continues to lash out intermittently at her father well into the third volume, but by then it is clear that the motif is peripheral.

It is also clear, disappointingly, that Miss Mathers has no genuine interest in childhood. The third volume conscripts a child for service as an emotional dummy. There is a snaky rival for Paul Vasher's affections who contrives to score over Helen by diddling the hero into marrying her. She and Paul have a son and, as he grows up, she neglects him and Paul spurns him as the offspring of an unwanted union. But Helen drenches him with all her thwarted love, apprehending him as a Paul-substitute. Since it is intolerable to keep the child at the middle of this ugly emotional nexus, Miss Mathers kills him off—thus achieving at one stroke a juicy piece of pathos and a neat symbol for an ended love affair. It is another book with an ending unbelievably distant from the gay irreverence of its beginning.

Both *We and the World* and *Comin' Thro' the Rye* challenge the didactic view of parent-child relations, the first with sober and tentative analysis, the second with unreflective abuse. What neither makes much use of is humour. Yet humour proved the most effective dissolvent of attitudes that were felt to be out-moded. We can see this by looking at three successful books which harked mockingly back to their more solemn precursors.

The first, F. C. Burnand's *The New History of Sandford and Merton* (1872), is the slightest. Parody usually provides a useful index to changing taste, but Burnand's book is not a real parody, merely a light-hearted squib. Day's egregious ideas offer plenty of openings for genuine satire, but Burnand neglects nearly all of them. He is content with simple reversals: earnestly upright Mr Barlow is replaced by a slyly avaricious humbug addicted to drink, cant and sadism; sweet-tempered Harry becomes a spiteful little fiend. Farce and horseplay define the comedy, with pepperings of doggerel and outrageous, rib-digging puns, Day's naive solemnity is what Burnand fixes on most. No doubt his own merriment represents in the main a healthy advance, but one cannot help suspecting now and then that he is laughing for the wrong reasons. Day's sentimentality about poverty and savages is hardly confuted by chirpy dismissals of charity or jibes about 'self-made Mr Merton' or giggles at the idea of an 'intelligent negro'. Still, the book does dissipate the pomposity of its original, and it indicates that by the 1870s Day's book seemed absurd enough to some to be written off without much attention.

F. C. Burnand was the editor of *Punch*, and for a time one of his colleagues on the staff was F. Anstey, who was invited to the magazine on the strength of his first book. That book was *Vice Versa*, the most artistically successful of the late-century counter-blasts to juvenile didacticism. Perhaps also the most commercially successful: on publication in 1882 it became an instant best-seller and it has never been out of print since. None of Anstey's subsequent books repeated its extravagant triumph.

Vice Versa is a landmark in the decline of Victorian patriarchy. The idea behind it is simple but brilliant: by accident a magic stone makes a father and son swap physical appearances yet retain their original minds and feelings. Most of the book traces the fortunes—or misfortunes—of the father, Paul Bultitude, at his son's private school, as he abortively attempts to make his real position known. With the peremptory and inflexible manner of an irascible, middle-aged merchant, but the appearance and reputation of his fourteen-year-old son, Mr Bultitude lurches desperately from one humiliation to another.

In a sense Paul Bultitude's adventures sum up a tendency of the century: he is forced to discover childhood. 'He had no knowledge of boys,' we are told, 'nor any notion of acquiring an influence over them, having hitherto regarded them as necessary nuisances, to be rather repressed than studied.' Having taken the place of his son, Dick, he has to see everything afresh. He experiences sneaks and bullies from Dick's angle and he encounters the privations of school life—the cold and the confinement, the bad meals. There are also miseries of his own making. His lofty unconcern for his son's little doings now afflicts him as a dismal handicap. And his ungenerous interferences in Dick's life recoil upon him depressingly:

> It was by no means the least galling part of Mr. Bultitude's trials, that former forgotten words and deeds of his in his original condition were constantly turning up at critical

seasons, and plunging him deeper in the morass just when he saw some prospect of gaining firm ground.

It is vexing to have Dick's headmaster, Dr Grimstone, threatening him with the injunctions of 'your excellent father—his own injunctions. Just as he had given Dick the benefit of some 'stagnant wisdom' about school-days being the happiest time of your life, so one of the masters, Mr Blinkhorn, begins to spoon out the same platitudes to him—but this time Paul rejects them angrily and brands them 'miserable rubbish'. To his dismay he discovers that the pets he found in Dick's room during the holidays, and ordered to be 'summarily destroyed', were procured for several boys at the school who gave money for them in advance. Faced with their belligerent demands, he quails. 'For the first time he repented his paternal harshness.'

Repentance, of course, is where it all leads. Paul Bultitude comes to know what sort of life his son lives. Though his body shrinks, his imagination expands. He regrets having given no thought to his son's existence, regrets having kept him short of money. When at last he escapes and makes the magic stone reverse its effects, 'a spirit of mildness' stays his hand: and this he does not regret. The book concludes:

> His experiences, unpleasant as they had been, had had their advantages: they had drawn him and his family closer together. . . . Mr. Bultitude would never after this consider his family as a set of troublesome and thankless incumbrances.

The pattern is didactic but, for a children's book, it is inverted; charting not the slow resipiscence of an erring child but that of an erring parent.

The title *Vice Versa* refers of course to the father-son exchange, but it also has a wider application. The book's impact depends on a familiarity with the conventions of hortatory children's literature. Its plot reverberates with sardonic echoes of earlier works. Dr. Grimstone, for instance: behind his posturing self-importance we can glimpse the lineaments of all the school-story headmasters who were the crown and zenith of earthly justice, who delivered their moral warnings with awesome gravity. In Grimstone's mouth the moral rhetoric is blown up till it pops: foaming with indignation he assembles the whole school for a frenzied tirade against peppermint-eating.

'Your innocent schoolmates . . . shall not be perverted with your pernicious peppermints, sir; you shall not deprave them by the subtle and insidious jujube. . . . I will not expose myself or them to the inroads of disease.'

The choice of words lends just the right emphasis to the innuendo that, whatever these headmasters may pretend to be denouncing, they really have but one thing on their minds. Like an overflexed cane the vocabulary of reprobation has at last innocuously splintered.

In Anstey the majestic dwindles to the absurd. He belittles with nicely-timed cynical murmurs. The headmaster commutes a sentence of expulsion to one of corporal punishment: the event was an emotional high-spot in *Eric*, but when it occurs here Anstey casually remarks:

Boys are not often expelled from private schools, except for especially heinous offences, and in this case there was no real reason why the Doctor should be Quixotic enough to throw up a portion of his income—particularly if he could produce as great a moral effect by other means.

The tone is knowing, sly, impatient of pomposity. Occasionally Anstey makes the element of parody explicit. He explains Mr Blinkhorn's character like this:

The fact was, he was an ardent believer in the Good Boy of a certain order of school tales—the boy who is seized with a sudden conviction of the intrinsic baseness of boyhood, and does all in his power to get rid of the harmful taint; the boy who renounces his old comrades and his natural tastes (which after all seldom have any serious harm in them), to don a panoply of priggishness which is too often kick-proof.

Anstey evidently regarded such tales as anti-childhood propaganda, and his own book fired one of the first salvos at the whole tradition of unassailable adult authority and moral earnestness. It also tipped upside down the Rationalists' preoccupation with facts. In place of the data-hungry juveniles of Day, we are presented with poor Mr Bultitude vainly trying to cotton on to the customs and lore of childhood, having literally to go back to school.

The freshness of all this has long since faded, or been smudged away by imitation. But one should estimate *Vice Versa* in its historical context, and even now it is an amusing book to read.

D*

Anstey wrote with suave lucidity and picked out the subjects for his satire with discernment. Not that the satire sticks entirely to literature. In his modest and genial autobiography (*A Long Retrospect*, 1936) Anstey reveals how much of it was based on fact. He did not enjoy school life, though he was no victim and had no particular hardships to endure. He began the first draft of *Vice Versa* when he was twenty-one (in 1877) and the 'local colour and details' were based on recent memories. Of the original of Grimstone, he says: 'The examples of his oratory in my first story are of course burlesqued to some extent, but he did fulminate very much on those lines.' But his autobiography also confirms what *Vice Versa* strongly suggests—that he was familiar with the didactic juvenile books. At school, he says, he read 'Dean Farrar's *Eric*, and *St. Winifred's*, which . . . I am afraid I accepted as lifelike presentments of what went on at public schools.' When he was younger he had read *Sandford and Merton* ('good in parts, whenever Mr. Barlow was out of the way'), and he gives a fascinating account of his early Sunday literature. 'There was a time when my mother read aloud to us from *The Fairchild Family*. But a spirit of irreverence came over us, and she and we laughed so much that I think the readings were given up.' Many years later Anstey returned to *The Fairchild Family*, with what remains the funniest and most penetrating essay on that work (reprinted in *The Last Load*). For Sunday reading there was 'also a book called *Ministering Children*, which always affected me with the profoundest melancholy'. *Ministering Children* got its come-uppance in Anstey's famous story 'The Good Little Girl' (also based on a Perrault tale), whose priggish little heroine, Priscilla, fond of exhorting and rebuking her relatives, is promised by a fairy that a jewel shall drop from her lips every time she passes an improving remark; the jewels tumble copiously out but, alas, they are found to be counterfeit. Priscilla takes the point (Anstey, 1892).

Anstey mentions in his autobiography that Butler 'knew and liked *Vice Versa*'. The book probably rates as the closest juvenile equivalent to *The Way of All Flesh*, but it lacks Butler's sourness and rancour (Anstey's parents encouraged him when he was writing it). Not all of its humour comes from turning the tables on parental pomposity. Some of its best passages grow out of the sheer incongruity of the positions Paul and his son find themselves in. Addressing Dr Grimstone, Paul sometimes relapses into a tone of blustering effrontery, to the hand-rubbing relish of his son's astonished schoolpals, and the stilted outrage of Grimstone himself. Paul's unconcealably middle-aged attitude also lets him down in his dealings with Dulcie, a young girl at the school who exasperatingly turns out to be both his son's sweetheart and Grimstone's daughter. He greets her fluttering attentions with a scandalised repulse. On the other hand there is the comic position of Dick, masquerading as the master of the house, going clownishly about his father's business, ebullient, childlike and absurd.

Ultimately, the book does not neatly bifurcate our sympathies for father and son. Since it is Paul's predicament that we attend to most of the time, we never regard him as simply a contemptible butt. At the end, indeed, when he escapes from the school, the suspense of the situation and the disagreeableness of Grimstone put us altogether on Paul's side. We want him to escape and we want him to recapture the stone. Anstey manages the denouement with psychological acumen, and makes the return to normality not a disappointment but a triumph. He knows when to fade out the escapism.

Anstey's brand of good-tempered mockery is less evident in Rudyard Kipling's *Stalky & Co.*, another attack on the old didacticism with the weapons of humour and farce. Published in 1899, *Stalky & Co.* probably did even more harm to the moralistic school story than *Vice Versa*. As John Rowe Townsend has said, it 'damaged the genre by making it appear naive' (Townsend, 1965). More significant, it was closer to future developments than *Vice Versa*. It rejected the child-squashing ethic of earlier works to replace it with a more callous and cynical code.

Surprisingly, Kipling regarded *Stalky & Co.* as 'a truly valuable collection of tracts'. He was not against didacticism as such, merely against hectoring and explicit didacticism. The exploits of Stalky, M'Turk and Beetle deliberately flout the stuffy conventions of previous boys'-school stories, and their conversation keeps alluding derisively to the works of Dean Farrar. But beneath the slangy and oblique style we can make out Kipling's own message. Kipling shared the common feeling at the end of the century that the best treatment for young people was judicious letting alone. The housemasters, the school sergeant and various prefects try to drill and lecture Stalky and Co., or catch them out in error. But the boys always merrily foil their superiors, making their plots boomerang and their sermons fizzle out. Only the headmaster

can outwit them and he does it by resorting to their own techniques. Knowing they have manipulated school procedures to
their advantage, he discards the customary interrogation and
simply canes them. 'I think we understand one another perfectly',
he says. And the boys admire him all the more for the 'howling
injustice' of his methods.

Up to a point *Stalky & Co.* supplies a useful antidote to the
tense and twitching morality of earlier works. It adds, however,
some nastier ingredients. Stalky and his chums roll about in
mirth, eyes streaming, at their triumphs over others, but only
the complacent could share all their laughter. Kipling is anxious
to cock a snook at the solemnities of those like Farrar, but
seems blind to the viciousness of his own gleefully conjured
pranks. Stalky gets his own back on a persecuting master by
inflaming a local carrier to hurl stones through the master's
window; the consequences include the injury of a small boy who
has sneaked—'Manders minor was bleeding profusely from a cut
on the cheek-bone.' Beetle reports this to the others howling and
gasping with hilarity: 'Manders minor's head's cut open.' Where
the early didactic books had contained finger-wagging admoni-
tions against cruelty to animals, Kipling's heroes have fun shoot-
ing a cat, cutting it up and letting its rotting body stink out a
rival dormitory. They also, at the instigation of the school
chaplain, inflict protracted torture on some bullies, finishing the
work 'all dripping with excitement and exertion'. In his book on
Kipling, J. I. M. Stewart defends this notorious episode as realism.
It is meant to show, he says, that 'violence breeds violence', because Beetle, who has himself suffered much mishandling when
younger, 'just stops himself from thus bullying for the sheer sake
of bullying' (Stewart, 1966). Surely, though, the episode, all
thirteen pages of it, is meant simply to be enjoyed. The chaplain
slyly congratulates the lads afterwards and they smirkingly reply:
'Don't forget our pious motives, Padre.' Mr Stewart also defends
the episode because he likes the way it is described; he calls it
'a masterpiece of sinister reticences'. This point may be more
readily conceded; the scene *is* effective, as torture scenes go.

Scorning cant about the 'honour of the house' is fair enough;
sadism and insensitivity are questionable extensions. *Stalky & Co.*
dispenses with stern sermons on 'the decency due to elders', but
is in danger of dispensing with moral thoughtfulness altogether.
It represents the furthest point in the gradual extension during

the nineteenth century of the range of permissible activity for young people.

It does not, however, represent the furthest point in emancipation from adults, for all its escapades are depicted as preparations for the adult world. Its last chapter, for example, points out at length how Stalky's schoolday ruses were to stand him in good stead for killing the natives in India. Emancipation from the adult world, as Gillian Avery has noted, reached its far point in the works of Kenneth Grahame. His children are morally casual and self-absorbed. In his prologue to *The Golden Age*, a book originally written for adults, he described how he perceived grown-ups when he was a boy. They were 'stiff and colourless Olympians' dragging out 'an aimless existence'. They were deluded in thinking that their political and social topics 'were among the importances of life'. The children felt themselves to be the 'illuminati' who 'could have told them what real life was' (Grahame, 1895). Grahame seems near to endorsing the child's view, to asserting that the child's life is in some absolute sense superior to the adult's. What is certain is that he would have upheld the conclusion to which the whole discovery of childhood had been tending: that the child's existence was important in itself, not simply as a preparation for maturity.

(iv)

The change that came over nineteenth-century children's books was partly due to the waning of simple didacticism. In Mrs Trimmer's journal the entry for 22 September 1785 reads (Trimmer, 1814):

> After a night of refreshing sleep, I awoke early, and offered up my prayers to God. I then looked over my manuscript of Fabulous Histories, and made an addition, which I hope has a tendency to do honour to my Creator, and inspire persons with right sentiments.

Compare Anstey's comment on *Vice Versa*: 'I was not a profound thinker; I had no message to deliver, no theories to propound, no cause to advocate.' But the change was not merely a matter of writers no longer wishing to teach: it was that they wished to teach different things. Anstey's unassuming comment shows how

far didacticism had gone out of fashion, for it fails to acknowledge the genuinely purposeful elements in his humour. The later
writers were didactic in a different way. They still had values
and assumptions, but they held them with less obsessiveness and
vehemence. And they were different values, different assumptions.
The chief focus of change was the theory of childhood. Both
Rationalist and Evangelical children's books arose from a growing
curiosity about childhood and a conviction of the importance of
early training; essentially, though, both regarded children as like
adults but smaller, as stunted and imperfect replicas. The Rationalist child was a small robot, incomplete until fully programmed.
The Evangelical child was a small soul, in need of unflagging
parental protection. As the child's nature was recognised as
different, the role of childhood changed—and with it the role of
parents. Even in children's books this change is evident; even in
a genre which, in the main, approached new ideas with caution.

Chapter IV

JANE AUSTEN AND DICKENS

'He had been very little cared for at any time by his
family, though quite as much as he deserved.'
                    JANE AUSTEN, *Persuasion*

'O! don't talk of duty as a child, Miss Summerson;
where's Ma's duty as a parent?'
                    CHARLES DICKENS, *Bleak House*

(i)

In some ways minor writers are peculiarly useful; lacking orig-
inality, distracted only slightly by imagination, they can offer, for
the chronicler of popular values, a most sturdy and accessible
source. This is what we find with children's books: though so
many are artistically penurious, they are also richly informative
about bygone tastes and assumptions. From major works, on the
other hand, it is harder to quarry ideas. Major writers are more
complex and more oblique, less reliant on cliché and custom;
their ideas bind organically into their work and can't be just
neatly plucked out. Nevertheless, major writers, too, illuminate
their age. Certainly, with parent-child relations, we may find that
the two major novelists from the beginning and middle of the
nineteenth century contribute valuable evidence about changing
attitudes. The shifts in outlook and sentiment recorded in previous
chapters are discernible, too, in the contrast between Jane Austen
and Charles Dickens.

Of course, this contrast must be treated with caution: there
are patent difficulties in approaching these writers for this kind of
evidence. In one sense, clearly, both Jane Austen and Dickens
were highly untypical people: it is not a representative activity
to turn out masterpieces. Then again, how should we compile
their ideas? It is difficult to extract a 'philosophy', a consistent
outlook on parents and children, from a writer so rich and contradictory as Dickens, so subtle and fine-woven as Jane Austen.
What is more, some unlikeness may well be explained by biographical facts. Dickens endured the blacking factory, while Jane
Austen's childhood was apparently serene. Dickens had an un-

happy family life (at least in certain important respects), while Jane Austen, except for some minor irritations (for example, her mother's hypochondria), appears to have lived in peace. Also they differed considerably in their personal knowledge of children. Dickens was head of a family of nine, while the only children in Jane Austen's life were her various nephews and nieces. (And her books: *Pride and Prejudice*, her 'own darling child'; *Emma*, her answer to her niece Anna's baby; *Sense and Sensibility*, which she could no more forget 'than a mother can forget her sucking child': Letters, 29 January 1813, December 1815, 25 April 1811.) Possibly, it may be argued, there is bound to be a difference, in their treatment of children, between a busy, cosmopolitan father of nine and a provincial maiden aunt.

There is something to be said for all these objections, but none of them is decisive. A writer may be extraordinary in talent, invention and artistic finesse, yet still be profoundly influenced by the values of his day. The critical problems, when fiction is read for insight into contemporary thought, are indeed formidable; with patience, tact and delicacy they can be overcome. The importance of personal biography is likely to vary from case to case; with Jane Austen and Dickens it is not sufficient to account for their difference as writers. What has also to be invoked is the contemporary climate of thought; and this chapter will argue that on the subject of childhood, as also on parental and filial roles, the contrast between Jane Austen and Dickens is not merely personal. It is symptomatic of a general shift in thinking and sentiment.

(ii)

In her treatment of parent-child relations Jane Austen is pre-Romantic. But she also displays a regard for children, a certain cautious tenderness, of a kind which, as argued in chapter I, developed in the eighteenth century.

It is sometimes maintained that we find in Jane Austen a conservative version of contemporary thought; recently she has even been stigmatised as a keen anti-Jacobin (Butler, 1975). But in her personal fondness for children, and her occasional focus on them in her books, she was rather advanced for her time. In the majority of eighteenth-century novels (*Camilla* is perhaps the most striking exception) children are nullities. The formative period in the lives of the characters is dismissed in a sentence or two: the needlessness of recording it is often remarked by the authors. Jane Austen shared some of these presuppositions, but she could also at times, as with Fanny Price, enter into the mind of a child. As Angus Wilson has rightly declared: 'The first novelist's description of a lonely child's neglect . . . is in that proto-Victorian novel *Mansfield Park*; . . . the childhood pages of Fanny's history are a prelude to the stories of Florence Dombey and Jane Eyre and Maggie Tulliver.' (Slater, 1970.) Likewise with parent-child relations: she certainly upheld the power of parents, but she didn't believe, any more than did Dickens, in their irreproachable wisdom. What is more, even her grimmest parents are comparatively mild. They do not, as in Richardson, curse their children, or goad them to marriage by the application of psychic cruelties (Lady Susan is a minor exception). And yet despite her temperateness, her mildly progressive approach to the young, her attitudes still contrast markedly with those of later writers. Her thoughts about children, and about their duties, would have been quite unacceptable to many Victorians.

On this subject Jane Austen was touched by transition. She was writing at a time when, among the middle classes, there were two competing views of the young. On the one hand they were seen as reprobates, their duty to learn and to obey their elders, their importance mainly financial. On the other, they were coming to be seen as darlings, pleasant and possibly even wise, deserving respect in themselves. What we find in Jane Austen is the first of these views—but refined by her own intelligence and qualified by the second. The tension between the two rival conceptions can sometimes be sensed in her fiction. But where it emerges most definitely is in the contrast, on the subject of childhood, between her life and her writing.

It is quite clear from the evidence of her life and letters that Jane Austen was fond of children. 'Dear itty Dordy', she writes to Cassandra, of her three-year-old nephew George. 'I shall think with tenderness and delight on his beautiful and smiling countenance and interesting manners till a few years have turned him into an ungovernable, ungracious fellow.' (27 October 1798.) *Young* children are obviously preferable, but even so we have here unexpected support for the doctrine of innocence. Sometimes Jane Austen would take this so far as to tolerate naughtiness. In 1809, when his son was born, she despatched to her naval brother

Francis some affectionate doggerel. Smilingly, she expressed her wish that the son would take after his father: 'Thy infant days may he inherit, / Thy warmth, nay insolence of spirit; / . . . So may his equal faults as child, / Produce maturity as mild.' (26 July 1809.) (The closest the fiction comes to this is when Mr Knightley decides that spoiled children can turn into excellent brides.) Repeatedly Jane Austen's letters reveal how she loved her nephews and nieces, how she entertained them, gave them advice, was always anxious to help. In return she remained their most popular aunt. 'Her first charm to children was great sweetness of manner', according to one niece, Caroline. 'She could make everything amusing to a child. Then, as I got older . . . she would tell us the most delightful stories, chiefly of Fairyland.' This account is confirmed by Anna Lefroy: 'Aunt Jane was the general favourite with children; her ways with them being so playful, and her long circumstantial stories so delightful.' (Austen-Leigh, 1926.) From purely biographical evidence there is very little warrant for regarding Jane Austen as unresponsive to children.

When, however, we turn to the fiction the climate of feeling has changed. The only children's book mentioned here is the one which Emma has read: 'Madame de Genlis' epistolary treatise, *Adelaide and Theodore*, a work in which fairy-tales for children are rejected because they 'stop the course of their reasoning'. In her fiction Jane Austen presents for approval her formal and public values; and these, on the role and duties of children, are rather less lenient. First of all she does not assign children a role of intrinsic importance. Secondly, with parent-child relations— whether the children be juveniles or young people in their twenties—she comes out strongly in favour of firmness, of control and supervision; she ridicules cosseting, or even marked fondness, and condemns premature independence. She leaves very little room for belief in the trappings of innocence: the values, tastes and perceptions of children are nowhere considered superior to those of the adult world. Put simply, what she requires from parents is firmly principled guidance. From children she requires submission and quiet; from young men and women, respect.

The unimportance of children in Jane Austen's fiction is shown by their ghostliness. Jane Austen herself had seven siblings and her fictional families are frequently large (Mr and Mrs Heywood in *Sanditon* have no fewer than fourteen children). But most of these shadowy juveniles only rarely receive any notice; their creator being indifferent to them, they remain in an artistic limbo. Catherine Morland has eight younger brothers and sisters: except for Sarah they are hardly seen. The Gardiners in *Pride and Prejudice* have a 'troop of little girls and boys': they are mustered for background merriment on Elizabeth's arrivals. A utilitarian attitude to children, either financial or social, remains a strong force in Jane Austen. She and her characters are acutely aware that children have to be kept. Whereas in Dickens (and other Victorians) children are a source of emotional enrichment, in Austen they are more bleakly seen as a long-term financial drain. One might cite the debate in *Mansfield Park* about the adoption of Fanny: expense and benevolence are weighed in the balance, and the cost of her upkeep is only made light of by wily advisers like Mrs Norris, who have no intention of paying. (Compare the sentences in *Emma* on the adoption of Mr Weston's Frank: 'From the expense of the child . . . he was soon relieved . . . the child was given up to the care and wealth of the Churchills.') What children provide in return for their keep is also utilitarian: not spiritual guidance or emotional wealth, but timely social diversion. As Jane Austen remarks of Lady Middleton's son, 'On every formal visit a child ought to be of the party, by way of provision for discourse.' Despite the note of sour irony, this is what happens elsewhere. After dinner at the Coles' party in *Emma*, 'the children came in, and were talked to and admired amid the usual rate of conversation'. Occasionally characters will chat about children to change an embarrassing subject.

This utilitarian approach to children—their use, by both characters and novelist, as pretext and convenience—may be seen from the episode in *Persuasion* when little Charles has a fall. A dislocated collar-bone, a twisted back, the victim a small defenceless child—one can easily imagine how all this might be handled in many a Victorian novel. In *Persuasion* the treatment is functional; the effect on engagements is the primary thing; the focus is not on the child. The 'first uneasiness' of Mr Musgrove is naturally 'about his heir': his eldest grandson will eventually inherit the Great House. The child's aunts, Henrietta and Louisa, arrive with frightened enquiries; but they soon revert to their genuine interests and depart 'apparently more full of Captain Wentworth than of little Charles'. Within a day the casualty's parents are both of a similar mind: they are willing to go out, and leave him at home, in order to meet the new visitor. The boy's mother, of course, on hearing the news, has enjoyed her obligatory hysterics; but after this her conception of maternal duty is severely limited:

> 'I hope I am as fond of my child as any mother—but I do not know that I am of any more use in the sick-room than Charles, for I cannot be always scolding and teasing a poor child when it is ill.'

Mary argues that since little Charles may worsen, her husband should not have left her alone; clearly she should have accompanied him, for the child is obviously safe. Here, as elsewhere in this episode, the satirical attack is transparent. But what, one may wonder, is the particular standpoint from which the attack is launched? After all, the finer characters, too, use the injured child as a pretext. At first Captain Wentworth, avoiding Anne, declines to come to the Cottage: 'he seemed afraid of being in Mrs Charles Musgrove's way, on account of the child'. Later, when he changes his mind, he sends advance warning to Anne; again his excuse is anxiety for the state of the injured boy. No one is concerned for the child himself; during the discussion of his condition each character reveals ulterior interests. This is true even of Anne herself. She offers to stay behind with the child and the 'sincerity of her manner' soon persuades the boy's father to accept. Nevertheless, as we learn later, 'the little boy's state' was really a 'pretence for absenting herself' from Captain Wentworth. Later still she stays away again 'under the mixed plea of a headache of her own and some return of indisposition in little Charles'. Unlike the others Anne genuinely helps the boy, but like them she makes use of him.

One might notice, moreover, the kind of help that Anne is shown to offer. She stands in for Mary because she knows she can be 'of the first utility to the child'. She looks back with fondness on Uppercross because of 'her usefulness to little Charles'. Mary Musgrove's maternal negligence is criticised not from an emotional, but from a purely practical standpoint. Despite the exposure of ulterior motives, there is no suggestion that the circle of adults ought to have responded more emotionally to the plight of this miniature person. Emotion, in the form of Mary's hysterics, is shown to be utterly useless.

The adults aren't concerned with the child himself but this, it appears, can be no great sin, for neither is Jane Austen. For her, the child's fall is a plot convenience. It defers Anne's meeting with Captain Wentworth and thereby heightens suspense; it prepares for Louisa's concussion at Lyme and the proof of Anne's capability. After the accident has served its purpose it is scarcely mentioned again.

But though children themselves are not important in Jane Austen, their education is: she is interested less in what children are than in what they might become. A great deal has been written on Jane Austen and education—on schooling, on 'accomplishments', and, recently, on her putative view that effective tuition depends on the power of love (Devlin, 1975). Actually her opinions on upbringing were fairly conventional. Except for the biblical substantiation they resembled those found in the *Christian Observer*, discussed in chapter II. Training and discipline must begin early and should be consistently maintained; neglect, indulgence, too early independence were likely to lead to harm. But the fundamental premise of this education (in its secular aspect, as Jane Austen adopts it) is that children should be *socialised*: pulled out of their native anarchy and brought into society's rules.

Jane Austen believed that unpleasantness of temperament, and the consequent need for a careful training, could emerge very early in life. In 1817 she told Fanny Knight that the daughter of another niece, Anne Lefroy, 'has a very irritable bad Temper'. She added: 'I hope as Anna is so early sensible of its defects, that she will give Jemima's disposition the early and steady attention it must require.' (13 March 1817.) At this date Jemima was seventeen months. In the fiction Jane Austen is fierce about children who have failed to receive such attention. An egregious offender is Annamaria Middleton, a sly squalling monster of three. Embraced by her mother, this 'pattern of gentleness' emits 'violent screams' when slightly scratched. A sarcastic description of her sufferings follows:

> Everything was done . . . in so critical an emergency, which affection could suggest as likely to assuage the agonies of the little sufferer. She was seated in her mother's lap, covered with kisses, her wound bathed with lavender-water . . . her mouth stuffed with sugar plums. . . . With such a reward for her tears, the child was too wise to cease crying.

Writing in 1894, Alice Meynell objected to this passage. 'The lack of tenderness and of spirit is manifest in Miss Austen's indifference to children', she complained. 'The novelist even spends some of her irony upon a little girl of three. She sharpens her

pen over the work.' (Meynell, 1921.) But Jane Austen's spoilt
children are not the bright 'pickles' of late Victorian fiction; they
are more like wild animals. Elinor Dashwood confesses drily that
when at Lady Middleton's, she never thinks of 'tame and quiet
children with any abhorrence'. The Price children at Portsmouth
in *Mansfield Park* are likewise 'quite untamable'. They chase each
other up and down the stairs, 'tumbling about and hallooing'. The
youngest horror is five-year-old Betsey, injudiciously indulged by
her mother and 'trained up to think the alphabet her greatest
enemy'. The Musgrove children are also indulged and are consequently greedy and have damaged the furniture.

The scars of spoiling are visible, too, in the adult wastrels and
villains. Nearly all those who go around flirting and jilting, or
otherwise acting without due care, have been spoon-fed or
flattered when young. Lady Susan admits that in her infant years
she was so much indulged that she was never obliged to attend
anything. The voluble, conceited Tom Musgrave in *The Watsons*
has been given 'rather an unsettled turn' by inheriting, 'when he
was very young', eight or nine hundred a year. Willoughby is
another casualty of 'too early an independence and its consequent
habits of idleness, dissipation and luxury'. Even Edward Ferrars,
whose parent is a harridan, falls prey to permissiveness. He complains that if only he'd been forced by his mother to adopt an
'active profession', he would never have fancied himself in love
with the spiteful Lucy Steele. Significantly it is Mrs Ferrar's
negligence, rather than her threats and her bullying, which does
Edward positive harm. Henry Crawford has been ruined by bad
example (the Admiral's rears and vices), but also by 'early independence' and overmuch lenience: 'Few fathers would have
let me have my own way half so much.' Julia Bertram is better
than her sister Maria mainly because she has been 'less flattered
and less spoilt', but both have been made complacent by their
mother and puffed up by Mrs Norris. The elopement of Lydia in
Pride and Prejudice demonstrates 'the mischief of neglect and
mistaken indulgence towards such a girl'. The negative part of
the fault is her father's, the positive part her mother's. It is only
by 'proper attention and management' that her sister Kitty is redeemed. Mr Darcy was also, by his own account, spoilt by his
parents who, though good themselves, never taught him to correct
his temper. They 'allowed, encouraged, almost taught me to be
selfish and overbearing, to care for none beyond my own family

circle, to think meanly of all the rest of the world'. Perhaps he is being too hard on himself (and also on his parents). According to Mrs Reynolds, his housekeeper, 'he was always the sweetest-tempered, most generous-hearted, boy in the world'. Mr Collins is a curious example: brought up in subjection by 'an illiterate and miserly father', he originally possessed 'great humility of manner', but this has been unhappily counteracted by 'early and unexpected prosperity'. As a result we have the inimitable 'mixture of pride and obsequiousness'.

Bad adults in Jane Austen have been badly brought up, or have failed to obey their parents. Some of them indeed betray their badness by their lack of filial respect. Edward Stanley, the meretricious hero of *Catharine*, is unpardonably rude to the heroine's aunt and inattentive to the father who has spoilt him ('He then got out of the chaise & entered the house without waiting for his Father's reply'). Tom Bertram is coarsely unfilial and so is his ne'er-do-well friend John Yates, who has 'never been with those who thought much of parental claims' and who considers Sir Thomas 'infamously tyrannical' for cutting short *Lovers' Vows*.

If cosseting weakens the moral fibre, strictness can strengthen it: Jane Austen assumes throughout her work that, in the treatment of young people and children, firmness is necessary. All her more sensible characters take over this assumption. Henry Tilney has little time for Catherine's plea that when 'poor little children' are learning their letters, instruction can amount to torment. Perhaps, he retorts, it is 'well worth while to be tormented for two or three years of one's life, for the sake of being able to read all the rest of it'. Catherine's mother is similarly stoical about her daughter's expulsion: 'It is always good for young people to be put upon exerting themselves' (the same truth, more severely expressed, is eventually acknowledged by Sir Thomas). Although John Knightley is a home-loving husband, and a conscientious and affectionate father, he wants his children to be 'active and hardy' and his parental precepts are brief: 'Do not spoil them and do not physic them.' Mr Knightley himself, as mentioned above, eventually softens towards spoiled children, but here we see the mellowness of recent betrothal, for one of the things he has liked about Emma is her no-nonsense manner with children: with them, unlike adults, he asseverates, she is not 'under the power of fancy and whim'. The sternness assumed to be fitting for children is sometimes remarkable. When Lady Susan's daugh-

ter, cruelly neglected, attempts to run away from school, even
the kindly Mrs Vernon believes that at sixteen she 'ought to
know better' and receives sympathetically the mother's announcement that in future the girl will have to be treated 'with some
severity': 'All this sounds very reasonable.' When Mrs Vernon
actually sees the girl, she immediately goes back on this—but her
initial assumptions are telling.

In Jane Austen the ability to take charge of children is a good
clue to character. The first gallantry performed by Captain
Wentworth, which leaves Anne 'speechless' and 'overcome', is
when he relieves her of a two-year-old boy who has fastened on
her back. The more worthless adults, on the other hand, are
querulously weak. Mary Musgrove complains that her children
don't mind her and blames her mother-in-law. Mrs Price is
abruptly defied by her children and like Mary she is also incompetent in keeping control of the servants (the historical
association of domestics with children is explored by Philippe
Ariès). Mr Price is strident but ineffectual: he recommends flog-
ging but is quite ignored. Lacking firmness, he also lacks dignity.
In Jane Austen it is rarely commendable for an adult to descend
to the level of a child—like Mrs Bennet wrangling with the Lucas
boy, or Mrs Norris relating her 'triumph' over the pilfering
attempts of Dick Jackson.

Mrs Bennet, Mrs Norris and Mrs Price—all of these women, in
their treatment of young people, are partial and capricious. Mrs
Norris is determinedly cruel to Fanny and mean to her god-daugh-
ter Susan; she is, however, oozingly obsequious with her two more
privileged nieces. Mrs Bennet is a weak and whining parent and
often overindulgent; but she can also be petulantly imperative—
as when she tries to use her husband's authority to coerce Elizabeth into expedience ('Oh! Mr Bennet, you are wanted immediately. . . . You must come and make Lizzy marry Mr Collins') or
force Lydia and Wickham into line ('When you get to town, find
them out, wherever they may be; and if they are not married
already, *make* them marry'). Poor, draggle-tailed Mrs Price is
certainly well-meaning, but she, too, exposes the need for a parent
to be consistent and firm.

Indeed from Jane Austen's treatment of parents we can infer
the same views about education, and about the relations between
the young and the old, as emerge from her treatment of children.
In nearly all cases what she attacks is the failure to maintain

authority, to guide, supervise, keep in order, to preserve an impartial detachment. Only rarely does she also attack excessive
severity.

There are very few *good* parents in Jane Austen, and even these
are criticised to some extent. Possibly the best is a minor character, Sir Reginald in *Lady Susan*. His letter to his son is both firm
and considerate, candid but courteous. All the same he is rather
too easily appeased by patent rationalisations. Likewise Mr and
Mrs Morland are in some ways exemplary. 'It is impossible', as
Catherine says, 'for parents to be more kind, or more desirous of
their children's happiness.' Mrs Morland's forbearance is proof
of this: she does not 'insist on her daughters being accomplished
in spite of incapacity or distaste'. And yet although the Morlands
are kind they are also imperceptive: they fail to suspect, on their
daughter's return, that her mooning is due to love. Mr and Mrs
Musgrove are similar: in contrast with Sir Walter Elliot they are
warm and friendly, not overambitious but genuinely tolerant;
they accept their daughters' marriages even though they have
reservations. Despite this they trust their daughters too much
and are generally too doting. They are guilty of neglect and
indulgence—the two overriding weaknesses of parents in Jane
Austen.

Mr and Mrs Musgrove are negligent when they let both Louisa
and Henrietta encourage Captain Wentworth. Just as children
have to be disciplined, young people have to be given advice—
and they need to be guided especially on points of propriety.
This is where Mrs Allen falls down, with her lazily tolerant
recommendation, 'Do just as you please, my dear.' Even more
sluggish is Lady Bertram, who fails to take measures against the
play and gives Fanny only one piece of advice—to accept the
proposal from Henry Crawford—in the course of eight years
and a half. But the prince of the irresponsible parents is probably
Mr Bennet: he basks in the thickets of embarrassment that have
sprouted from his own neglect. Concise, sardonic, intelligent, he
lacks executive strength; and Elizabeth sees how his ironies have
usurped his awareness of duty: 'Her father, contented with
laughing at them, would never exert himself to restrain the
wild giddiness of his youngest daughters.' Even after the elopement and the chase to London, his self-reproaches are brief. He
is too satirically sensitive to the comic-moral side of his own
situation and his incapacity to mend.

However, Mr Bennet can at least acknowledge—even if he does little to rectify—his family's infirmities. As he states with characteristic wit, 'If my children are silly I must hope to be always sensible of it.' In this respect he is superior to that gaggle of blindly indulgent parents who stray through Jane Austen's work. A prize example is Mrs Thorpe, the beaming mother in *Northanger Abbey* who dilates on the talents of her sons and the beauty of her daughters. Her dearly-loved oafish offspring John reveals he is a 'dutiful and affectionate son' by greeting his mother with a hearty handshake and enquiring, 'Ah, mother! how do you do? Where did you get that quiz of a hat, it makes you look like an old witch.' This address satisfies her fondest wishes, and she receives her hopeful hobbledehoy with 'delighted and exulting affection'. Elders who dote on their children's looks are always absurd in Jane Austen. They are present even in the juvenilia (Mr and Mrs Dudley in *Catharine*) and crop up quite often thereafter. The contentment of Mrs Edwards in *The Watsons*, 'complacently viewing her daughter's good looks', anticipates that of Lady Bertram, aroused to a fit of family pride by Fanny's effect on Crawford: 'And looking at her complacently, she added, "Humph, we certainly are a handsome family".' Jane Austen herself was never so partial; she believed that even praise of one's baby should not be irrational. As she wrote to Cassandra, of a sister-in-law: 'Mary grows rather more reasonable about her child's beauty, and says she does not think him really handsome.' (8 January 1799.)

The book that has the ripest child-indulgers is *Sense and Sensibility*. This novel opens with a stark illustration of the dangers of liking small children. Old Mr Dashwood bequeaths his fortune to the people who need it least. This is because he has fallen in love with an infant nephew, who on occasional visits

> had so far gained on the affections of his uncle, by such attractions as are by no means unusual in children of two or three years old; an imperfect articulation, an earnest desire of having his own way, many cunning tricks, and a great deal of noise, as to outweigh all the value of all the attention which, for years, he had received from his niece and her daughters.

Emotional susceptibility, the temporary eclipse of rational judgement, the resulting damage to others: surely we have here the first example of the book's predominant theme. Even before the main plot has begun, the perils of sensibility—with a cautionary case of fondness for children—have been insinuated.

Almost all the parents in *Sense and Sensibility* are foolishly indulgent, but the ironies against them range from the savage to the almost affectionate. Sir John Middleton, who delights in noisy youngsters, is merely an amiable buffoon, but his wife who, though coldly formal with adults, allows her children to attack the guests, is rather more repellent. She is a bit like a person with a dangerous dog, patting its head and praising it to the terrorised visitors. By contrast the motherliness of Mrs Jennings is never worse than a foible; eventually, poured out on the Dashwood girls, it becomes a real source of strength. The old lady dotes on her daughter Charlotte, in whose former room, near the mantel-piece, there still hangs 'a landscape in coloured silks' as proof of her schoolgirl performance. Expectably, when Charlotte has a baby, it is not until a fortnight has elapsed that her mother feels it 'no longer necessary to give up the whole of her time to her'. But when Mrs Jennings, as a mother-substitute, determines to remain with the ailing Marianne, she reveals a sterling kindness of heart 'which made Elinor really love her'.

Mrs Dashwood herself is a good-hearted woman, but she too is overindulgent. She is 'perfectly satisfied' that Marianne should remain alone with Willoughby, and again, when the glamorous fraud has decamped, 'perfectly satisfied' that Marianne must have got engaged to him. She refuses simply to ask the girl for fear of forcing her confidence; she would not, she declares, presume to exploit her daughter's 'sense of duty'. Elinor thinks this is overstrained, considering her sister's youth—but 'common sense, common care, common prudence, were all sunk in Mrs Dash-wood's romantic delicacy'. This passage might well be juxtaposed with an episode in *Mansfield Park*. When Sir Thomas is pressuring Fanny to marry, she reflects on his limitations: 'He, who had married a daughter to Mr Rushworth: romantic delicacy was certainly not to be expected from him.' Mrs Dashwood has a false and Fanny a true conception of romantic delicacy; both passages, though, afford parents a good deal of latitude. Insensi-tivity does not consist in questioning or advising about marriage partners—only in dictating.

In Jane Austen weak or indulgent parents are usually imper-ceptive. They are unable to detect their children's faults or anticipate their misdeeds. Adults soft-hearted towards the young are often also soft-brained. Old Mr Woodhouse is characteristic, with his misty conviction that Emma is perfect and his vacuous approval of his grandchildren: 'They are all remarkably clever; and they have so many pretty ways. They will come and stand by my chair and say, "Grandpapa, can you give me a bit of string".' Isabella Knightley likewise assumes that everyone is pleased to see her brood, and Mr Weston is so full of his Frank that he fails to scent his falsity. But perhaps the fondest reality-benders are Mr and Mrs Musgrove, who dote on their youngest, 'the lingering and long-petted Master Harry', listen with rapture to their daughters' performance (and with 'total indifference to any other person's') and mournfully idealise their dead son Dick, 'whom alive nobody had cared for'. Mrs Musgrove's 'large fat sighings' have aroused the compassion of critics like Mudrick, who wish to be seen to be charitable, but this reaction exaggerates Jane Austen's own ruthlessness. Captain Wentworth, after all, evinces 'the kindest consideration for all that was real and unabsurd in the parent's feelings'. In any case, a sharp view of facile nostalgia (evident too in the portrait of Benwick) tenders a valuable qualification in a book so concerned with regret.

If elegiac matrons are comical, so too are apprehensive ones—mothers who are jumpily solicitous for the health of their little dears. Given the contemporary juvenile death rates, such solicitude might seem reasonable, but Jane Austen usually sketches it as mildly ridiculous. A doctor who visits Marianne Dashwood, by 'allowing the word "infection" to pass his lips, gave instant alarm to Mrs Palmer on her baby's account'; 'within an hour' the potential victim has been swept by its mother from the house. Isabella Knightley is similarly obsessed with embrocations and maladies, and when Mrs Weston has a baby it need only be 'not quite well' for a minute for her thoughts to turn towards Perry. But presumably these flutterings are preferable to the fake concern of Lady Susan, who uses the risk of influenza as a means of getting rid of her daughter.

Lenience, solicitude, a permissive partiality—these are the characteristic faults of parents in Jane Austen. But of course not all the inadequate parents are neglectful or indulgent. There are also the more traditional villains, the cruel, stern or mercenary mentors, the familiar dragons and tartars. It is interesting, though, that in this category the main examples are from earlier books: Lady Susan, Mrs Ferrars, the blustering General Tilney. Very few parents in the later novels are guilty of excessive severity. The point is that Jane Austen was adopting a convention: despotic parents and prearranged marriages, the young romantically defying the old—things like this had been popular subjects for at least two centuries. It is arguable that from the very beginning Jane Austen distrusted such clichés. Defiance of paternal authority, in the cause of passion and liberation, was a feature of the sentimental novel which even at the age of fourteen, she attacked and ridiculed. *Love and Friendship* contains 'tyrannical' parents like those in, say, the novels of Charlotte Smith; but they emerge as considerably more generous than the aggrieved and gurgling lovers. 'No! Never shall it be said that I obliged my father' is the boast of the story's noble hero, and the heroine reduces to absurdity this stereotyped contempt: 'I must inform you of a trifling Circumstance . . . which I have as yet never mentioned.— The death of my Parents a few weeks after my Departure, is the circumstance I allude to.' Later Jane Austen made borrowings from the cast of the sentimental novel, but caricatures like General Tilney remain chiefly functional.

One parent from a later book might seem to disprove this thesis: Sir Thomas Bertram is surely censured for his ill-advised coldness towards his children, his inflexible severity. To some extent, of course, this is undeniable. Sir Thomas is 'not outwardly affectionate' and his reserve represses his daughters' spirits. To them he represents external restraint and his absence is therefore welcome. Jane Austen is clearly supporting the calls, increasingly frequent from the end of the century, for a closer connection between fathers and children, a more intimate and trusting bond. But although Sir Thomas is too remote, he is not too authoritative: he never acts better than when, without rancour, he puts an end to the play. Even his remoteness is less damaging than his mercenary ambition. Sir Thomas is certainly not a tender man, but this is not a major failing. Mr Price also lacks 'tenderness', but Fanny dislikes him, and pines for Mansfield, on revealingly different grounds. At Mansfield there is quiet and orderliness: 'If tenderness could be ever supposed wanting, good sense and good breeding supplied its place.' For Jane Austen there were better things than tenderness for the moral education of the young.

Indeed, one might state the case more strongly: in Jane Austen those who feel tenderness for children, or express pointed concern for them, are nearly always hypocrites, or transparent self-deceivers. Lady Susan, in her very first letter, curries favour by praising her hostess's children, while the dependent Margaret Watson is careful to gush about the niece she has left in Croydon (' "Sweet little darling!" cried Margaret. "It quite broke my heart to leave her" '). Another parasite, Mrs Clay, makes a point of inserting a flattering tribute to Mary's 'fine little boys'. No hypocrites, however, could outstrip the Steele sisters, who arrive at Lady Middleton's with a coach-load of playthings and then meet her children 'in continual raptures, extolling their beauty, courting their notice, and humouring all their whims'. Affection for children is often no more than a cover for self-interest. Fanny Dashwood disguises her appalling meanness as concern for the inheritance of her child, while her husband tells Elinor that he hasn't called because 'we were obliged to take Harry to see the wild beasts at Exeter Exchange' (a menagerie in the Strand). Emma, too, deceives herself, dandling her sister's smallest child as a means of mollifying Mr Knightley, and crying up the claims of 'little Henry' (her nephew, and heir to the Donwell estate) when she hears that her lover might marry. In Jane Austen's last work, *Sanditon*, Diana Parker, supposedly sick, bursts into her brother's house and immediately demands, 'Send for the children —I long to see them', before she has even begun to explain her unexpected arrival. From first to last the approvers of children are silly or insincere.

Taken in conjunction with all the wet doting, the implication of this is clear: no person who had reached the age of reason could wish to pay much attention to children; those who do so are soggy or sly. On the other hand it is almost impossible to be a *filial* hypocrite. Regard for parents, unlike love for children, is simply an individual's duty, and if duty prevails over inclination, this is not reprehensible. The few examples in Jane Austen's work of filial hypocrisy occur when characters pretend to affection as well as respect for their parents. Frank Churchill leans lovingly on the word *home* and Miss Bates, among others, succumbs: 'I do congratulate you, Mrs Weston, most warmly. He seems everything the fondest parent could—'

If we turn to the passages in Jane Austen that deal with the rights and duties of children, the picture is complete. Nearly all of them imply a great demand for respect, discretion and obedience, for deliberate self-effacement. A considerable tribute of attentiveness is expected from young people. Lady Bertram simply 'cannot do without' her Fanny who is eventually replaced by her sister Susan as 'the stationary niece'. A couple in *Lady Susan* require their son 'to keep up our spirits these long winter evenings', while fathers like Mr Watson and Mr Woodhouse need their daughters as nurses and slaves. So long as young people remain unmarried their parents' word is law. Elinor and Marianne stay on in London, despite their private preferences, because their mother has wished it. When Elizabeth Bennet, threatened with marriage, attempts to escape from Mr Collins, her mother insists that he must be heard: needless to say, 'Elizabeth would not oppose such an injunction.'

None of the heroines would dream of opposing: all of them are paragons of filial obedience. It is not, however, that their parents are particularly wise or good. On the contrary most of them are unsound and some are deplorable. But the heroines have to deplore them in secret: the mildest expostulation is the most they may openly risk. Fanny Price, Eleanor Tilney, Elizabeth Bennet and Anne Elliot are all on occasions deeply ashamed of what their parents do. But though they can't love their mothers and fathers, they accord them unfailing respect. Anne Elliot can see her father's faults—she has 'a knowledge, which she often wished less, of her father's character'. However, when he sneers at her for visiting her poor friend Mrs Smith, although she longs to say something back, 'her sense of personal respect to her father prevented her. She made no reply'. Later, when she is shown a letter in which Sir Walter is called a fool, 'Anne could not immediately get over the shock and mortification of finding such words applied to her father.' Presumably she would also be mortified by reading the book in which she appears, for Jane Austen is quite happy to describe the man as 'a foolish, spend-thrift baronet'. An odd fact about Jane Austen's books is that, for the most part, the heroines are discouraged from framing those explicitly critical judgements which the author herself, in writing such books, both enjoys and shows the need for.

Dutifulness is often, in fact, a sign or a test of virtue. Miss Bates's sterling character is revealed by her kindness to her aged mother—she even nips out from the ball at the Crown to help the old lady to bed. The theatricals in *Mansfield Park* are partly a test of duty. Edmund opposes because 'it would show great want of feeling on my father's account', while his sisters 'were not in the least afraid of their father's disapprobation'. Emma Watson is a dutiful girl: unlike her sisters she is 'delighted' to keep her father company and is greatly distressed when her imprudent aunt is spoken of disrespectfully. Mr Howard, whom Emma was eventually to marry, recommends himself early on by his charity to her father: he helps the old man, with his gouty foot, up a rather steep flight of steps. The relations in this work anticipate the situation in *Emma*. Whatever her other faults, Emma Woodhouse is a patient and generous daughter. Her adhesive loyalty is taken so far that, immediately after Mr Knightley's proposal, she forms a 'most solemn resolution of never quitting her father. She even wept over the idea of it, as a sin in thought'. Emma, moreover, judges other people largely by their kindness to this selfish old man. John Knightley's occasional 'want of respectful forbearance' is, in her eyes, his greatest fault, but she feels she can accept the Coles' invitation when they send to London for a folding-screen to protect Mr Woodhouse from a draught. Mr Knightley, so attentive to her father at Donwell, so willing to live with his father-in-law, is clearly the man to marry. It is notable that Mrs Isabella Knightley, despite her 'maternal solicitude', puts filial duty first. Her enormous indulgence towards her children stops short, we are told, at the point where it might disturb the old gentleman's peace.

As a rule only dubious characters complain of their relatives. Mary Crawford commits a grievous offence by referring to her uncle the Admiral (according to the author, 'a man of vicious conduct') as not her 'first favourite in the world'. 'Very wrong—' pronounces Edmund, 'very indecorous.' Oddly, however, Edward Ferrars, who speaks sarcastically about his mother, is seemingly not condemned.

Given the dictates of filial duty, what happens when there is a genuine clash between a parent and child? As we might expect, the answer depends as much on the sex as on the cause of the disaffected young person. A young man, in pursuit of what he himself wants, may sometimes defy his parents. When Catherine is banished from Northanger, she wonders what Henry Tilney will think, but assumes that he will not dare to speak to his irate, unreasonable father. But Henry abruptly ignores the General; he follows Catherine to her home and offers her his hand. However, this unusual show of independence is qualified by two facts. The first is that Henry is secure of a fortune by marriage settlements. The second is that Mr and Mrs Morland, despite the ferocity of the General's conduct, insist on obtaining his consent before they can vouchsafe theirs. A patriarch is a patriarch, even if he is mad.

Because of the laws of inheritance, and the smaller opportunities for independence, young women in Jane Austen's work are considerably more submissive. The heroine of the early story *Catharine* repeatedly employs a 'tone of great humility' to cope with her red-faced aunt. The plight of Susan Price is instructive, in the Portsmouth sections of *Mansfield Park*. A girl of fourteen with better judgement than her mother, Susan is right to see faults in her home life, but wrong to protest so shrilly. Fanny tries to teach her by example 'juster notions of what was due to everybody, and what would be wisest for herself'. In other words, a respect for one's parents is enjoined not only by duty but by prudence: Fanny can see 'all the obligation and expediency of submission'. A girl is not likely to have much power to amend her relatives' faults. Anne Elliot, having been told the truth about her scheming cousin, considers it a 'vain idea' to pass on the news to her family.

One of the most disputed questions on Jane Austen is how far Anne Elliot should have been guided by the advice of Lady Russell. The case presents a fundamental disagreement between a young person and her parent-figure (Lady Russell, we are told, had 'a mother's rights') and is clearly crucial to our understanding of filial obligation. A detailed discussion of this dispute would pull in almost every part of the book, but what we may briefly emphasise is the rather startling upshot: that although Lady Russell's advice was wrong, Anne was right to accept it. In the course of this novel one may notice a shift from the claims of romance to those of prudence, from passion to filial duty. Compare, for example, Anne's observations at the beginning and end of the book (the passages occur in chapter four and in the penultimate chapter). In two respects Anne maintains her opinion: that Lady Russell was in fact wrong and that, in similar circumstances, she herself would not give such advice. But in two other ways, by the end of the book, Anne's assessment has importantly changed. In the earlier passage she feels 'she should yet have been a happier woman in maintaining the engagement'; later she thinks the opposite. Then again, she believes at first that it would have been better to maintain the engagement even without any certainty of Captain Wentworth's success—'without reference to the actual results of their case'. Later she reverses this view, asserting

E

that the situation 'was, perhaps, one of those cases in which advice is good or bad only as the event decides'. The main effect of these changes of mind (as of, among other things, the character-contrast between Anne and Louisa Musgrove) is to give a retro-active justification of Anne's submission to duty. Lady Russell was certainly wrong, but the author doesn't wish to undermine the authority of an elder (even as it was, one contemporary critic complained about the moral of the book, 'which seems to be that young people should always marry according to their inclinations and upon their own judgment'). This impression is confirmed by a change in the text: in the final chapter in the book as it stands one sentence contrasts Anne with Lady Russell, to the latter's disadvantage:

> There is a quickness of perception in some, a nicety in the discernment of character, a natural penetration, in short, which no experience in others can equal, and Lady Russell had been less gifted in this part of understanding than her young friend.

Originally this read much more bluntly—and much more sub-versively (Chapman, 1926):

> A young woman proved to have more discrimination of character than her elder—to have seen in two instances more clearly what a man was.

Persuasion was Jane Austen's last complete novel, but similar alterations may be detected in even her earliest work. Among the erasures in the manuscript of *Catharine* is a piece of mild impertinence from the heroine to her aunt.

Jane Austen, then, insinuates throughout her work consistent approval of filial duty and parental authority. Her view of parent-child relations is profoundly pre-Romantic. She reveals in her fiction little belief in the wisdom or innocence of children and what she prizes most in young people is obedience and re-spect. Most important of all, the subject of childhood is not an emotional one for her; she has, indeed, only amused contempt for people who find it so. She can therefore see little to agitate her in the feelings or grievances of the young. In this she contrasts revealingly with later writers like Dickens.

But of course if we sum up her ideas like this, we are likely to flatten her tone. Her pervasive humour prevents her opinions (except for one or two notable lapses) from assuming that blunt and didactic shape which they take on in resumé. Although she endorses parental power, she is very far from adopting a pose of solemn exhortation. Indeed she mocks the contemporary taste for trite parental advice. She tells us that when Catherine Morland left home no warnings flowed from her mother's 'wise lips', while the father in her burlesque *Plan of a Novel* dies after 'four or five hours of tender advice and parental admonition to his miserable child'. Only a booby like Mr Collins would apologise for having accepted his dismissal from the woman he proposed to instead of from her mother, and only a crackpot like Sir Edward in *Sanditon* would start spouting an 'unrivalled address to parental affection' from Scott's *Lady of the Lake*. The claims of parental authority are never piously preached over: they are effectively implicit. Moreover, there are one or two bits in Jane Austen through which we can glimpse children happy or free— Catherine Morland at the age of ten 'rolling down the green slope at the back of the house'—or which indicate an affection for children of the sort that we find in her letters. Captain Harville makes toys for his children (as Jane Austen's brother Francis did) and Admiral Croft, surrounded by the Musgrove brood, proposes to carry them off in his pocket—an appropriate gesture, in this writer's work, for a pleasant-natured eccentric. Perhaps the most favoured child in the corpus is the little boy at the ball in *The Watsons*—Charles Blake, who is given a few remarks which suggest the power of innocence, and whose emotions and conversation are keenly, if briefly, evoked. But as a rule it is the adult world which fascinates Jane Austen. Children are nothing in themselves, and even when they are with their parents they rarely rate equal attention. To this there is perhaps just one exception: the uncharacteristic vignette in *Persuasion* of the family Christmas at Uppercross, with three groups of children present:

> On one side was a table, occupied by some chattering girls, cutting up silk and gold paper; and on the other were tressels and trays, bending under the weight of brawn and cold pies, where riotous boys were holding high revel; the whole completed by a roaring Christmas fire, which seemed determined to be heard, in spite of all the noise of the others. Charles and Mary also came in, of course, during their visit; and Mr Musgrove made a point of paying his respects to Lady Russell, and sat down close to her for ten minutes, talking with a

very raised voice, but, from the clamour of the children on his knees, generally in vain. It was a fine family-piece.

Even here it is the adults, rather than the children, who are picked out as individuals, but this was the closest Jane Austen ever came to creating a noisy and disorderly, but contented family scene. In this passage, uniquely, we are moving towards the domestic vision of Dickens.

(iii)

Christmas, hearthsides, boisterous children—perhaps it would be preferable to say that these are the usual ingredients in the popular memory of Dickens. It is in fact a highly selective memory, reliant on the Christmas books and stories, the festive merriment in *Pickwick Papers*, and a collection of rosy cameos that crop up in later works. Such radiance undoubtedly expressed the ideal, but the norm was strikingly different. Few husbands and wives are happy in Dickens, even fewer parents and children. Consider, for example, *Little Dorrit*: the antique honour of Old Nandy, the decency of the Chiverys—these things, beside the claustrophobic tensions of the Dorrits, the Calvinist ferocity of Mrs Clennam, emerge as minuscule. Painful family relations are the rule in Dickens. The suffering eclipses any flashes of domestic bliss.

The Marshalsea Prison in *Little Dorrit* may serve to remind us of Dickens's own childhood: his father's imprisonment for debt and his own longer term at the age of twelve as a 'drudge' in the blacking warehouse. The latter event in particular had a permanent effect on Dickens. His regard for the thoughts and emotions of children arose from a knowledge of their miseries; hence the bleakness, as well as the ubiquity, of his writings about the young. Likewise his shock at his mother's indifference affected his feelings about parents in general and inspired, as Edgar Johnson has said, 'that long sequence of rejected children, fatherless or motherless, neglected or abandoned, who move through almost all Dickens's stories' (Johnson, 1952). Indeed the ordeal may have cut even deeper than has always been suspected. Recently John Carey has convincingly shown how, again and again throughout his work, Dickens re-assembles the blacking factory, and places in the ruin a sad, lonely child uncorrupted by the murky surroundings (Carey, 1973). However, as Angus Wilson has observed, there are two common features of Dickensian childhood suffering—Calvinist gloom and factual cramming—which are not at all clearly discernible in the novelist's own childhood (Slater, 1970). Dickens of course helped to shape his age, but he was also influenced by it. As an heir to the Romantic poets and essayists, he adopted, extended and popularised the cult of juvenile innocence. As a generally progressive novelist, he absorbed those ideas about the treatment of children which had steadily become more acceptable since the end of the eighteenth century. His particular thoughts about upbringing were neither unique nor novel: what was sensationally new to fiction was his close and emotional focus on children, their centrality in his books. In fiction Dickens was the most persistent and the most influential champion of the young. His work therefore contrasts usefully with the writings of Jane Austen.

Interestingly, though, in his earliest work the contrast is not so great. The intensity of Dickens's concern for children—if not always, as noted, the particular forms—certainly derived from his personal experience, but this didn't mean, at least in his fiction, that his rage and concern were more intense the closer he was to his childhood. In fact the opposite seems to be true. In his earliest work his great empathy is obscured by a mask of convention. Anxious to conquer his degradations, to screen them from the eyes of his admiring public, he assumes a resilient, cheery persona, a tone of amused assurance. Part of this persona, robustly Georgian, is an attitude to children which is not his own: a heartily external attitude, a traditional smiling disdain. In *Sketches by Boz* and *Pickwick Papers* children are predominantly comic or vicious. Typical of the *Sketches* is the fourteen-year-old, scrutinised in 'Criminal Courts', who has disappointed his 'poor old mother' by his idleness and crime. The children in *Pickwick* are laughable gargoyles, selfish, greedy and dim: the Fat Boy, the ridiculous Master Bardell, the youngsters imprisoned in Sam Weller's humour —a smothered baby, a boy bled to death, a poor child who swallowed his sister's necklace and had to be muffled in the hospital because he rattled too much. This conventional jollity at the expense of children, a mixture of comedy, indifference and contempt, carries over into some of the later novels, especially when the subjects are low-bred. Simply in *David Copperfield*, for instance, we may laugh at the gangling Wilkins Micawber, the 'orfling', a comic maid who snorts, or David and Dora's impossible page, a chronically tearful, weak-headed orphan who gets transported for stealing a watch—'expatriated', as David facetiously rephrases it, ' "up the country" somewhere; I have no geographical idea where'. Dickens's sympathy for children, arising out of pity for himself, was sometimes startlingly limited. Normally, however, he was less self-centred and even in his earlier work his feeling for children, his compassion for and delight in them could not be entirely suppressed. *Sketches of Young Couples* (1840) has a withering portrait of doting parents which Jane Austen might have appreciated, but despite his attempt at disapproval Dickens's account of the spoiled infants—dabbling their fingers in damson syrup, waving their legs and spoons in the air—is aglow with happy indulgence. Similarly, in *Pickwick* and *Sketches by Boz* there are one or two tremulous deathbed scenes through which Dickens's emotions about maltreated childhood are given some relief.

In his apprentice fiction, then, Dickens largely disguised the feelings that sprang from his own early years. Among these feelings were his sympathy for children, but also his resentment of his parents. He began by adopting a conventional stance, regarding young people loftily as lower forms of life. Gradually, though, and overwhelmingly, he revealed his identification with them, and then, more slowly and cautiously, he went on to satirise parents. At the same time, however, he held up for approval a cosy ideal of domestic contentment—parents and children in unison—which he personally had seldom enjoyed. As a result there is a curious dichotomy in his presentation of family life. Though frequently extolling filial affection, he is rather reluctant to portray it. Nor, when he does so, is there any real doubt about where his true powers reside. The merriment is flaccid compared with the pain: it is the difference between a deeply felt experience and a nebulous aspiration.

In his early books we can watch Dickens working out the implications of what he had known. He builds on the notion of childhood innocence, rejects the usual adult attitudes, and eventually comes to concentrate on the irresponsibility of parents. *Oliver Twist* enlists sympathy for the child by depicting him as a defenceless victim. There is no attack on parents, for Oliver is an orphan, but what we may observe in the early chapters is something like a bullying conspiracy of the old against the young.

As far as children are concerned, sprucely respectable parish officials and sadistic boors like Gamfield the sweep are shown to be in gruesome collusion; the only blessing invoked upon Oliver comes from little Dick. But though Oliver is innocent, he is also passive. The figure we recall is the recipient of oppression, the lugubrious waif of Cruikshank's etchings. At this stage childhood innocence is merely a negative quality, affording a moral immunity-pass to its fortunate possessor.

Persecution is one concomitant of Dickensian childhood innocence; another is premature death. In Jane Austen there is only one juvenile death—that of Mary Price in *Mansfield Park*—and it takes up about five lines. But for Dickens the connection between goodness and graves was something extremely important. Oliver Twist himself survives (he becomes a contented legatee), but the death of his tortured friend little Dick points forward to the future pattern. In *Nicholas Nickleby* childlike innocence again leads to the grave. The victim is this time the plaintive Smike, a 'listless, hopeless, blighted creature' who, during his first conversation with Nicholas, comes up with the question, 'What faces will smile on me when I die?' Many of his sufferings are a replay of Oliver's: ill-used in an oppressive institution, he is rescued, kidnapped and recovered; he even awakes, while dozing in the country, for a glimpse of horror from the past. In this book, however, in apportioning blame, the author can be seen to be edging towards a partial indictment of parents. Smike turns out to be Ralph Nickleby's son, and although Ralph's paternity is primarily a plot convenience, the revelation is significant: in *Nicholas Nickleby* parental exploitation is a minor but definite theme. The parents are shown to be using their children for various selfish ends. Apart from the egocentric demands of Mrs Nickleby herself (a portrait, of course, of Dickens's mother), there are Mr and Mrs Kenwigs showing off their daughter's dancing skill and Vincent Crummles putting the infant phenomenon through her paces. Mr Snevellicci uses his daughter's honour as a pretext for indulging in tipsy threats, while Mr Bray uses Madeline as both a mediator for his sponging and a butt for his rancour. Even Squeers betrays warped parental pride, commending the feeding at Dotheboys Hall by poking at his corpulent son.

All the children here are exploited in some way, but not all are exemplars of innocence. In *The Old Curiosity Shop*, however, the equation of youthfulness with virtue is taken to its hopeful limit. In this book all the adult-child relations are based on Dickens's firm rejection of the doctrine of depravity. Nell, of course, is 'guiltless of all harm or wrong', but so is Kit Nubbles; so is the Marchioness; so is the schoolmaster's favourite pupil; so is Miss Edwards at Miss Monflather's academy; so is the bereaved youngster who requests Nell not to become an angel; so, even, is Quilp's boy, who despite his matiness with the malignant dwarf, is never treated as genuinely evil, merely as ebullient and jokily anarchic. One consequence of this optimistic vision is that children need little restraint. Adults who ignore this are depicted as tyrants: the imperious Miss Monflathers, the repellent Sally Brass (a sadist who, in a cancelled draft, was more clearly the Marchioness's mother). In contrast we have the indulgent vignettes of liberated children: the whooping pupils of the schoolmaster, the urchins with the bachelor. The suggestion is that children, like the Garlands' pony, will respond only to mildness.

Thus far *The Old Curiosity Shop* is merely extending what was always implicit in Dickens's previous books. But it also introduces something new: the idea that children have moral authority, that they are the genuine teachers. Nell, unlike her virtuous predecessors, is not only a Victim but also a Guide: in character she alternates curiously between a timorous, vulnerable maid and a managing little mum. When her grandfather regresses to infancy, becoming a helpless or mischievous brat, Little Nell takes charge of him. Likewise Kit Nubbles looks after his mother, sustaining her spirits with compliments but also, when the occasion demands, dispensing a brisk moral lecture. This role-reversal was used by Dickens in several subsequent books. Children who have to take care of their parents, or even—like the work-weary Jenny Wren— berate them for their naughtiness, are among his most favoured fixtures.

Such ministering children might possibly remind us of the heroes of Evangelical tracts: those youngsters, too, on account of their virtue, were allowed to enlighten their parents. But apart from the comedy of Dickens's conception (Kit Nubbles preaches *anti*-puritanism), the types are different because virtue in Dickens is made to depend not on Christian conversion but on youthfulness itself. This is one reason why, in Dickens's work, so many of the children die. Death is almost indispensable as a moral preservative. John Forster, in his biography of Dickens, claims credit for the death of Nell: he successfully urged Dickens to kill her off 'so that the gentle pure little figure and form should never change to the fancy'. Nell is too good for this world and therefore departs for the next.

The dying child in Dickens is also intended, as Philip Collins has rightly observed, to indict the adult world. But in the case of Nell, as in previous books, it is not the victim's mother and father who end up in the dock. Creating a series of pitiful orphans, Dickens held back in his earlier work from roundly condemning parents. With the appearance of *Barnaby Rudge*, however (the first of his novels to be conceived), such hesitation ceased. The book is a comprehensive attack on paternal delinquency.

The children here are not juveniles but young people on the verge of leaving home. There are five sets of filial relationship and in all except one the father is seen as a bully or exploiter. Sir John Chester is a character who seems to have arisen from Dickens's indignant (and careless) perusal of Lord Chesterfield's notorious *Letters*. An icy, imperturbable hypocrite, he casts off his son in a scene which looks forward to that between Charles Darnay and his uncle the Marquis in *A Tale of Two Cities*. Sir John also has an illegitimate child, the anarchic centaur Hugh of the Maypole, whom he systematically exploits. Even after discovering his paternity, he is happy to let his son hang. John Willet, the blockheaded innkeeper, flanked by his deferential cronies, likewise relies on the services of his quick and obliging, long-suffering son, though he also enjoys exposing him to public humiliation. Eventually the frustrated Joe Willet rebels: after hurling one of the goading toadies head foremost into a heap of spittoons, he runs away to join the army, which, as the remarks of the sergeant suggest, is attractive partly for the freedom it offers from the conventional respect for fathers (contrariwise, when Joe says goodbye to Dolly, she dismays him by asking after Mr Willet, 'that dear old gentleman'). The galloping murderer Mr Rudge ungraciously curses his offspring twice, once before and once after birth. By stabbing someone just before Barnaby is born, he endows the baby with idiocy and a blood-red spot on the wrist. Later, when his son is fully grown, he threatens to kill him, exploits his good nature, but eventually shuns him as an unpleasant symbol, making off to the gallows with no further message than a vicious imprecation. By contrast Mr Haredale, Emma's uncle, seems a positively mellow guardian, but even he, before finally winning her praise as the kindest possible father-figure, colludes with his life-long enemy Chester in stopping her love affair. The only forbearing and genial father is the sturdy Gabriel Varden. He spoils his daughter Dolly, but is none the worse for that: nor, ultimately, is she. He is willing to forgive his strutting apprentice, the one rebel against paternalist authority whose revolt is unjustified.

Most of the fathers are callous or despotic, most of the children oppressed. But although each case is notably different, the book forges links between the fathers, as also between the sons. Rudge attacks Edward and strikes Joe Willet, as well as threatening his idiot boy. John Chester, on arriving at the Maypole Inn, impresses Old Willet by his favourable contrast with the rude and unruly young. Conversely, when Joe is collared by his father, Chester delights in his public disgrace. The sons are similarly associated, for Joe conveys messages for Edward, they break from their fathers in consecutive chapters, they emigrate on the same day. The tendency of these and other linkings is not difficult to discern. By establishing conspiracy among the parents, and solidarity between the sons, the book questions the authority of the older generation and celebrates the younger.

What is more problematical is the link between these filial antagonisms and the social and political events: how does Dickens relate the riots to the abuses of paternal authority in the earlier parts of the book? Clearly there is likely to be some connection between a writer's opinions on filial duty and his general social views. Mrs Trimmer, we remember, feared that unbeaten children might grow up to dance the *carmagnole*, and Jane Austen's appreciation of discipline is of a piece with her social values. With Dickens, too, there is a genuine connection between his— for the most part—radical politics, his distrust of established authority, and his treatment of family relations. But in *Barnaby Rudge* the two ends of this tie-up are not satisfactorily joined. If the novel proposes, as is often alleged, an 'analogy between society and the family', it is surely incoherent. There is little equation of parental severity with the misuse of power on the part of the rulers, and even less of a relation between the filial rebellions and the social insurrection. Chester, one of the tyrannous fathers, finds it convenient to foment the riots, while Joe and Edward, filial victims, are prominent in opposing them. Joe fights on the colonialist side in the American War of Independence, while Hugh, cruelly used by both his father and society, lashes out violently against the one and succumbs to the wiles of the other. To substantiate the point would take much longer, but crudely one could say that in *Barnaby Rudge* the family and society, far from being analogous, are almost separate spheres. In the home, authority is largely abused. In society, attacks on authority are largely unjustified.

The critique of parents in *Barnaby Rudge* is, then, only loosely related to the vision of society. But Dickens soon became far more skilful in the assimilation of domestic scenes to social analysis. More and more he assailed the pre-Romantic, utilitarian approach to children, and more and more he aligned this approach with larger public evils. In *Dombey and Son* what poisons parent-child relations is the notion of children as personal property. Dombey is estranged from both daughter and son because of his purse-pride, his unyielding belief that all life can be cast into commercial terms. He thaws a little towards his son because a boy is an asset, an addition to the firm, a reassuring extension of his own ego; a girl is 'merely a piece of base coin that couldn't be invested'. Dombey's attitude permeates all society, for both Mrs Skewton and Good Mrs Brown use their offspring as possessions. In *Hard Times*, likewise, filial conflict represents something far more insidious than a mere clash of temperament. It is a *systematic* psychic cruelty that Gradgrind inflicts and the evil is in the system, not the man. The philosophy he uses in training his children pervades education and industry too. The book broadens out from the school to the home to the northern industrial city: in each the same dogmas are paramount: the belief in self-interest as the cardinal motive, the apotheosis of the quantifiable. Gradgrind's mechanical treatment of his children is refuted by the titles of the separate volumes: 'Sowing', 'Reaping' and 'Garnering'. Since learning is rather an organic process, the father reaps and garners what he has sown. Hence the first volume ends with Louisa's marriage; the second with her collapse at her father's feet; the third with Tom's disgrace.

Increasingly, then, in his indictment of erring parents, Dickens has some larger evil more directly in mind. He attacks Calvinism, Benthamism and commercial inhumanity, and the parent-child relationship provides a useful container for putting the abuse on display. The nature and causes of parental misconduct are shaped by the themes of the individual book. One might compare Mrs Jellyby and Mrs Matthew Pocket, who both allow their children to tumble into mischief unchecked. Their reasons are significantly different: Mrs Jellyby is preoccupied with misdirected and over-systematised social philanthropy; Mrs Pocket preens herself as too much of an aristocrat to tackle mundane domestic tasks. Both failings connect with the wider themes of *Bleak House* and *Great Expectations*.

One assumption, however, remained constant in Dickens, his legacy from the Romantics: that childhood is a special and better period, that its innocence and spontaneity should never be heartlessly quenched. Such a view could not fail to have repercussions on parent-child relations. Admiration for the purity of smaller children promoted a general respect for the young, and this in its turn meant that mothers and fathers, even those whose offspring were no longer juvenile, were expected to behave with greater forbearance, to demonstrate greater concern. Even—perhaps especially—the humblest child deserved some affection and care. In Dickens the adults are often 'placed' by their attitudes to the young. Consider, for example, the cast of *Bleak House*. Esther Summerson is naturally affectionate with children, popular and entertaining. Inspector Bucket, on the other hand, merely pretends to be keen on them when he arrives to arrest Mr George. The apparently implacable nature of Gridley is suddenly given a new complexion by his gentleness with the orphans. Perhaps most strikingly revealed are those who have dealings with Jo: Chadband, who treats him as a springboard for a sermon; Skimpole, who betrays him; Guppy, casually uninterested; Snagsby, kind but uninvolved and ineffectual, always ready with half-a-crown, 'that magic balsam of his for all kinds of wounds'. Responsiveness to children is the soundest test of a character's moral standing.

The doctrine of the natural goodness of children entailed a number of other beliefs which, throughout the Victorian period, were increasingly proclaimed. Three in particular may be specified, all of them common in Victorian thought. Each contradicts the approach of Jane Austen; each finds its consummate embodiment in the novels and stories of Dickens.

The first is the conviction that, children being innocent, the wickedest thing one can do to them is to rob them of their childhood. 'Spoiling' seemed far less pernicious to Dickens than imposing maturity. He himself had almost been cheated of his childhood, and as early as his sketch 'A Visit to Newgate', he delivered a passionate threnody for youngsters 'who have never

known what childhood is. . . . The thousand nameless endearments
of childhood, its gaiety and its innocence, are alike unknown to
them.' The lament continues into the novels, which are crammed
with the victims—Jenny Wren, 'Charley' Neckett—of enforced
prematurity. Half the case against Mr Dombey is the way he
wants to hustle Paul into adulthood—'Dear me, six will be changed
to sixteen, before we have time to look about us.' (Compare
Alderman Cute in *The Chimes*: 'We shall have this little gentleman in Parliament . . . before we know where we are.') The
effects of such treatment are engraved on those adults—Edith
Dombey, Arthur Clennam, Mr Jackson in *Mugby Junction*—who
sadly or bitterly recognise that they never had a childhood. On
occasions, though, Dickens will blame the victims, implying they
have somehow perversely chosen to dry themselves up. We recall,
for example, the etiolated Smallweeds, who have acquired a
wizened worldly shrewdness from living in an imaginative
drought. Similar monsters feature in *Martin Chuzzlewit*: Jonas
has an old head on young shoulders (Dickens declares he would
like to knock it off), Ruth Pinch's rude and sneaky pupil is
a thirteen-year-old with 'nothing girlish about her', and the
Misses Mould, daughters of the undertaker, have ripened into
prematurity 'sporting behind the scenes of death'. Significantly,
though, in this novel, Dickens does not train his sarcasm on the
premature knowingness of Young Bailey. Such swagger and
bravado he finds engaging, even when, as with the Artful Dodger,
they indicate some genuine corruption. At least these youngsters,
for all their toughness, have preserved a measure of whimsy: the
wayward fancifulness of childhood has not entirely withered.

Dickens's belief in the sanctity of childhood determined his
attitude towards juvenile reading—his insistence that fiction and
fairy-tales must displace tracts and treatises. The Evangelical
approach to children, cautionary and stained with expedience, is
mocked in many of Dickens's novel, while his opposition to the
Rationalist books, chock-full of indigestible data, is everywhere
apparent in *Hard Times*. In 1869 he recalled his reading (in an
article reprinted in *The Uncommercial Traveller*) of Thomas Day's
Sandford and Merton. He depicted Mr Barlow as an 'instructive
monomaniac', patiently removing the magic from life:

If he could have got hold of the Wonderful Lamp, I knew he
would have trimmed it and lighted it, and delivered a lecture

over it on the qualities of sperm oil, with a glance at the whale fisheries.

Barlow, for Dickens, is the enemy of clowns and pantomimes, a purveyor of abstruse technical information: Barlow, quite clearly, is Gradgrind.

A second corollary of juvenile innocence (not a strictly logical one) is the notion that adults, too, to be virtuous, would need to resemble the young. This notion of course contrasts with Jane Austen, who acknowledges little or no distinction between the childlike and the childish. In her work adults who remind us of children are deficient or risible. Mr Woodhouse, poring over Mr Knightley's curios, is, we're told, 'fortunate in having no other resemblance to a child than in a total want of taste for what he saw, for he was slow, constant and methodical'. Charles Musgrove is sometimes petulantly puerile and when he books a box at the theatre for his mother, he exhibits an undignified childish delight: 'An't I a good boy? I know you love a play. . . . Have not I done well, mother?' Admittedly, in literature before Jane Austen, there was also a tradition of childlike virtue—it was available, for example, in Sterne. But Dickens took it further than ever before. His pantheon is crammed with a soft-boiled array of credulous infantile adults. Mr Pickwick, Tom Pinch, Trotty Veck, Captain Cuttle, Mat Bagnet, Mr George, Joe Gargery, Jarvis Lorry, Mr Boffin, Mr Crisparkle—the list of those approvingly likened to children, either explicitly or by implication, is almost interminable. Many of the female characters, too, are closely akin to children: Little Dorrit, or Ruth Pinch, or the winsome, wifely Dot Peerybingle, the heroine of *The Cricket on the Hearth* ('I'm such a silly little thing, John, that I like, sometimes, to act a kind of Play with Baby, and all that: and make believe'). Dependable adults are not only like children, they also remember their childhood. Esther Summerson, like Dickens himself, continually dreams of her tender years, while Jarvis Lorry in *A Tale of Two Cities* declares they no longer seem very far off although he is nearing eighty. Tom Pinch, too, discovers that his boyhood is still ineffaceably with him: as he gazes into a children's bookshop in Salisbury, phantoms from the past swim delightfully into his mind. Corrupt adults, on the other hand, have long burnt their bridges to youth. Casby, for instance, in *Little Dorrit*: 'Perhaps there never was a man . . . so troublesome for the imagination to picture as a boy.' Moral renovation is frequently sealed by a sudden reversion to childhood: the apparently dying Sir Leicester Dedlock 'like a child' in trooper George's arms, old Anthony Chuzzlewit 'crying like a little child', penitent at the last. Perhaps the most successful regression is Scrooge's: magnificently wrinkled and crabbed at first, broken down by visions of juvenile jollity, eventually converted into a benevolent nursling ('I'm quite a baby. Never mind. I don't care. I'd rather be a baby'), he ends up patting children's heads and playing 'wonderful games'.

Adults less fortunate than Scrooge, unable to turn into jubilant children, may at least be refreshed by their presence. In Jane Austen children are usually kept separate, they can please but not edify their elders, and they have to be maintained. In Dickens it is quite otherwise: a third offshoot of the doctrine of innocence is the idea that contact with the young will enrich and regenerate. This theme, which received its classic formulation in George Eliot's *Silas Marner*, is also ubiquitous in Dickens, though the treatment is far more insipid. Arthur Clennam, perked up by the girlish Pet Meagles, is only restored to total vigour by the juvenile Little Dorrit. Dr Manette is revived by his daughter, while Jane Gradgrind testifies that Sissy Jupe (adopted from the childlike circus people) has greatly improved her complexion. In the Christmas stories children are continually required to rejuvenate the jaded. The gruff Englishman in *Somebody's Luggage* is melted by a cuddlesome girl he adopts—an orphan endowed with a 'little fat throat' and the obligatory dimpled hands. The grey, lonely clerk in *Mugby Junction* keeps himself cheerful by borrowing Polly, his former sweetheart's daughter. Also pining for juvenile contact is the faded hero of *The Poor Relation's Story*, who befriends Little Frank and weeps when a stranger mistakes the child for his own.

Since children and young people have so much to offer, one might expect adults to court their company and treat them considerately. But except for a few forlorn bachelors, such affection rarely occurs in Dickens—which is fortunate, for when it does the writing degenerates. Among the admirable characters there are very few happy and successful parent-child relationships. There are, of course, numerous vapid vignettes of lower-class family affection. The Nubbleses in *The Old Curiosity Shop* swarm round in a thin haze of merriment—the family 'all strongly alike', red-cheeked and laughing in concert. Dickens was listlessly fond of such scenes: this corporate mirth is set in motion again with the

Toodle family in *Dombey and Son*, the Bagnet 'light infantry' in *Bleak House*, the Cratchits in *A Christmas Carol* and the Tetterbys in *The Haunted Man*. Filial affection is also permitted when either the parent or the child is incapacitated. Occasionally, as with Wemmick and the Aged P., the dependent party is the older one, but more often it is the younger. Unlike the majority of children in Dickens, cripples can count on affection. Tiny Tim is beloved by his family, Barnaby Rudge by his mother. 'Lamps' the railwayman in *Mugby Junction* and Caleb Plummer in *The Cricket on the Hearth* have both devoted their lives to their daughters, who are, respectively, crippled and blind. Dr Marigold adopts a deaf-and-dumb child, Caddy Jellyby gives birth to one: in both cases the infirmity ensures sustained affection. Likewise Master Humphrey, who is horribly deformed, recalls how, in his earliest childhood, his mother would dote on him.

The only filial relationship of any length in Dickens which appears to prosper despite the fact that both partners are sound of body and mind, is that between Bella Wilfer and her father in *Our Mutual Friend*. Even this is evidently fabricated as a quaint curiosity: 'It was always pleasantly droll to see Pa and Bella together.' But Dickens does manage to communicate much of their reciprocal enjoyment and affection. He does so by distorting their expected roles. Bella acknowledges the distortion when she refers to her father as a brother, but the reader may dispute her diagnosis. She is not so much a sister to him as a mother-cum-lover. She takes benevolent charge of him, instructing him to buy a new suit of clothes or babying him at his meals. But there is also a sensuous undercurrent in her fondness for twining her fingers through his hair, acting delightedly as his 'beautiful woman', meeting him for liaisons he must keep secret from his wife, or 'stopping on every separate stair to put the tip of her forefinger on her rosy lips, and then lay it on his lips'. Her two characters are fused when she gives him a wash:

> Bella soaped his face and rubbed his face, and soaped his hands and rubbed his hands, and splashed him and rinsed him and towelled him, until he was as red as beet-root, even to his very ears.

It is as if he is being handled by a faintly erotic nanny.

Despite its oddity the relationship does not come across as twisted or suspect. It is appropriate that we should sense Bella's physical presence, and the time she treats her father as if he needs a nappy is when her thoughts are full of the baby she is going to have. Nevertheless even this happy relationship depends on the daughter rather than the father being the dominating figure. Love must flow mainly from the child's side rather than the parent's.

Apart from cripples and the lower classes, there are two other areas in Dickens's work where, in contrast with the usual pattern, parents and children harmonise. The first comprehends those episodes where Dickens expresses belief in the force, the unerring mystic semaphores, of the blood relationship. To Jane Austen the notion seemed laughable, as witness the outburst in *Love and Friendship* when the heroine spies an old gentleman descending from a coach: 'At his first appearance my Sensibility was wonderfully affected . . . an instinctive Sympathy whispered to my Heart, that he was my Grandfather.' But in Dickens such awestruck communions are common between parent and child. In *Barnaby Rudge* the gaze of Hugh keeps locking with that of the evil Chester, while Barnaby himself, attacking a robber, has only to hear the words 'I am your father' to fall back aghast, and then spring forward, in a warm embrace of the murderer. *Bleak House* contains two such reunions which pay homage to the ties of nature. The first is when Esther claps eyes on Lady Dedlock: 'Shall I ever forget the rapid beating at my heart occasioned by the look I met as I stood up!' The second is between Mr George and his mother, when the trooper regresses like a born actor: after clasping his parent round the neck, he goes down on his knees before her, folds his hands together in prayer, 'and raising them towards her breast, bows down his head, and cries'. In *A Tale of Two Cities* Lucie Manette, confronted at last with her jail-broken father, simply lays her hand on his arm: 'A strange thrill struck him when she did so, and visibly passed over his frame.' These *frissons* are plainly delightful to Dickens, but the language, hackneyed and histrionic, betrays his real disbelief. Parental neglect, exploitation, oppression are cogently dramatised in his work. When he aims to communicate filial concord, he whips up a synthetic lather.

There is, however, one exception to this rule: if both parent and child are corrupt or unpleasant, Dickens is usually highly successful in conveying their ghoulish agreement. He enjoys demonstrating how dutiful children can learn all too well from their evil elders. Oddly this pattern begins with a pair who are scarcely evil but are, one might say, morally unorthodox. Sam Weller and his father Tony, equipped with the same deflating humour, the same Cockney smartness and talent for roughstuff, enjoy, despite their sarcasms, a perfectly trusting rapport. The father boasts to Mr Pickwick that he has taken great pains with his son's 'eddication', allowing him to shift for himself in the streets. The son owns to a high sense of filial duty: he would always ask his father to give him a thing before he proceeded to steal it. Parents and children of this kidney continue to flourish in Dickens's work, but after the Wellers they become corrupt: Dickens is intrigued by how easily a vice can be handed on. That obedience can compound villainy is a prominent theme in *Martin Chuzzlewit*, a book which, as one of its chapter headings has it, 'Exhibits filial Piety in an ugly Aspect'. While Martin takes after his grandfather, Jonas reduplicates old Anthony's foibles: trained to think of everything in property terms, he now regards his father gloomily 'as a certain amount of personal estate' which would be safest 'banked in the grave'. After taking steps towards this end, he pays 'dutiful attention' to his father's terminal symptoms. The funeral arrangements, says the undertaker, are the most 'filial' he has seen. The pattern repeats itself in *Bleak House*, where old Smallweed congratulates Bart on his scrounging, while the grand-children are waiting for the old man to die. Eventually his financial wiles are wiped out when they avariciously betray him. Other mentors who live to regret their own products include Mr Gradgrind (with his children and Bitzer) and Miss Havisham (with Estella). Sometimes the unsavoury filial duos resemble each other not only in character, but also in appearance. Juliana MacStinger in *Dombey and Son*, a forceful man-catcher like her mother, is 'already the image of her parent'. Mrs Heep, in *David Copperfield*, is 'the dead image of Uriah, only short'. The culminating couple in this convention are Jerry Cruncher and his son, the characters in *A Tale of Two Cities* who bear 'a close resemblance to a pair of monkeys'. Jerry's boy, 'a grisly urchin of twelve, who was his express image', is eager to follow his father's profession of digging up dead bodies. He reveals his obedience early on, for when Jerry throws boots at his wife for praying, instructing his son to keep an eye on her and call him if there are 'any signs of more flopping', the child—'whose head', as Dickens remarks, 'was garnished with tender spikes'—maintains the required watch on his mother and makes her life miserable. Jerry comes to feel that his lively boy will yet be a blessing to him.

All told, this parade of eccentrics and crooks, so horribly efficient in transmitting their flaws, is hardly a shining advertisement for filial obedience: if receptiveness can lead to this, rebellion might be better. Not, of course, that Dickens is being subversive: characters who fail in filial duty, like the young, unregenerate Martin Chuzzlewit or the blustering Bounderby in Hard Times ('There's no family pride about me, there's no imaginative sentimental humbug about me'), are always firmly condemned. But since Dickens chooses to concentrate not on contented families, but rather on delinquent parents and guardians, those who exploit or neglect their charges, he ends up by making obedience seem a virtue that leads to corruption.

Usually, then, in Dickens's work, the parents are miserable failures; those who are not tend to succeed in warping their children's minds. His portrayal of adults is scarcely tender: habitually their treatment of the young is foolish or cruel or both. These impressions were based on his personal experience: he remarked in a letter of 1844 that to him most parents seemed selfish with their children. His vision of the young, on the other hand, is basically optimistic: they at least have the potential for good and he celebrates their freshness and innocence in a manner which in previous centuries would have ranked as preposterous. He believes that childhood is valuable, not a period to be completed in anxious haste. He admires grown people who have childlike qualities and suggests that the company of the young can be morally invigorating. He deprecates sternness in upbringing (he was always against corporal punishment), abhors any utilitarian approach, and the process of induction to the adult world he regards as quite often disastrous. In all these respects he is, of course, diametrically opposed to Jane Austen.

But perhaps our conclusions should not be so sweeping, for Dickens was a multifarious man whose opinions not only underwent change but were sometimes inconsistent. One area where he partially revised his assumptions concerned childlike innocence. In his later books he shows how this popular virtue can easily be faked: characters like Bishop in Little Dorrit, or (a particularly skilful portrait) Harold Skimpole in Bleak House, embody the abuse of juvenile innocence, its artificial and artful protraction for the sake of personal gain. Moreover, after the earlier works, it is offered as a vulnerable quality, no longer a simple talisman which guarantees success. When Sissy Jupe's 'childlike ingenuous-ness' affords her a victory over Harthouse, the confrontation, though close to the mawkish, is a marked improvement on similar scenes in Dickens's earlier books: for example, in *Nicholas Nickleby*, where Kate's stinging purities make Ralph stagger back, or a whole nest of villains can be plunged in consternation 'by the presence of one young innocent girl!' In his treatment of innocence the turning-point was probably *David Copperfield*, a novel which, as Q.D. Leavis has shown, reveals how the retention of trustfulness can prove to be a disability. David's mother succumbs to the black charm of Murdstone, while the hero is enamoured of the feckless Dora and captivated by Steerforth; likewise the basically good-natured Micawber is duped by Uriah Heep. The most disastrous example of credulity is no doubt Little Em'ly's (Steerforth, she believes, will make her a lady), but even Betsey Trotwood, we learn, was hurt by her innocence earlier in life, trusting a husband who broke her fortune and nearly broke her heart. However, it would be a mistake to exaggerate the consistency of the rigorousness of this critical reappraisal. David says his childish love for Em'ly was purer than anything in later life, and although in the main he is wryly objective when recalling his spooney responses to Dora, he also has moments where he praises them for their 'purity of heart'. What is more, the odd sub-plot with Dr Strong runs feebly counter to the general pattern, the old scholar's soft, blinkered trustfulness being grandly vindicated. Similar ambivalence may be detected in the book's critique of undisciplined affection, particularly that of parents. Certainly much of the parental love has swollen and deformed itself into fixation—Mr Wickfield's adoration of Agnes is 'diseased' (when Heep starts to talk about marrying her, the father rises from the table with a scream), and similar feelings fester within the possessiveness of Mrs Steerforth. But again there appears to be a sentimental exception: the throaty devotion of the wronged uncle, Daniel Peggotty. Mrs Leavis has argued that this, too, 'without any possibility of denial or conjecture', is clearly meant to be morbid. It is admittedly impossible to deny that—in the eyes of a modern reader at least—there does seem something a bit strange about Mr Peggotty's attachment. When he first hears that Em'ly has run off with Steerforth, blood springs out of his mouth. Later, after finding the fallen woman, he heaves as he

gives an impassioned account of how he has just come from
spending the night with his niece's arms round his neck. To be
sure, these are not, as Mrs Leavis remarks, feelings which would
normally be understood as 'creditable to a worthy uncle'. But her
contention is that Dickens himself emphatically intended a dis-
turbing effect. If so, it is difficult to know what to do with David
Copperfield's unwavering praise for Mr Peggotty's mission : David
keeps insisting on his 'rugged eloquence', his noble 'steadfastness
of purpose', his 'patient gravity'. David, of course, is not Dickens;
but when he makes misjudgements, as he often does, they
are always plainly presented as such. There is no evidence whatever that we are meant to disengage Dickens's view of Mr
Peggotty from David's. We are informed that the fervently
affectionate uncle, after delivering the second of his travel mani-
festos ('I'm a-going to seek her, fur and wide' etc.), disappears
into 'a glow of light'—not, surely, an hallucination of David's.
The idealisation is Dickens's own, and if we can scarcely believe
that the author, in his treatment of Emily and Mr Peggotty, could
condone the odd sexual undercurrents, we need only notice what
wins his approval elsewhere in the book. David winds up with a
sister-wife, Annie Strong with a father-husband. Even Peggotty
might be spared some concern : Barkis may be willin', but one
wonders whether he is able.

Dickens continued, then, to revere childlike innocence, as also
the power of untutored affection, even though he became, in his
later works, more alert to their limitations. A somewhat surer
consideration, for closing the gap between him and Jane Austen,
is his attitude to care and discipline. Despite his belief in natural
goodness, he still thought that children should be superintended,
and despite his opinion of the majority of parents, he worshipped
obedience. The first point is evidenced by the fact that increasingly
neglect, rather than oppression, is stressed as the hurtful force.
The early books have cruder bullies and exploiters : Squeers,
Willet, Sally Brass. But Dombey is seldom actively hostile, merely
chillingly unresponsive, while David Copperfield, though beaten
once, is far more woundingly ignored. Even in *Hard Times*,
although Tom and Louisa are 'crammed with all sorts of dry
bones and sawdust', the reader mourns chiefly for what they
have missed : their condition is defined repeatedly in terms of
loss, starvation, blindness—images of privation (compare the
description of Bitzer's skin : 'unwholesomely deficient in the natu-

ral tinge'). Of course, blatantly oppressive parents continue to crop up in later works (Rogue Riderhood, for instance, in *Our Mutual Friend*), but in the main, with the later mentors, it is not so much what they do to their children as what they leave undone. That neglect is an evil is also apparent from those youngsters who, wholly abandoned by society, remain quite uncivilised. Jo in *Bleak House* is primordially decent, but the brutish little boy in *The Haunted Man*, and the hideous 'Deputy' in *Edwin Drood*, are striking examples of juvenile jetsam created by adult neglect.

As for filial obedience, Dickens's admiration for this is almost as great as Jane Austen's. True, he has warmer affection for children and is therefore more indulgent. But he also prizes submissiveness, particularly in girls. Florence, Nell and Little Dorrit are all adoringly loyal to their elders, though undervalued and spurned. Louisa is sometimes wearily sullen, but she still comes back to her father's house when her marriage has finally collapsed. Even the young men in *Barnaby Rudge*, who do go so far as to break from their fathers, are almost heroically deferential, in view of their provocation. The fact is that Dickens himself, as a parent, was not only kindly but highly demanding, insistent on neatness and punctuality, and anxious to determine his sons' careers. He felt deeply that children should not be ill-treated, but there was seldom any question that they ought to obey. When *Barnaby Rudge* was serialised, his own three children were all very small, so his sympathy for youthful liberation, heavily qualified though it may seem, was safely theoretical. As his children increased in size and number, so, it seems, did Dickens's grievances: he became more and more perturbed by their drifting, annoyed by their lack of grip. Certainly by the time of Tattycoram, the runaway foundling in *Little Dorrit*, Dickens is detectably less tolerant of youthful recalcitrance. When the fiery girl returns to Mr Meagles, humble and penitent once again, she still receives a grey lecture on duty, Little Dorrit being cited as a virtuous model she would do well to emulate. In *The Dickens Theatre* Robert Garis, assuming—like most readers—that Dickens himself is sponsoring these worthy sentiments, remarks that this 'sermon' is 'worse than inept': redundant after the girl's full account of her conversion, and inappropriate from Mr Meagles. Mrs Leavis, however, with her customary vigour, has accused Mr Garis of missing the point: Dickens is not endorsing the Meagleses, but completing the case against them:

for instance, their simple moralising habits which have been shown as driving Tattycoram to run away and which, when —the alternative represented by Miss Wade proving even more intolerable—she is driven to return, are still forced on her, thus showing that a Meagles can learn nothing.

This certainly sounds a convincing defence, a plausible interpretation. The only thing wrong is that it rewrites the book. Tattycoram doesn't run away because of the Meagleses' 'moralising habits': she does so because she is jealous of Pet and because she feels people try to shame her. It is debatable, anyway, whether the Meagleses really are in the habit of moralising: they are certainly less disposed to it than Dickens himself (see, for example, his outbursts on behalf of the heroine). Nor does Tattycoram return to Mr Meagles as the lesser of two evils: her speech of contrition makes it quite clear that she has recognised Miss Wade's moral perversity and now feels her former resentments were unjust. Can we even say that the sermon is 'forced' on Tattycoram? She herself has already volunteered a highly moralistic account of her case and Mr Meagles summons her to him 'gently'. Of course, Mrs Leavis is perfectly right to defend the book's general presentation, sustained over many successful chapters, of Mr and Mrs Meagles: Dickens does indeed both appreciate their virtues and yet firmly acknowledge their faults. But when we come to the final lecture, a dreadful simplicity takes control. That the author is endorsing this exhortation is not, as Mrs Leavis suggests, a mere foolish misreading from Mr Garis, but the clear implication of Dickens's text. What she ignores is the crucial sentence, shortly before the concluding lecture, 'Father and Mother Meagles never deserved their names better, than when they took the headstrong foundling-girl into their protection again.' It is strictly incredible that this express praise of the Meagleses' parental benevolence should be used to usher in an episode designed to confirm their parental weakness. What we have is a study of family friction that relapses suddenly into sententious cliché. Dickens was a pre-eminent Victorian not only in his energetic liberalism, but also in his strong attachment to duty, and his fondness for obedience.

In some respects, then, on parent-child relations, Dickens is not entirely different from Jane Austen. He is quite often sceptical of natural goodness (he had no belief whatever in 'The Noble Savage') and he shares her respect for parental supervision and for filial obedience. But even allowing for such qualifications, the distance between them is still immense. It is true that they both attack neglectful parents, but their motives are usually different. In Jane Austen such parents are criticised because they have failed to give discipline—or guidance, or stricter control. In Dickens, however, the commonest faults are neglect of imaginative stimulation, a careless unawareness of the offspring's virtues, or simply a failure to love. The assumptions, ideals, and, most important, the relative assessment of parents and children are significantly disparate in their work, and the changes correspond with those also apparent in articles and children's books. Jane Austen and Dickens are both major novelists who deal with education and upbringing, but their values and even the nature of their feelings are partially conditioned by the climate of their age. In its simplest terms what separates them is the gulf between the 'Puritan' attitude to children and the later 'Romantic' one.

Chapter V
BUTLER AND GOSSE

'Young people have a marvellous faculty of either dying
or adapting themselves to circumstances.'
                SAMUEL BUTLER, *The Way of All Flesh*
'There gushed through my veins like a wine the deter-
mination to rebel.'
                EDMUND GOSSE, *Father and Son*

(i)

For anybody who wishes to study the rise of childhood in the
nineteenth century, there is, among works of fiction alone, an
almost embarrassing quantity of relevant evidence. On the rights
of young people, and on parent-child conflict, Bulwer, Meredith,
Trollope and Thackeray could all be valuably analysed, not to
speak of the Brontës, George Eliot and James. If, however, we
restrict the subject to rejection of paternal authority, two books
in particular stand out. Samuel Butler's *The Way of All Flesh* and
Edmund Gosse's *Father and Son* have long been cited as historical
landmarks, works which, anticipating Shaw and Strachey, signified
the end of Victorian values and especially of 'the Victorian Father'.
It is true that these books have historical importance, but not
quite of the kind described. Their importance historically is
mainly symbolic, for attacking as they do the 'Puritan' ethos in
the cause of what is clearly a 'Romantic' one, they epitomise that
change in attitudes to children which, as noted in previous chapters, gathered pace in Victorian writing. But neither book may be
said to have exposed the typical Victorian father. First of all the
very notion of 'the Victorian Father' is probably a myth. If it
postulates a figure who, as paterfamilias, was unprecedentedly
severe, then it goes against much of the evidence on domestic
developments. In the Victorian period the trend was towards a
greater humanity in attitudes to children and also, by the end of
the century, some impugnment of the power of parents: in
literature the two works under discussion are the culmination of
this trend. To this extent, then, it is wrong to describe them as
works which are anti-Victorian. They are, on the contrary, in
many respects quintessentially Victorian.

A second thing wrong with the orthodox view is its hidden assumption that Butler and Gosse were undoubtedly typical cases: that the family situations they describe represented middle-class life. The assumption is an extremely dubious one, even though, as we shall see, these works do have connections with much other literature. Why should we give credence to *The Way of All Flesh* rather than to more contented works? Why should we generalise from the story of Gosse when his father was so palpably odd? From fiction and autobiography we may learn how people lived in the past, what they thought, what they felt, what values they had—we may even catch sight of some general trends in behaviour and belief. But while the information thus received is so often vivid and concrete, it can never be more than approximate as regards typicality. How many people lived like this, what classes and areas were involved, how long this kind of behaviour held sway—such questions, after reading literature, must remain for the most part unanswered. Literature, in short, is not to be used as a substitute for sociology. The family situations of Butler and Gosse may have been typical in certain ways, but we cannot assume this without other proof; their books describe Victorian fathers, but not 'the Victorian Father'.

This question of the representative value of *The Way of All Flesh* and *Father and Son* is not a mere methodological detour, but a problem provoked by the books themselves: it is crucial to their impact. For although both works are highly personal productions—direct or fictionalised autobiography—they also claim to transcend the personal, to offer not only subjective reminiscence but objective social reporting. Neither author saw himself as recording simply his personal experience; both men believed that their sufferings and conflicts related to matters of general importance, to social mores and historical development and maybe even to science. As a result, their works fluctuate in content, contract and expand in focus. Sometimes the author will concentrate on the individual and particular, the autobiographical; at other times personal feelings and memories are purposefully put into a wider perspective, subsumed into grander themes. What is more, this shift in subject-matter carries over into the tone. Ironic detachment, in both Butler and Gosse, alternates oddly with indignation; the tone responds accordingly to analysis or attack. The books are both of them curious mixtures—at once intensely personal memorials and sweeping, documentary statements, works of cerebral investigation and of passionate resentment. But though the books have this conflict in common, their achievement is not on a par. Whereas in Gosse the attempt at detachment is balanced and sharpened by emotional memory, in Butler the latter, the starting point, is finally eclipsed by the former. One author escapes from theoretical composure; the other escapes into it.

(ii)

Samuel Butler (1835–1902) was the son of a clergyman; he was always rather ashamed of the fact, but never quite got over it. A quirky, iconoclastic man, resentful of his family and his up-bringing, he nevertheless hankered after acceptance and craved for security. Goaded by his parents into radicalism, he was also profoundly conservative, so although he was attracted by novel ideas, he would drain them of threatening import. As a result he wrote revolutionary satire which he then went on to undermine with evolutionary theory.

The initial impulse of *The Way of All Flesh* was personal indignation. Butler began it when the death of his mother was ascribed by his father, at her funeral, to the publication of *Erewhon*. That was in 1873 and he worked on the book for a year. Then came a four-year interlude when Butler was occupied with business activities and the writing and publication of *Life and Habit*, his first book on evolution. He returned to the novel in 1878, shortly after his father had let him know that he had 'purposely refrained' from reading any of his works (Silver, 1962). He revised the novel during 1878 and extended it to chapter 60 (the one which ends with Ernest's arrest), but then abandoned it again in order to attack Darwin and his followers, who he felt had wilfully snubbed him. His final period of work on the novel was between 1882 and 1884. At the beginning of 1885 a friend of his, Miss Savage, died; she had long been his literary confidante, and had always encouraged him in writing the book. After her death he did nothing more to it.

He always recognised, however, 'that it wanted a great deal not only of rewriting but of reconstruction' (Keynes and Hill, 1935). At the end of 1883 he wrote (Jones, 1919):

My own idea is that the first vol. is the best of the three, the second the next best, and the third the worst—but then they have been rewritten just in this order, the first having been ten years in hand, the second five, and the third only one.

Butler is correct about the book's decline in quality—and correct about this having something to do with its strangely prolonged composition. He is incorrect, though, to ascribe the decline to inadequate revision. There is a more fundamental un-evenness, a loss of momentum and inspiration, a relapse from the sureness of memory and satire into speculation and theory. The revisions, indeed, tend to weaken the book, for Butler cannot leave well alone. While the early parts, both comic and savagely satirical, are nourished by his personal experience, the later parts dwindle into exegesis, a trickle of shallow nostrums. The customary charge against satirists is that they are too 'negative'. Butler's fault is the opposite: he needs must explain, dogmatise, introduce his current obsessions. The bitterness of money-loss seeps into the book's atmosphere; tracts on evolution disrupt the narrative; the pages are filled with pickings from the 'Notebooks'—aphorisms, drolleries, wordy reflections, most of them untransmuted. The targets change. Reviewers had ganged up on him, so they must be wheeled into the line of fire; the scientific quacks, too, the 'Darwin clique'. The Church, on the other hand, might not be so bad: at least it was opposed to his enemies. The attack grows diffuse, the emotions bland, the irony loses direction. Worst of all, inveigled by evolution, Butler begins to theorise—but his theories topple the satire. The book finally fails because its moral assumptions—sometimes untenable in themselves—are ruinously inconsistent.

The primary theme of *The Way of All Flesh* is the attainment of independence. Ernest struggles for personal freedom, believing that 'absolute independence' is 'his only chance of very life itself'. Independence has three main aspects: religious, financial and—most important—filial. Butler's whole philosophy of life is packed into what he says in this novel about Christianity, Money and the Family. But what he says is contradictory. Offering both criticisms and recommendations, he vacillates first about their scope and secondly about the values they imply.

Sour attacks on marriage and parents pervade *The Way of All Flesh*. What, one may wonder, is the scope of the criticism—is it simply a record of Butler's experience or a wholesale indictment of the family? Certainly the book is autobiographical—especially up to chapter 60. Theobald, Christina and Charlotte are drawn from Butler's parents and sisters, and while Butler's friend, Henry Festing Jones, may have gone too far, in his admiring *Memoir*, in defending the accuracy of Butler's portraits, only one biographer, Mrs R. S. Garnett, has denied them any truth at all. Mrs Garnett's case was hardly convincing: formerly a close friend of Butler's younger sister, she argued, in 1926, that Butler's father was not an ogre, but 'a kind-hearted, humorous genial old man'; that even if Butler did not like him everybody else did; and that, in any case, physical punishment has never been bad for boys. Citing Canon Butler's jocular doggerel, written to his wife in baby-talk, or the poetry full of 'fun and sparkle' produced by the younger sister, May (sample: 'Never a drop of whiskey/To keep the frost away,/Nor e'en a single biskey/To cheer the bitter day'), Mrs Garnett strove hard to dispel Butler's laughter, but perversely contrived to confirm it (Garnett, 1926). The family correspondence, published in the sixties, indicates what we might expect: that although Butler spotlit, in his portrait of his family, their more derisory and less amiable features, he did have genuine cause for complaint and plenty of material to work on.

The family relations in *The Way of All Flesh* are, then, based on Butler's own; but did he regard them as symptomatic of a more comprehensive malaise? The novel supplies an uncertain answer. Sometimes the diagnosis is quasi-historical:

> It must be remembered that at the beginning of the nineteenth century the relations between parents and children were still far from satisfactory. . . . The parents in Miss Austen's novels are less like savage wild beasts than those of her predecessors, but she evidently looks upon them with suspicion, and an uneasy feeling that *le père de famille est capable de tout* makes itself sufficiently apparent throughout the greater part of her writings. In the Elizabethan time the relations between parents and children seem on the whole to have been more kindly. The fathers and sons are for the most part friends in Shakespeare, nor does the evil appear to have reached its full abomination till a long course of Puritanism had familiarised men's minds with Jewish ideals as those which we should endeavour to reproduce in our everyday life.

As an historical explanation, this account has its weaknesses, but it *is* an historical explanation, and its implications are amply confirmed by passages elsewhere. Recurrent phrases like 'in those days' and 'life some fifty years ago' suggest that the author is appraising the past from a more enlightened period, looking back on bad old times. He is merely claiming that Christina and Theobald are typical of the clerical parents of their age. But sometimes the qualifications are dropped: the couple are typical of all clerical parents, or perhaps of all parents whatever. The indictment seems to be growing wider and when Butler adds biological perspective (prompted by his musings on evolution), it swells to the all-embracing. Ernest Pontifex remarks that 'there is no inherent love for the family system on the part of nature herself'. He invites us to 'poll the forms of life' and comments with relish on the ants and bees who 'sting their fathers to death'. The narrator, Edward Overton, laments:

> Why should the generations overlap one another at all? Why cannot we be buried as eggs in neat little cells with ten or twenty thousand pounds each wrapped round us in Bank of England notes, and wake up, as the sphex wasp does, to find that its papa and mamma have not only left ample provision at its elbow, but have been eaten by sparrows some weeks before it began to live consciously on its own account?

In the novel the sphex wasp takes human form as Towneley, a gleaming repository of gifts and virtues, the finest of which is that when he was two, his mother and father both fell out of a boat and bequeathed him an enormous estate. The best place for parents is out of the way. Ernest himself believes this. He puts his children away from him on the grounds that parental unkindness is inevitable. Elsewhere we learn that, for biological reasons, the hero's own parents are incorrigible and that he could only wait till they died 'and be thankful when they did so'. At times, undoubtedly, Butler felt sure that his own case was not only typical but also universal. When Ernest, after narrowly escaping a beating, comes to realise that he has for both his parents 'a cordial and active dislike', this is proof, according to Overton, that he is 'reaching man's estate'. Apparently, growing to hate one's parents is part of the natural process.

These biologically-prompted conclusions (emphasised by the novel's title) are, of course, incompatible with the historical diagnosis. They also go against the more modest suggestion (made, for example, in chapter 44) that the parent-child relationship *could* be successful if only a few small abuses were removed. What is perhaps even more perplexing is the fact that quite often the book does recommend some form of parental guidance. Ernest is likened to a foal in need of assistance from its mother, and Edward Overton, like Aunt Alethea, behaves as a surrogate parent. Festing Jones tells us in his *Memoir* that Butler, despite his blood-stained childhood, knew of course that not all fathers were capable of cruelty. But only one part of Butler knew this. He wished both to plead for more gentle parents and also to reject them completely.

Butler also vacillates in his treatment of marriage. In his own life he preferred a prostitute to a wife, remarking that if you could buy your milk there was no need to keep a cow. The novel, too, takes a pretty bleak view of holy matrimony. When Theobald is placed under wedlock and key, Butler evokes his state of mind with a marvellously lurid image: '. . . the drop had actually fallen, and the poor wretch was hanging in mid-air along with the creature of his affections.' But Theobald, we're told, is not an exception: 'by far the greater number' of newly-weds suffer similar mental anguish. Ernest's marriage is instructive, too: although he has to get a separation, he is apparently 'much happier in his married life than people generally are'. The reason seems to be that for most of the time his wife kept out of the way. No one, Overton glumly opines, can have a 'reasonable certainty' that marriage will bring him peace. Yet despite the fact that at the end Ernest seems certain not to marry again—to Overton's pride and delight—he is still quite happy that his daughter, Alice, should grow up to marry Jack Rollings. Moreover, even the glorious Towneley suddenly turns up married. The novel's sprightly cynicism limps off into compromise.

Butler, then, is uncertain about the scope of his criticisms. He is even more uncertain in his moral assumptions, for here he is torn between his feelings and his theories, the memories of his early years and the researches of his later ones. Let us leave the theories aside for a moment and concentrate on his feelings. Emotionally Butler was quite convinced that his father had done him wrong: flogged him as a child, exploited him as a young man, browbeaten him as an adult. 'Those who have never had a father', he wrote, 'can at any rate never know the sweets of losing one. To most men the death of his father is a new lease of life.' (Keynes and Hill, 1951.) As for his mother, Butler believed that like Christina she had crushed her son's natural affections by her grovelling subservience to her husband.

In *The Way of All Flesh* the hero's parents are seen as not only ridiculous but also contemptible. One source of derision is animal imagery, which in the 1870s and 1880s came readily to Butler's mind: he was reading the literature on evolution and his head was swimming with insects, chickens and decapitated frogs (the sphex wasp, mentioned earlier, has flown in from *Life and Habit*). Butler delights in dehumanising Theobald: he is an ass, a sheep, a 'clever bullfinch', a decoy elephant. Likewise Christina is repeatedly pictured as a bulging, voracious fowl. She is a 'Barbary hen', a 'ravenous young cuckoo', an owl pouncing silently on her son's remarks in order to 'bring them up in a pellet six months afterwards' (the pun deftly fuses the sense of 'missile' with that of 'regurgitated food'). Also making against the couple are images of violent assault. Theobald actually beats Ernest, but his psychological bullying, too, is described in physical terms. Harried by his father's hectoring accusations, Ernest is 'being kicked when he was down'. When he is called on to answer questions, 'the thumbscrews were instantly applied'. Ernest's education, Overton says, was 'an attempt not so much to keep him in blinkers as to gouge his eyes out altogether'. Butler uses all the resources of his satire to render Theobald ridiculous—oblique or direct mockery, the ruinous clause in the middle of a sentence, the jibe that jabs out at the end. Even when the father acts decently, his motives are undermined. If he is punctual in paying his debts, it is only because of his 'constitutional timidity'. If he is agreeable to Ernest's friends, it is only out of sly self-justification. Butler pummels Theobald remorselessly, leaves him felled or floundering. Black and scowling in a bad mood, smug and vapid in a good, Theobald is damned with faint praise or denounced as lying and credulous. On the whole, Christina comes off better, being allowed at least a dignified death. But she too is mostly a ludicrous character. Lost in egocentric dreams, contentedly snobbish or wheedling and spiteful, she seems less culpable than Theobald but even more pathetic.

Here, however, the reader must pause, for Butler has an interesting twist. According to the novel's moral theory, there are no grounds for condemnation. Right, says Butler, is what makes you happy; wrong is what makes you sad. The earliest and fullest statement of this doctrine occurs in chapter 19. The previous chapter has just concluded with the death of George Pontifex, Theobald's father, a character presented as richly repulsive in almost every respect. Mean, priggish, lying, despotic,

he has beaten his children on any pretext; oozing bogus benevolence, he was, to those who knew him better, a cantankerous
old glutton. How strange, then, to find his conduct excused; but
Overton explains:

> Having lived to be seventy-three years old and died rich, he
> must have been in very fair harmony with his surround-
> ings. . . . He has spent his life best who has enjoyed it
> most. . . . The world has long ago settled that morality and
> virtue are what bring men peace at the last.

It begins to appear as if old George Pontifex must be forgiven
because beating his children gave him satisfaction; and this,
indeed, is the conclusion drawn. Overton says that parental unkindness is not usually followed by inconvenience; therefore 'it
shows no great moral obliquity' if parents, 'within certain
limits, . . . make their children's lives a burden to them'. This is
normally taken to be hugely funny, a typical Butlerian irony.
But the sentiments are lifted almost verbatim from a sober passage
in the *Notebooks*, the main difference being that the note begins,
'I am sorry to have to admit it, but . . .' (Bartholomew, 1934).
Butler thought he was facing a tough but inescapable fact of life.
If success and happiness are the sole foundations of morality, a
successful and happy man cannot be bad. George Pontifex was
not an exalted character, but 'judge him according to a fair
average standard, and there is not much fault to be found with
him'. Overton adds that what he has said:

> should go without saying in modification of the verdict which
> the reader may be inclined to pass too harshly not only upon
> Mr George Pontifex, but also upon Theobald and Christina.

This, surely, is rather a mild caution to set against all the im-
putations of fatuity and viciousness, all the talk of thumbscrews
and eye-gouging.

Several points need to be made here. First, the whole of this
chapter is a late addition to the manuscript. It is an example of
how Butler, as he grew more opinionated, could not refrain from
obtruding his theories, even when they stultified much of his
satire. It shows he was wrong to believe that revision would
always lead to improvement.

Secondly, it will be noticed that two moral criteria are being
advanced: that right is what gives pleasure; and that right is the
practice of the majority ('a fair average standard'). Both of these

connect with Butler's views on evolution. For Butler, there is no
moral absolute, life being a process of continual change. The
only ultimate test of a thing's value is whether it conduces to
survival. On Butler's theory, organisms adapt themselves to their
environment and pass on the knowledge to their offspring. After
many generations the knowledge becomes unconscious, instinctive.
Instinct, for Butler, is Memory. We have an Unconscious Memory
of what has happened to us in the person of our ancestors, so
we know instinctively what is good for us (this is why Ernest is
often saved by the intervention of his unconscious). Whatever
gives pleasure is likely to be good, to be an evolutionary asset.
Likewise, survival goes by majorities. What the majority feels to
be right or wrong, good or evil, true or false, is likely to be trust-
worthy—at least the *successful* majority. George Pontifex is moral
on every count: 'in very fair harmony with his surroundings',
happy, wealthy and similar in outlook to the majority of successful men. Despite all the satirical attacks on him, he cannot be
condemned.

As well as containing flaws in itself, this theory cripples the
novel. First of all it infects the language with evasion; under-
standably embarrassed by his own ideas, Butler equivocates. The
doctrine is plastered with slippery provisos: 'within certain limits',
'for most men and most circumstances', 'I speak broadly and
exceptis excipiendis'. But a satirist cannot afford to dither about
his moral standpoint. Then again, Butler's pleasure-morality was
handicapped by his nature. It partly evolved out of exasperation
with the tiresome Christian insistence on duty, exhortations to
which he found loathsome. He associated 'duty' with bores, and
dreary Sabbaths, and life being uphill all the way. The prospect
was intolerable. All the good characters in *The Way of All Flesh*
are determined to seek their own comfort. Overton hungers for
'peace at the last', Ernest for a quiet life of self-indulgence,
Alethea to 'make the rest of her life as happy as she could'. What
is strange is how drably dispirited these declarations sound. There
was little in Butler of the epicure; he once recorded that if he
were richer the only two things he would care about were 'a few
more country outings and a little more varied and better cooked
food'. To this note he added a few years before his death: 'I have
long since obtained everything that a reasonable man can wish
for.' (Keynes and Hill, 1951.) Butler was not naturally a pleasure-
seeker; his hedonism was theoretical. In the novel he tries gamely

to hold to his theory, but difficulties keep arising. Why, for example, should Alethea devote herself to Ernest? It will mean giving up her London home and moving to Roughborough. Butler pauses, turns the question over; he outlines the 'excellent reasons' against such egregious altruism. Finally Alethea is vindicated on the ground that 'she wanted someone to leave her money to'. The attempt to excuse her generosity is fumbling and strained. Elsewhere the problem is simply ignored. Ernest helps the banished Ellen, or gives money to a poor woman in his parish, and Butler forgets that in the book's own terms his decency is at best mere caprice, at worst a deplorable lapse from self-interest.

Or perhaps Butler didn't so much 'forget' as simply not mind the confusion. He has, after all, protected himself against charges of contradiction. One of his arguments is that a completely consistent system of thought is impossible, so we might as well embrace inconsistency: the only thing we must always be is flexible and moderate. But this aspiration was itself inconsistent with Butler's own emotions. Butler had a craving for temperance, a tireless hatred of zealous endeavour; he would go to almost any lengths to attack extremism. These tangled responses had no doubt been spawned in his father's rectory; certainly he associated his relatives with a graceless puritanism. The necessity for effort and dogged adherence to principle—this was the cant of parents and the Church. Butler, as always, took over such pieties and stood them on their head. 'Nothing is well done nor worth doing,' pronounces the dying Alethea, 'unless, take it all round, it has come pretty easily.' Later it seemed that evolutionary theory justified moderation. Those who intended to survive would have to adapt to circumstances, to blend with their environment, to accept the status quo. Moreover, instinct rather than reason was 'the ultimate court of appeal'. As Ernest ruminates in prison, he comes to feel that it matters little what doctrines people profess; the important thing is to follow instinct, to live by generous compromise, to avoid dogmatic extremes.

It is easy to see why such a stance appealed so strongly to Butler. This kind of 'perfect gentleman's' code, apparently sanctioned by evolution, negated the dreary dogmatism of his father and family. It could therefore supply a good deal of satisfaction—a good deal, but still not enough. After all, it was not only his family's opinions that Butler wished to negate: his revulsion from his parents was not merely mental, but emotional and moral. The

theory did not allow for this; counselling urbanity and compromise, it failed to accommodate Butler's feelings about his miserable
childhood. In the novel, theory collides with emotion. Immediately
after Ernest's praise of 'charitable inconsistency', his lapse into
'amiable indifferentism', he is spurning his parents with flashing
eyes, hysterical in his resolve. The trouble is that, in response to
his parents, Butler wants things both ways: he wants all the
gestures of renunciation, the relief of savage satire; but he also
wants to flaunt his suavity, his belief in moderation. In itself
each ideal is acceptable, but brought together they clash. Butler
was convinced, as Ernest is, that 'we become persecutors as a
matter of course as soon as we begin to feel very strongly upon
any subject'. But unfortunately Butler did feel strongly, especially
on the subject of his family. He certainly wanted to satirise, but
satire implies moral standards; and he did not want to moralise.
As a result there is, in *The Way of All Flesh*, a continual shift of
tone. Sometimes, as above, we find that the theory is dissipated
by powerful emotion, but more often we find the reverse. An
indignant satirical attack will drain away into a plea for sang-
froid, a dramatic scene will be interrupted by a mumbling
excursus. Butler palliates his satire, almost apologises for it. The
treatment of George Pontifex is one example; another is the
treatment of Ernest's beatings. When Theobald flogs Ernest, then
rings the bell for prayers 'red-handed as he was', Butler's personal
indignation is unmistakable. But very soon afterwards the adult
Ernest is reflecting breezily:

> What a fool . . . a man is to remember anything that hap-
> pened more than a week ago unless it was pleasant. . . . If I
> had to be born again I would be born at Battersby of the
> same father and mother as before, and I would not alter
> anything that has ever happened to me.

An even more flagrant reversal occurs in the presentation of
Dr Skinner. Ernest's headmaster, when first introduced, is drenched
in a hailstorm of stinging invective, but the adult Ernest says
sunnily that if ever he meets the old buffer again, 'there is no
one whom I would shake hands with, or do a good turn to more
readily'. Butler himself was as eager as Ernest to adapt to his
environment. He hated Shrewsbury, the original of Roughborough,
but later in life he attended its speech days for twelve consecutive
years.

It may be the case, as Butler claims, that all philosophies con-

tain contradictions, but this does not pardon the creative confusion
at the heart of *The Way of All Flesh*. Repeatedly the emotional
thrust, the autobiographical element, is deflected by Butler's
theories. Sometimes he writes with a wish to reform; children, he
warns, who have suffered at school may one day expose their
teachers: 'If even two or three schoolmasters learn this lesson
and remember it, the preceding chapters will not have been
written in vain.' But he argues elsewhere that pre-natal influences
so mould a man's character that it is 'hardly possible' to escape
their consequences. Frequently—again inspired by evolution—he
insists that motives are unimportant; yet he treats Christina less
harshly than Theobald for the very reason that she 'meant well'.
Even Theobald's motives, though, are not entirely clear: usually
he acts with deliberate malice, but sometimes Butler exonerates
him and suggests he is merely misguided.

This double focus in *The Way of All Flesh*—one moment a
heatedly personal response, the next a pose of detachment—is
evident especially in the character of Overton, who, as Miss
Savage shrewdly remarked, is both 'an impartial historian' and
also 'a special pleader'. When Overton lays out the correspondence
between Theobald and George Pontifex, he explains that it was
found by Ernest

> among his father's papers written on gilt-edged paper, in
> faded ink, and tied neatly round with a piece of tape, but
> without any note or comment. I have altered nothing.

But after this flourish of factual authenticity, Overton drops all
pretence: he recounts conversations he could never have heard
and thoughts he could only conjecture. After the marriage of
Christina and Theobald, the factually scrupulous narrator declares, 'What they must have felt during their first half hour the
reader must guess, for it is beyond my power to tell him'; but he
then proceeds to tell not only what they felt, but what they
said and did, and how they looked, and even calculates that a
particular thought came to Theobald 'about three and a half
miles after he had left Crampsford'. Butler has tangled two modes
of narration—not an important fault in itself, but one which
damages Overton by making him seem somewhat biased. It isn't
simply that Overton looks into the minds of Christina and Theobald; the trouble is rather that he always discovers such dis-
creditable thoughts there. By being so hostile he invites us to

question the dubious authority of his accounts. So too when he reports a conversation: belittling details, like 'said Theobald impressively', draw attention to his role as prosecuting counsel—and remind us that he has no evidence for his niggling accusations. At other times, though, when Butler is less heated, is attempting in fact to appear detached, Overton is given alternative employment as the author's defence attorney. For example, Butler felt rather ashamed of having made public his mother's correspondence (in the guise of a letter by Christina). He was therefore, according to Festing Jones, 'particular to insert' near the end of the book a solemn justification. Overton states that, despite his misgivings, Ernest has reassured him: Christina herself would certainly have wished to see the letter published. But what we may wonder, of the scathing commentary with which the letter was followed? Would Christina, or would Butler's mother, have wished that, too, to be published? The strategy—mockery and then explanation—is characteristic of Butler. Seeking to display his gentlemanly standards, to make his satire respectable, he lapses into hypocrisy or portentous equivocation.

The independence which Ernest attains is not only filial but also religious, and eventually financial. The handling of Christianity, however, follows the usual pattern. At first the condemnation is severe. Ernest reflects in prison that most of his ills have been due to the influence of Christian teaching, and this bears out what the reader has seen. Theobald is not only a bully, but a clergyman: ringing the bell for prayers after beating his children, relieving in private the tensions set up by his public role as 'a kind of human Sunday'. Ernest is confirmed on Guy Fawkes' Day, and it is cleverly implied that the true turning-point for him is not the confirmation ceremony at midday, but the burning of Theobald's effigy in the afternoon. The main climax of the book occurs when Ernest, having set out to convert Miss Snow, is interrupted by the intrusion of Towneley, who is not concerned with her soul. 'Deeply humiliated' by the contrast with Towneley, Ernest slinks off 'Bible and all' and back in his room, converted himself, he pushes the Bible away from him and kicks it into the corner.

Sure enough, the equivocations soon follow. Ernest, says Overton, was really trying to give up his parents 'for Christ's sake'. True, he would have thought he was giving them up because they hindered his happiness: '. . . but what is this if it is not

Christ? What is Christ if he is not this?' Debating-tactics of this
nature came readily to Butler; he would often try to promote
his opinions by dressing them up in a surplice. Also, after his
quarrel with Darwin, he softened towards the Church. Ernest
comes to feel that, for all its 'mistakes', the Church contains
much 'valuable truth' and is preferable to Huxley and Tyndall—
two scientists with whom, when he wrote this section, Butler was
at loggerheads. It is clear from his letters that, in Butler's opinion,
the 'valuable truth' preserved by the Church was that which
resembled his own beliefs on the theory of evolution. The novel
begins with a firm attack on the cruelties, follies and self-decep-
tions engendered by Christian teaching. It ends with Ernest's bland
suggestion that we all should be 'lukewarm churchmen'. The
glib change of mind is typical of the novel's whole procedure. At
first: pungent satire, pressured by personal resentment. Later: a
conformist compromise, motivated partly by topical obsessions,
but largely by the author's desire to appear easy-going and
urbane.

This man-of-the-world philosophy tinctures, too, the novel's
theme of financial independence. Like most respectable Victorian
heroes, Ernest receives an enormous bequest and by the end his
main worry is that 'do what he would he could not get through
more than about fifteen hundred a year'. Butler's admiration for
money, however, went far beyond the conventional. For him it
was a fundamental fact of life, almost an aspect of biology; like
Overton he regarded poverty as 'a quasi-embryonic condition'.
Inheritance was a process of nature—in his own case, one which
was morbidly clogged by his father's longevity. But although he
had years of financial strain, he never lost faith in Mammon. The
novel sometimes reads like a ledger-book: it contains long accounts
of debts and investments, assets and legacies. Butler despises the
presumptuous poor—Badcock and the Simeonites; he cannot, however, dilate enough on the merits of the opulent Towneley. Overton is ready continually with the nostrum of the five-pound note.
He slips one immediately to John the Coachman when it turns
out that he, rather than Ernest, is the legal husband of Ellen; and
for Ellen herself there is a pound a week 'to be paid so long as
she gave no trouble'. Another pound a week is offered to the couple
who take in Ernest's children. This is equally successful: 'they
jumped at the offer', says Overton. Children themselves are easily
bribed: despite his ostensible defence of them, Butler tends to

view them as commodities, or rather perhaps as obsequious servants, hanging around for their tip. Overton, Alethea and eventually Ernest all win the friendship of children with money, for, as the narrator smilingly puts it, 'Boys are very like nice dogs in this respect—give them a bone and they will like you at once.' But then—for Overton, everybody is a nice dog in this respect.

It is plain that Butler's worship of money was partly a reaction against his parents—a reaction against their puritanism and against his need for their aid. He felt that his father had financially tricked him and in *The Way of All Flesh* he takes his revenge: 'got up regardless of expense', emboldened by his huge bequest, Ernest returns to his parents' house, 'with an air of *insouciance* and good humour upon his face', to visit his dying mother. As his father stands stammering with disbelief, he genially announces the new situation—and quickly quenches Theobald's wrath with a few words of blistering reproof. Such scenes are certainly laughable, even though they fall short of their purpose. But Butler's desperate worship of money not only leads into puerility, it also conflicts with another theme—the more Romantic defiance of parents, the praise for simplicity and nature. Ernest is saved by atavism: his emancipation is often portrayed as a return to the life of his great-grandfather, a country carpenter, a builder of organs, a lover of the sun. Ernest, too, derives sustenance from the sun and takes to building organs; he determines to move into some occupation in which he will be 'kissing the soil'. Throughout the book the life of nature represents an ideal or a favourable contrast. Immediately after Theobald has beaten Ernest, he is put to shame by the maternal kindness of a local cottager's wife. Ernest, predictably, wants his own children 'to be brought up in the fresh pure air'. He himself is certainly responsive to nature: when he goes abroad on holiday, he cannot pass a peasant or a 'bank of opening cowslips' without 'drinking it all in with an enjoyment too deep for words'.

In a book that reveres material wealth, such rhapsodies sound rather suspicious. If Ernest has such a thirst for simple nature, it seems odd that the plot should be contrived to leave him as a London writer with more money than he can spend. It is not that millionaires can't like cowslips. What grates is the assumption that Ernest's life of leisure, depending on vast sums of money supplied and invested for him by others, has anything to do with the life of rural crafts and simple integrity represented by Old

Pontifex. The praise of nature is pure game, a holiday indulgence. When Ernest gets a job selling second-hand clothes, he is supposed to be kissing the soil 'with a vengeance'. The equation of commerce with commitment to nature is strange enough in itself. But in any case Overton always makes sure that while his young friend is kissing the soil, he does not stoop too low. To stop Ernest cutting himself adrift 'from music, letters and polite life', he takes over the first-floor flat. The moneyed life or the life of nature? The book attempts to recommend both and finally brings them together. Praise of nature and respect for money jostle each other comically when the wealthy Ernest goes with Overton to visit his children near Gravesend. It is, of course, 'a lovely April morning' and the bargeman's children, laughing and romping, are 'flaxen-pated little folks'. The visitors dole out 'oranges and sweeties', give away shillings instead of pennies, and everything is satisfactory. Ernest chats for a while in 'the fine bracing air', expresses his approval of the simple outdoor life, and then, reminding Mr Rollings to say when he needs any money, makes off to his rooms in the Temple to carry on writing and spending. The whole episode, with its awkward, perfunctory elation, exposes the incongruity of two of Butler's ideals. Financial independence and natural freedom—both were escape-routes from the rectory, but, as Butler conceived of them, they led into different worlds.

Each theme, then, in *The Way of All Flesh*—the filial, the religious, the financial—slides off into some discordance; each aspect of the novel's satire—its scope, its values, its alternatives—betrays prevarication. Again and again the intention changes, the targets are redefined. To denounce all parents, to denounce some parents, to denounce some parents some of the time. To denounce and to tolerate, denounce and commend. To give up Christ and give up for Christ's sake. Warring ideals are espoused by the author, strange contortions achieved: grappling urbanity to indignation, praising nature and capital investments, kissing the soil at the Stock Exchange. Why is *The Way of All Flesh* so confused? The first and most obvious explanation is that, being written over several years, it was stultified by its revisions. Just as in *Erewhon* the earlier satire is marred by the changes of 1901, so here the original fictional framework, set up to release Butler's indignation, is weakened by its use as a vehicle for evolutionary dogma. 'There are no end of delightful little bits,' Miss Savage

wrote to Butler in 1883, 'but you must not convey the idea that
Ernest is only a peg on which to hang your theories and fancies.'
It is indeed rather disconcerting when not only Overton but
Ernest, too, begins to pronounce on evolution; and not only
Ernest, but a doctor whom Ernest consults. As the book goes on,
more and more events are ground into Butler's creaking theories,
all grist to the evolutionary mill: even Ellen's relapse into
alcoholism is described as a kind of resumption of feral charac-
teristics. When Theobald dies, Overton lectures about life being
death and death being life—this, too, taken from Butler's theories.
Evolution leads up to such writing as this: the straining, barren
paradox, the rickety aphorism. But evolution may also explain
many flaws: the exculpations that follow the satire, the claim
that those satirised could hardly be reformed. And the frequent
appeals to evolution must be a later refinement. They could not
have assumed the forms they take in the book until after the
writing of *Life and Habit*. They must have gained admittance
during the second stage of composition.

Evolution is the cause of particular muddles, but the basic
causes should probably be sought in Butler's own character. It
was partly that he found it difficult to come to terms with his
childhood: feelings of anger, of indignation, of protest against
his parents' injustice conflicted with a wish to forget it all, to
establish a peaceful life. Psychologically, the study of evolution
seemed to promise satisfaction for both of these drives: attractive
at first for its subversiveness, its apparent opposition to his father's
religion, it could also be used, in Butler's opinion, to justify
tolerance and moderation, acceptance of things as they are. But
the radical excitement soon wore off: the theories that Butler
came to adopt left little room for his childhood emotions—which
continued, however, to assert themselves without his intellectual
approval (hence the vacillation in *The Way of All Flesh* between
satire—moral, emotional—and detached analysis). But another
cause of muddle was that Butler's childhood, not rationally absorbed into his adult personality, continued to assert itself in a
totally different way. His father's rectory retained its hold; Butler
could never quite shake off the doctrines on which he had been
reared. Unlike Ernest, he never broke from his family. He wanted
to wound them, but in private, without their knowledge. He was
going to publish *The Way of All Flesh* as soon as his father died;
but when his father did die, he decided he could not publish it

while his sisters were still alive. He was desperate to keep the book
secret from his family. In November 1873 he wrote to his sister
May to contradict 'a report that I have written a book in which I
have introduced my father'. He has written no such book 'and
shall never do so'; he has not 'the faintest conception of what the
present report can allude to'; he wishes to 'contradict it unre-
servedly' (Howard, 1962). Despite his attacks on the Family,
Butler always found domestic harmony attractive. *The Fair Haven*
(1873) contains an idealised portrait of a father. Late in life Butler
wrote an immensely long and laudatory biography of his grandfather. Finally, in *Erewhon Revisited*, father and son, husband and
wife, clasp hands in a positive debauch of good cheer. On Butler's
opinions, too, his family background retained its hold. Cogitating
on evolution, Butler got rid of God; but later, with the aid of
Lamarckian theory, he smuggled the deity back again, though
shorn of His propensity to preach. He attacked the Church, then
became 'a Broad Churchman', began, in his own phrase, by tearing
open the wounds of his Redeemer, and ended up defending the
Lamb of God from the bloodthirsty 'wolves' of science. So too
with sexual morality. Butler went to a prostitute for twenty
years, but thought that no gentleman would have written *Mrs
Warren's Profession* (Muggeridge, 1936). In *The Way of All Flesh*
the hero wavers about the morality of 'living in sin', but at the
end he publishes essays—including one on marriage laws—whose
conclusions, we learn, are 'conservative, quietistic, comforting'.
Overton, too, is just as anxious to preserve propriety: telling how
he saw Alethea at Roughborough and 'spent a few days with
her', he hastily adds, 'though of course staying at the Swan'.
Butler said that if he had not already alienated so many sections
of society, he would have liked to take up 'the sexual question'
(Jones, 1919). But it is doubtful whether his proposals would have
been very radical. In his book *Shakespeare's Sonnets Reconsidered*
he sees fit to offer the most profuse and impassioned apologies
for Shakespeare's character because, according to Butler's reading
of the poems, Shakespeare had once been on the verge of undress-
ing for Mr W. H.

Butler hated commitment. His mind was too whimsical and
protean to be perfectly suited to satire. However, many of his
confusions may be traced to his upbringing. Treated by his father
with severity and, he believed, with injustice, the child had a
double response: he wished not only to retaliate, but also to

be loved and accepted. The result, in the writings of the adult Butler, was a mixture of satire and apologetics, the former being potent, and often hilarious, until overwhelmed by the latter. Having embarked on *The Way of All Flesh* as a means of expressing his personal resentment, of defending children and childhood, Butler ran aground into compromises, vague disquisitions, comforting theories, hints that possibly, after all, the traditional notions were best. In many ways, all too successfully, he adapted to his environment.

(iii)

When Edmund Gosse was a boy of five his mother wrote a book on parental duties: it was called *Abraham and His Children.* Mrs Gosse argued that although, in the past, parents had often been too severe, the contemporary failing was the opposite of this: '. . . we are in danger of losing all parental authority in our fear of exercising discipline on our children.' Rule, discipline, duty, subjection—these words wind familiar patterns through her prose. But Gosse's mother is optimistic: if a child is brought up correctly, she says, he will undoubtedly be 'just what we make him'. And if a child grows up differently—if he refuses to go the way he has been trained? In that case, Mrs Gosse concludes, the parents must have acted amiss.

The conflict between Edmund Gosse and his father was peculiarly intense. Since Edmund's mother died when he was only seven, the boy and his father were thrown very close together; and since Philip Gosse happened to be an extreme Calvinist, disagreement over the doctrines and the role of religion, a common domestic heartache in a time of changing beliefs, was in their case distressingly acute. Edmund had to fight hard to survive. His memories of the struggle, ostensibly so serene, are just discernibly shaken by the agitations of the past.

Father and Son was first published anonymously in October 1907. In scope it is a strange and pioneering work, a blend of biography, autobiography and social and religious history. As Gosse himself states in the first chapter, 'This book is the record of a struggle between two temperaments, two consciences and almost two epochs.' At first sight there seems to be a contradiction here: is the book intended to be an individual portrait or is it a representative case history? When concentrating on the clash of temperaments, Gosse stresses the singularity of the protagonists; when dealing with the clash of epochs, he points out their typicality. Thus he and his father were 'unusual' people, his father was a 'unique and noble figure', his own state 'was, I should think, almost unique among the children of cultivated parents'. Yet the book purports to be 'the diagnosis of a dying Puritanism', 'the record of a state of soul once not uncommon in Protestant Europe'. The two perspectives seem inconsistent, but on a closer look they coalesce. Gosse's point is that his parents were exemplars of a way of life, and a mode of thought, which by the mid-nineteenth century had almost entirely disappeared. His father was 'perhaps the last surviving type' of the Puritanism of the seventeenth century; he was unique by being an anachronism.

Father and Son is not, then, an exposé of 'the Victorian Father'. Some of Gosse's childhood was extraordinary by the standards of any age. His physical isolation, for a start, was protracted and extreme. His parents scarcely ever received visitors; they seldom took him out. At first he was quite incurious about other children and never spoke to one until after his mother's death. He was half way through his eighth year when he was first 'thrown into the society of young people'—his older cousins at Clifton. It was not until he was nearly ten that he 'made acquaintance' with a boy of his own age.

Apart from this oppressive isolation, his experience was severely circumscribed by a rigorous censorship. Anything savouring of entertainment was taboo: tobacco, story-books, the sights of London, Mr Punch—all were placed under a pious embargo. There were, it is true, a few anomalies in his father's prohibitive scheme: Scott's novels were proscribed, but not his poems, while Dickens was permitted for the curious reason that he 'exposes the passion of love in a ridiculous light'. And if the boy's life was censored, so was his parents': they voluntarily submitted themselves to similar deprivations. But although they were content, the boy was compelled to live in an 'intellectual cell'. Again and again Gosse describes his condition with images of confinement: he is a prisoner, a trapped bird, a thwarted flower or plant.

One thing, however, Gosse is willing to acknowledge: the loneliness of his childhood was what made it memorable. On several occasions he observes how his life, as soon as it ceased to be solitary, ceased also to be distinct. Solitude, suffering even, made possible his spiritual autobiography. Quite probably they also accounted for his personality in later life. Gosse was always a smooth and assiduous socialite, and perhaps his patient coaxing and cultivation of the eminent was a reaction against the solitude and humbleness of his childhood—the constricted social opportunities, the unstimulating company of the drawling Oddicombe 'saints'. Likewise, as an adult, he would always make a point of letting his fondnesses show. In his childhood, of course, demonstrations of affection had mostly been austerely eschewed.

'In his childhood'—but that, in an important sense, was a privilege he never enjoyed. One aspect of Gosse's upbringing which does seem to have been representative was the puritan refusal, on the part of his parents, to acknowledge that the workings of a child's mind were different from those of an adult. His father 'had no vital sympathy for youth, which in itself had no charm for him'. Like many Evangelicals, he regarded childhood chiefly in terms of its potential, of what it could be turned into when its peculiarities had been erased. 'He was in a tremendous hurry to push on my spiritual growth', says Gosse, whose own thinking on the subject of childhood is evidently Rousseauistic: 'He did not observe the value of negative education, that is to say, of leaving Nature alone to fill up the gaps which it is her design to deal with at a later and riper date.' The grotesque incongruity of his father's tuition is well conveyed by Gosse in the paragraph which tells how 'hand in hand' the two of them tackled the eschatological obscurities of the Book of Revelation. Edmund was led tenderly into the brimstone. In later life Gosse could not underrate either the limitations of a child's mind or its quirkiness and inscrutability. He believes that 'we attribute . . . too many moral ideas to little children' and that the development of a child's mind often 'defies adult definition'. Gosse himself had three children, and though, according to his biographer, his attitude to them was 'correct rather than impulsive', he was always careful to ensure that their upbringing didn't duplicate the gravity or isolation of his own. (Charteris, 1931. Compare Tadema, 1929.)

Gosse's parents made little allowance for the capacities of the juvenile mind; unconcerned with what it was capable of assimilating, they encouraged their son to swallow wholesale their own intellectual fare: abstruse natural history, antinomian hymns, pungent chunks of rare theology that he was completely unable to digest. Bit by bit, however, their syllabus was supplanted by reading which Edmund found more congenial: by fiction, by poetry, by the tempting products of the secular imagination. His discovery of 'profane' literature was a major factor in the enfranchisement of his mind. Its attractions deflected him from the wishes of his parents. On this theme the narrative of *Father and Son* has at times an almost symbolic neatness: 'I used to be told that having met all invitations to repeat such words as "Papa" and "Mamma" with gravity and indifference, I one day drew towards me a volume, and said "book" with startling distinctness.' The thoroughness with which Gosse records the various stages of his discovery of literature—a sensational novel found in the garret, Scott, Coleridge, *Tom Cringle's Log*—makes *Father and Son* almost a *künstlerroman*, an account of the development of an artist. Among the taboos, the tightness, of home, literature meant a glorious enlargement of perspective. And here as elsewhere Gosse's early experiences helped to determine his later taste. He tended to like euphonious nature-romance, the lyrical, the aesthetic, the picturesque—anything that promised an imaginative escape from the Scripture-sodden dourness of his father. To some extent he used literature as a substitute for religion, unwittingly fulfilling Matthew Arnold's famous prediction; and, also like Arnold, he grew up to deprecate Hebraism and to elevate Hellenism in its stead. His quotations frequently refer to the Greek gods, and he describes how he pored with furtive rapture over steel-engravings of their statues. His father attempted to engraft Christianity; the graft simply would not take. By temperament Gosse was always more inclined to be a man of letters than a biblical scholar. One of the central motifs of the book is the contrast between the whipped-up ardour of his religious devotions and the spontaneous ecstasy of his response to literature.

Even Gosse's father, though, was not only a biblical scholar. He was also an eminent marine zoologist: as well as being a minister in the Plymouth Brethren, he was a Fellow of the Royal Society. The balance was a very precarious one, and eventually the dangerous conclusions of science were suppressed by the statements of God. The main crisis in Philip Gosse's career occurred when he published *Omphalos*, an attempt to square geology with Genesis which exposed him to public scorn. He himself, however, saw no incongruity; he regarded his labours as a unity, and in some respects he was right. The brooding microscopic intensity which he brought to his study of anemones and corals he would apply also to his theological work, focusing on niceties of Calvinist doctrine for a minute dissection of their meaning. From zoology to theology was a short step: similar methods of analysis were used, similar delimitations of subject. 'He saw everything through a lens,' his son remarks, 'nothing in the immensity of nature.' But Philip Gosse's religious beliefs pervaded not only his professional work but also, as we might expect, the whole of his private life. For example, he believed that all ailments and mishaps were tokens of God's retribution. Even when Edmund trapped his nose in the door, it was taken as a sanctified affliction. Religious significance was also detected in every public event. Reading through the foreign news in *The Times*, Gosse's father would find vindications of biblical augury: 'If there was a custom-house officer stabbed in a fracas at Sassari, we gave loud thanks that liberty and light were breaking in upon Sardinia.' Likewise Gosse tells how his father, at breakfast, read out the news of a victorious battle and 'he and my Mother sank simultaneously on their knees in front of their tea and bread-and-butter, while in a loud voice my Father gave thanks to the God of Battles'. Gosse frequently captures, with urbane amusement, this mingling of the holy and the mundane. He talks, for instance, of his 'wet and glorious footsteps' after his baptism; or of the penitent Mrs Pewings, who reappeared 'with a face that shone with soap and sanctification'. The juxtapositions are neatly effective for playing off two opposed views of life: the dramatically religious view of the saints, the wryly rationalist view of the narrator.

Gosse injects subtle comedy into his sentences, writes up the oddities of his childhood experience with a suave retrospective smile. Yet his apparent ironic poise is perhaps misleading: a cultivated front rather than a deep assurance of attitude. There is evidence, particularly when he is writing about his father, that he is less coolly detached than he wishes to appear. It is true that, for much of the narrative, he seems completely self-possessed, seems calmly judicious and mature. In one of his poems, 'On Certain Critics', Gosse declares that while we are still wrapped up in the present (Gosse, 1911),

> *We know not what is false or what is true;*
> *But in the firm perspectives of the past*
> *We see the picture duly, and its faults*
> *Are softly moulded by a filmy blue.*

This is how *Father and Son* appears to be written : with the wisdom of reflective hindsight, in a mood of serene retrospection —'all this is long over, and done with'. The impression is achieved partly by Gosse's style. He excludes anything raw or rebarbative or banal, he tends to prefer phrases that are exotic or refined. He introduces flashes of endearing self-mockery, he looks back with condescending amusement on his toils and troubles of long ago: 'this ridiculous act . . .', 'this absurd little incident . . .', 'my life was made up of very trifling things'. His appraisals are expressed with civility and wit; he favours for his occasional strictures a tone of mild expostulation. And yet . . . here and there we sense something more intense: a discrepancy of judgement, a telling lapse of tone, a hint that not everything about his past has been so successfully subdued. We sense, surviving over the years, an animus against his father.

Traditionally this aspect of *Father and Son* has been almost wholly ignored. The book has convinced generations of readers of its calm objectivity. Harold Nicolson's response is characteristic: 'Sir Edmund Gosse's detachment . . . is indeed amazing; . . . he is never sentimental, never angry, never intense . . . essentially the book is scientific.' (Nicolson, 1927.) The only dissent from this orthodox view has been made for inadequate reasons. In his curious introduction to the Oxford edition (1974) James Hepburn argues that Gosse's account is in fact highly coloured. He offers as proof the fact that Gosse wasn't treated as badly as Alton Locke—even though Gosse's parents were just as extreme, as regards their fanatical religious beliefs, as the mother in Kingsley's novel. Moreover, Gosse admits to not having enjoyed the Plymouth Brethren's conference in London, when we know, from the *History of the Brethren Movement*, that one young girl from a similar background did enjoy such conferences. We cannot dismiss Philip Gosse, says Hepburn, because in the last decade it has been acknowledged that the men of the Victorian period 'possessed extraordinary character' (Gosse himself, as it happens, was also Victorian—for slightly longer than his father). This fact is clear from the photograph reproduced on the cover of the Oxford edition, where Gosse's father looks 'so powerful', while the son appears 'so pale'. Most of Mr Hepburn's other arguments are of a comparable standard.

If we wish to maintain that Gosse's account is not so impartial as it might appear, we shall need less eccentric reasons. In his preface Gosse asserts explicitly that his book is 'scrupulously true'. As regards fidelity to observed and accepted fact, this appears to be no empty claim. When writing *Father and Son* Gosse not only rehearsed his memory but carefully checked his sources. Many of the details of his parents' life he had professionally investigated several years earlier while writing his father's biography; these details find their way into *Father and Son* with no apparent contamination or adornment. Indeed his general attitude to his father in the earlier book is remarkably similar to that in *Father and Son*; there is no question of a laudatory official biography being followed by an anonymous stab in the back. The earlier biography is also useful for containing an appendix by Eliza Gosse, Philip's second wife, on 'Reminiscences of my Husband'. This is, of course, less critical than Gosse's account, but it bears out many of his statements (for example, the statement that Philip Gosse, always expecting the Second Coming, was at the last 'bitterly disappointed' by its failure to save him from death).

Gosse also seems to have had before him as he wrote a pamphlet produced by his father after his mother's death, entitled 'A Memorial of the last days on earth of Emily Gosse'. Several portions of the narrative of *Father and Son*—those dealing with the death of his mother—are based on this remarkable work. It is remarkable for what it reveals about Philip Henry Gosse: it is not a conventional memorial at all, crammed with panegyric and bathed in nostalgia, discreet in its avoidance of awkward or painful facts. It is a scientist's ruthlessly detailed account, relieved only by dogged adoration of God, of the agonies of his wife's last illness. A large part of it consists of a vivid description, harrowing in its clinical exactitude, of the surgery performed on her cancerous breast, before the excision of her tumour. Philip Gosse describes the cavity after the operation: 'a mass of raw fungoid flesh, on which a fetid pus copiously formed'. The publication by Gosse's father of this account alienated many of Mrs Gosse's friends and increased his loneliness after her death (Gosse, 1890). Edmund, however, based some of his text on its more reprintable details.

As far as can be confirmed from other sources, then, *Father and Son* is both accurate and honest. But not everything in the estimation of character is capable of objective verification, as Gosse himself would be the first to admit. Subjectivity must intrude— and especially when a writer is communing with his own past,

trying to explore the springs of his personality and give an account
of episodes in which he was once deeply involved. In this case
we should not be surprised to find some more personal indica-
tions: some wavering, some uncertainty, some sharp unpolished
edges of emotion. And this, or something like it, is what we do find
in *Father and Son*.

Perhaps the crucial question is: how far did Gosse intend the
book to be an attack upon his father? Almost certainly he would
have replied that he did not intend an attack at all. Sir Evan
Charteris relates that after *Father and Son* was first published,

> Quite a common criticism on the book was, 'How much
> better the father comes out of it than the Son'—this, said by
> way of disparagement, happened to be the criticism Gosse
> most desired to hear, since it implied a recognition that he
> had succeeded in one of the purposes he had in mind in
> writing the book.

And Charteris goes on to quote from a letter written by Gosse in
1924 in which he stated that:

> The book is a monument to the memory of my father, an
> extraordinary man. It is not of the same order as the lying
> epitaphs in churchyards, but I hope it is something better,
> the exact portrait of a good and even great man, whose
> character was too powerful not to have its disconcerting
> sides.

Yet if Gosse's intention was to salute his father, many people
misinterpreted the gesture. He received insulting letters about the
book, attacking it as useless and destructive. Lytton Strachey,
after a grumbling review by Gosse, alleged that his rival biographer had 'spent all his life saying disagreeable things about
other people (his father included)' (Holroyd, 1968). Some allowance
must be made here for polemical hyperbole and for the incautious-
ness of private correspondence; also, perhaps, for the tendency
to relate everything to one's own professional concerns. Possibly
we can dismiss the insulters, too, as mere irritable biased mis-
readers. 'No one would now be found', said Charteris, 'self-
righteous enough to criticise the book on the score of its unfilial
revelations.' Probably not—one is duly warned off; but it is still
permissible to ask if the tone of the book is quite compatible
with its author's intentions.

One can note certain gradations in Gosse's hostility. There is,
on the most publicly acceptable level, the direct and candid

disapproval: his parents are arraigned with great respect and sometimes even with sorrow. 'Yet there was also narrowness, isolation, an absence of perspective, let it be boldly admitted, an absence of humanity.' Or: 'I think that, with all his justice, he had no conception of the importance of liberty.' Nothing could sound more reasonable than this: temperate judgements, free of irony or rancour, straightforward disagreements about important values in life.

More frequent, though, are phrases with just a tinge of censure, oblique implications of excess or imbalance. 'I will not dwell here on their theories, which my mother put forth, with un-flinching directness, in her published writings.' Better, the dry suggestion is, if she *had* flinched from publishing such stuff: the word hints at a certain arrogant disregard for average educated opinion. 'Any such guttering theological rushlight as Miss Marks might dutifully exhibit faded for me in the blaze of my Father's glaring beacon-lamp of faith.' 'Glaring' works almost like a trans-ferred epithet, suggesting a surplus of truculent zeal. Similar in its effect is Gosse's account of his father's indifference to money: 'He had some dim dream, I think, of there being just enough for us all.' The word 'dim' tends to attach itself to the dreamer as well as the dream. Cumulatively, such words have a powerful effect, a persistent subterranean persuasion.

Sometimes Gosse allows the hostile tone to glint through the cut-glass of a polite irony. 'He prayed with fervour and animation, in pure Johnsonian English, and I hope I am not undutiful if I add my impression that he was not displeased with the sound of his own devotions.' In this case the understatement is perhaps a little overstated—the sentence comes uncomfortably close to a schoolmaster's cumbrous sarcasm. More feline is Gosse's descrip-tion of his father's influence on his stepmother: 'Over her wishes and prejudices my Father exercised a constant, cheerful and quiet pressure. He was never unkind or abrupt, but he went on adding avoirdupois until her will gave way under the sheer weight.' Effectively this presents his father as a gentle but relentless bully.

Very rarely, there will be a thrust of overt hostility, its impact all the more jolting amid the general blandness of mood. Such moments occur most frequently in the book's Epilogue, but earlier slight shocks are felt when Gosse calls his father a 'task-master' and 'high-handed', and particularly when he tells how his father put questions to him 'in a loud wheedling voice'.

But all this, it may be objected, is simply a matter of tone; admittedly there seems good reason to feel that Gosse is against his parents; all the same, his hostility does not distort facts, and he acknowledges their virtues as well as suggesting their faults. In reply to this, two points should be considered. The first is that, though Gosse doesn't knowingly distort facts, there is evidence that he is often eager to believe the worst. And secondly, what is notable about his occasional expressions of praise is how frequently they are cancelled or contradicted by statements he makes elsewhere.

Confronted with memories of his parents which are doubtful, shifting or unsure, Gosse tends to prefer the most unflattering interpretation, the one that puts their actions and motives in a murky, unfavourable light. For instance, he writes: 'I do not quite know how it was that neither of my parents took me to any of the sights of London, although I am sure it was a question of principle with them.' It is rather strange to be sure about something that really you do not know. A minor example, perhaps; but take his account of how the readings from *The Merchant of Venice* were discontinued at school:

> I was in the seventh heaven of delight, but alas! we had only reached the second act of the play, when the readings mysteriously stopped. I never knew the cause, but I suspect that it was at my Father's desire. He prided himself on never having read a page of Shakespeare, and on never having entered a theatre but once. I think I must have spoken at home about the readings, and that he must have given the schoolmaster a hint to return to the ordinary school curriculum.

In this passage one can feel the conviction growing firmer: the readings stopped 'mysteriously', he 'never knew the cause', yet he 'suspects' his father—it 'must have' been due to his father. But the supposition seems somewhat flimsier when we remember that, a couple of pages before, Gosse says himself that the schoolmaster was 'frank and modest, deferential to my Father's opinions *and yet capable of defending his own*' (my italics). Sometimes, through his eagerness to embrace an unfavourable fact, Gosse's recollections are hardly to be reconciled. Was his father so obtuse as to overlook the development of his interests? The answer is yes:

> The slender expansions of my interest which were now budding hither and thither do not seem to have alarmed my

Father at all. His views were short; . . . My Father, not a very subtle psychologist, applied to me the same formulas which served him well at the chapel.

And did his father also betray absurd fears about these developments? The answer is yes, again:

The growing eagerness which I displayed for the society of selected schoolfellows and for such gentle dissipations as were within my reach exercised my Father greatly. His fancy rushed forward with the pace of a steam-engine, and saw me the life of a gambling club, or flaunting it at the Mabille.

These quotations, it should be noted, are only a few pages apart.

It is discrepancies of a similar kind that alert us to the elusiveness of Gosse's good will, the precariousness of his esteem. As regards the life of his father and mother, the book is full of merely nominal admissions of merit, strategic concessions in a climate of dispraise. A favourite device is the unconvincing disclaimer. Gosse will carefully assure us that his life was not too bad, then allow us to conclude the opposite from other information he provides. He says, for example, early in the book:

It is so generally taken for granted that a life strictly dedicated to religion is stiff and dreary, that I may have some difficulty in persuading my readers that, as a matter of fact, in these early days of my childhood, before disease and death had penetrated to our slender society, we were always cheerful and often gay.

This is hardly the impression we receive elsewhere. Even at this time of his life, Gosse was having to sing hymns 'drearily and slowly' and to read Newton's *Thoughts on the Apocalypse*, 'a book of incommunicable dreariness'. The delicate, happy glow of an early period is evoked by Gosse to strengthen the contrast with the darkness of his life thereafter; for 'dreariness' is one of his most insistent terms in defining the general mood of his childhood. We remember the 'dreary street' at Oddicombe, the 'dreary light' of their drawing-room, the 'dreary little Latin book' that his father set him to study, the apparent 'dreariness and sterility' of school life, with its 'dreary' morning prayers. Gosse ensures that his little wisp of happiness is swiftly negated and crushed.

Similarly, he says that he does not for a moment regard his mother as a Mrs Jellyby, yet he at once adds drily that 'she developed an unexpected gift of persuasion over strangers whom she met in the omnibus or in the train, and with whom she courageously grappled'. The hilariously equivocal last word surely restores some of the ridicule that has been solemnly waved away. Or consider the fair-minded defence of his father's character which crops up towards the end of the book: 'My Father, let me say once more, had other interests than those of his religion. . . . He was no fanatical monomaniac.' This is followed by a couple of pages that relate his father's religious obsessions, and then Gosse comes out with what is really on his mind: there is surely something 'horrible' in the 'fanaticism' of his father's ideas. The attempt at a balanced and charitable assessment founders on the surviving splinters and shards of Gosse's irritation. Gosse simply does not believe that his father 'was no fanatical monomaniac'. He has already described his book *Omphalos* as 'this curious, this obstinate, this fanatical volume'. He has stated that his parents' faith was 'so strenuous that many persons might have called it fanatical'. And he has told how his father was greatly influenced by the 'fanatical' Mrs Paget, who was 'a parody of his own central self'.

Gosse's gracious little leniences impress the reader as somehow superficial; they seem like attempts to tone down intense emotions and embalm them in the repertoire of an after-dinner raconteur. For they refuse to hold steady: Gosse turns his temperate sentences, and brings in some sober concession of merit, only to find his phrases wriggling away, his civility mutating to scorn and annoyance. This is particularly the case when he is recalling his father, but it tends to happen with the whole Puritan ethos. With the Burmington sisters, for example: Gosse politely introduces them as 'excellent people', then adds that one of them was 'insignificant, and vulgarized by domestic cares'. With his father the shift is even more abrupt: old emotions well up and spill over the page and spoil his professions of approval:

> My Father was very generous. He used to magnify any little effort that I made, with stammering tongue, to sanctify a visit; and people, I now see, were accustomed to give me a friendly lead in this direction, so that they might please him by reporting that I had 'testified' in the Lord's service. The whole thing, however, was artificial, and was part of my Father's restless inability to let well alone.

In a like manner Gosse quotes a passage from Archbishop Leighton about the difference between a merely verbal and a heartfelt assent to religious belief, the second being 'saving faith'. This, he says, exactly defines the difference between his father and himself. But he goes on: 'He did indeed possess this saving faith, which could move mountains of evidence, and suffer no diminution under the action of failure or disappointment.' Gosse cannot resist the temptation to mock, to slip a banana-skin beneath his praise, and once again filial humility is trippingly turned into jest.

Sometimes he will come to an episode which is important enough to necessitate a mention, but which also seems quite unequivocally to redound to his father's advantage. In such a case, reluctantly, and often with some noisy murmurs of surprise, he will brace himself and then condescend to give a stiff acknowledging nod. After describing the gaps in his education, he tells how his father took care to put them right: 'My Father grudged the time, but he felt it a duty to do something to fill up these deficiencies.' Gosse grudges the concession, but feels it a duty to admit the fact into his narrative. Likewise he reveals how, when at last he acquired some friends, his father allowed him to keep them:

> It was a remarkable proof of my Father's temporary lapse into indulgence that he made no effort to thwart my intimacy with these my new companions. He was in an unusually humane mood himself.

This refers to the period after his father's second marriage, when —as Gosse puts it—with 'unwonted geniality' he read the poems of Walter Scott to his bride; and when he left his son to his own devices, being—as Gosse is again careful to add—'fully occupied with moulding the will and inflaming the piety of my stepmother'. When Gosse squeezes out a good word for his father, it is seldom unaccompanied by a reproachful scratch.

All this is not to suggest that Gosse *never* expresses genuine praise. The book does contain a few sincere tributes to his parents, with no sense of strain or empty good manners or cunning inversions of tone. Gosse movingly describes the courage they displayed as his mother declined towards death: 'Language cannot utter what they suffered, but there was no rebellion, no repining; in their case even an atheist might admit that the overpowering miracle of grace was mightily efficient.' On a less sombre occasion Gosse gives his father credit for his 'admirable' scheme of rationalising geography. But it must be insisted that much more often, when the book touches on commendation, we find something slightly disingenuous, a respectfulness fractured by resentment. Gosse recounts how he once felt furiously angry after his father had given him a beating:

> I cannot account for the flame of rage which it awakened in my bosom. My dear, excellent Father had beaten me, not very severely, without ill-temper, and with the most genuine desire to improve me. . . . I have to confess with shame that I went about the house for some days with a murderous hatred of my Father locked within my bosom.

What comes across most powerfully in this passage is the child's hatred, rather than the grown man's 'shame'; and surely one can feel some survival of quivering anger in the biting courtesy of that 'my dear, excellent Father'.

Even his father's occasional kindliness appears to have got on Edmund's nerves; he recalls, for instance, being spoken to 'in a tone of harrowing tenderness'. Looking back, he still finds it hard to believe in the authenticity of his father's goodwill; his descriptions of it are hedged around with suspicious qualifications. He remembers how his father would address him and his playmate 'with an air of great benevolence'. He hesitates, puzzled, when he recalls his father's gifts; fancy allowing him to have *Tom Cringle's Log*—'an indulgent act, for the caprice of which I cannot wholly account'. Or buying him a copy of Southey's poems—surely it wasn't such a kindness as it seemed:

> My Father presented me with the entire bulk of Southey's stony verse, which I found it impossible to penetrate, but my stepmother lent me *The Golden Treasury*, in which almost everything seemed exquisite.

Even an intentedly generous act can be preserved in a disparaging contrast.

To the reader of *Father and Son* it must become increasingly plain that, though the book is indeed 'scrupulously true' in its accurate rendering of objective facts, its narration of what events happened and when, it is, necessarily, by no means free from either the subjectivity of introspection or the personal bias of human judgement, the latter, indeed, being patently coloured by a close involvement with the people concerned, by a natural survival of keen emotion which betrays itself in edginess and irritation and refuses to be blandly incorporated into a mood of well-bred composure. The survival is most evident in the book's Epilogue. Here Gosse's language becomes shriller and less disguised, the disparity between his statements more marked. He begins, for instance, with an explanation of why the Epilogue has been attached: 'This narrative, however, must not be allowed to close with the Son in the foreground of the piece. If it has a value, that value consists in what light it may contrive to throw upon the unique and noble figure of the Father.' This sounds self-effacing and magnanimous enough. But then we turn over a few pages and discover how the narrative has in fact been allowed to close:

> It was a case of 'Everything or Nothing'; and thus desperately challenged, the young man's conscience threw off once and for all the yoke of his 'dedication', and, as respectfully as he could, without parade or remonstrance, he took a human being's privilege to fashion his inner life for himself.

The Son could hardly be more grandly in the foreground than this; the Father is not in the spotlight at all, but furiously writhing in the wings. And if we turn back to that first tribute—'the unique and noble figure of the Father'—we find it followed within a few lines by a picture which gives a quite different impression:

> He abated no jot or tittle of his demands upon human frailty. He kept the spiritual cord drawn tight; the Biblical bearing-rein was incessantly busy, jerking into position the head of the dejected neophyte.

With this the nobility is neatly annulled and we can only feel relieved that Gosse's father was 'unique'.

The Epilogue angrily heaps up phrases of nakedly embittered condemnation: 'the torment of a postal inquisition', 'uplifted Quixotism', 'exceedingly unfair', 'fanaticism', 'police inspection'. It also brings to a head what has been hinted at throughout— the violence and aggression of Philip Henry Gosse, despite his exterior of godly acquiescence. In the opinion of his second wife, Eliza Gosse, 'he was of a remarkably even disposition'; but this is hardly what we feel after reading Father and Son. Gosse's Father comes across as a volcanic character, prone to frightening eruptions of religious zeal. Emotionally, he was a man of tensely suppressed power; the God he worshipped was created in his own image—rigid and despotic, more just and jealous than merciful (no wonder Edmund, as a little boy, was apt to confuse the two); and having created this irascible God, he was capable of feeling anger against Him, of resenting His failure to order events as he himself would have wished. This happened after the scornful reception of *Omphalos*; but domestically, too, he was violent and angry, as his son reminds us throughout. In the Epilogue Gosse reduces his father to an intellectual pug: 'ready, nay eager, for argument . . . he would adopt a fighting attitude, and challenge me to a round on any portion of the Scheme of Grace'. Our final impression is of a man who, for all his belief in humility and love, desired omniscience and control: 'It was the prerogative of his faith to know, and of his character to overpower objection; between these two millstones I was rapidly ground to powder.'

Still, even here we can sense some rhetorical exaggeration, for doesn't the whole spirit of the book suggest that Gosse was not quite so easily pulverised? As he himself has already said, 'Through thick and thin I clung to a hard nut of individuality, deep down in my childish nature.' The point is that the Epilogue deliberately shapes events—letting in open disparagement and stoking up the emotional tone—so as to precipitate a convincing spiritual crisis and round off the book appropriately with the severance of father and son. The contrivance is apparent in Gosse's treatment of his father's letter: tiresome and intransigent it may well be, but there is nothing in it to indicate that it was 'furiously despatched' or that its purpose was a desperate challenge. There is external evidence, too, that Gosse and his father never broke so completely as would appear from *Father and Son*. They continued to argue and wrangle in letters for some time after Gosse was twenty-one; later they met and corresponded less often, but their cordiality increased. It does not seem to be true that, as Gosse states in the Epilogue, his father's character became 'more severely outlined, more rigorously confined within settled limits'. On the contrary, according to Charteris, by the 1880s 'the rigid framework of Philip Gosse's religious faith had relaxed. His beliefs . . . were now penetrated by a softer and more generous vision.' To some extent this softening was brought about by age; but even early in Gosse's life, when he left his father and went to London, there was no clean divorce of opinions. The last pages of *Father and Son* mislead—they appear to have misled Charteris himself, who exaggerates Gosse's emancipation at the time of his leaving home. He writes:

In his seventeenth year we find him settled in London lodg-
ings. The Throne of Grace so fondly and insistently figuring
in the ministrations of his father had become a shadowy
kingdom.

Just how shadowy we can judge from a reminiscence of Gosse as
a youth published by his friend George C. Williamson in the
London Mercury after his death. Williamson was 'eight or nine'
when they met, and Gosse was nine years older. The meeting
must therefore have taken place when Gosse had already left
home. Williamson's grandfather was a zoologist and Philip Gosse
had come to consult him about anemones. Williamson recalls
that he and Edmund went into the garden:

> How well I remember his stopping me with the imperative
> question as he pointed to my grandfather, 'Is he a be-
> liever?'. . . . What a cross-examination I underwent at his
> hands!. . . . 'Did my grandfather have Family Prayers?' 'Did
> he read his Bible?' 'Did he ever allow novels to come
> into the house?' 'Were my grandmother and my mother
> believers?' 'Did I read the Bible every day, and how much
> of it?'

Gosse went on to converse about the 'sea of fire' and to tirade
against the wickedness of cards (Williamson, 1928). One would
never infer from *Father and Son* that at this time he was still so
ferociously pious, that his ideas were still so deeply shot through
by his father's exclusive beliefs.

Father and Son, then, is not merely, as Gosse claims in its
preface, 'a genuine slice of life'. It is, rather, a sample of art, a
selective and organised piece of work, with all the literary skill
we might expect, all the customary narrative-moulding and
manipulation of the reader's response. At the same time it is a
deeply-felt personal history and the planned artistic pattern is
not always unruffled. In particular, when writing about his father,
Gosse sets out to adopt an attitude of detachment, but finds himself feeling more embroiled than he would wish. Filial tensions
are not so easily exorcised; Gosse condemns his father when he
means to understand him. But the evidence for this outlined
above—the inconsistent statements, the transitions of tone, the
conscious neatening of the narrative—should not be taken as
detracting from the book's achievement or as cavilling at Gosse
for failing to come up to some superhuman acme of compassion.
Gosse undoubtedly tries hard to be fair to his father, and to a

remarkable degree he succeeds; it is precisely because of his occasional malice that the book continues to enthral. We are gripped by the spectacle of a tolerant, civilised mind trying vainly to suppress all its flickers of annoyance and to square its very natural feelings of dislike with the conventional requirements of respect. Gosse's sympathy is balanced on a razor edge; if sometimes he lapses into personal resentment, at least he avoids being inhumanly aloof.

(iv)

It is clear that in many ways *Father and Son* is reminiscent of *The Way of All Flesh*. Admittedly, Gosse himself would be anxious to stress the extent of his difference from Butler. Once, in a review of Festing Jones's biography, he objected to the jaundiced acidity in Butler's view of his parents. He considered it obvious that *The Way of All Flesh* was not strictly autobiographical. Butler, he said (Gosse, 1922),

> disliked excessively the atmosphere of middle-class Evangelic-ism in which he had been brought up, and we must dislike it too, but we need not dislike the persons involved as bitterly as Butler did.

It is true that Gosse was less bitter than Butler, or at least more concerned to present for his readers a generous and accurate portrait. All the same, despite their different intentions, the two men have certain affinities. Both underwent the rigours of a puritan upbringing: grave, restricted and severe (one can scarcely believe that when Gosse was grown up, his father could talk about 'the unseemly levity that was possibly a hindrance to you in your childhood'). Both looked back on this time with irony— sarcasm quite often in Butler's case. And, most important, both found that their wished-for ironic poise, a balance of amused diffidence and curt rejection, a kind of cold-shoulder-shrugging wit, was continually in danger of being toppled by indignation, by a hot, sudden upsurge of something more intense. Artistically, however, in spite of this likeness, their achievement was not the same. In Gosse the intense or prickly moments invigorate the narrative. In Butler they are all too successfully assuaged by a story that reduces their significance and a theory that denies them.

But Gosse not only—in contrast with Butler—refrained from

erasing his childhood: he produced a history which, for all its uniqueness, relates to much else in Victorian literature on parent-child relations. There is, of course, the symbolic opposition between Philip Gosse's religious convictions and his son's Romantic aspirations: Gosse's escape epitomised a nineteenth-century trend. But Philip Gosse also, we are told at one point, admired *Sandford and Merton*—which shows how the Rationalist tradition of training could be biliously combined with its ostensible foe, with the bleak Evangelical approach to children which is the main target of *Father and Son*. What is more, Gosse's story bears a striking resemblance to many situations in Dickens—to, for example, the unhappy fates of Paul and Florence Dombey. Like Paul he was 'a preternaturally sedate small boy', a silent, ailing, lonely observer, propelled prematurely into contact with darker things. He was, quite genuinely, an 'old-fashioned' child—that figure so popular in the late Victorian press. Like Florence he would look wistfully out of his window at the other, happier boys and girls; and like her he found an ally in his stepmother. Indeed, the whole drift of Gosse's childhood was somewhat Dickensian: a brooding, introspective child, strictly brought up by a stern father and surrounded by adults who did not understand. Simply on a representative level (in literary terms, at least) the relationship between Edmund Gosse and his father was something of lasting importance.

And on a personal level . . .? Here, alas, its historical value was to prove of little solace. A time came, as Gosse says, when their minds were quite alien to each other and they only continued to keep in touch in obedience to 'the law which says that ties of close family relationship must be honoured and sustained'. But they did keep in touch, they did occasionally meet, and eventually the harsh friction between them, ultimately incurable, was at least alleviated by time. Gosse's father died on 7 August 1888; in the last year of his life he was described by his son in a letter to Hamo Thornycroft:

> My father . . . is very sweet and gentle, wonderfully mellowed at last by the softening hand of age; and I have felt an affection for him and a pleasure in his company, this visit, that I am afraid I never really felt before. And so, in the evening there is light.

CONCLUSION

Literary sources are frequently deceptive; what they describe and what they embody may well be two different things. One reason why children in the nineteenth century are so often assumed to have been treated more harshly, to have met with more troubles than ever before, is that all kinds of documents acknowledged such harshness, examined and pondered such troubles. Articles were written on the problems of young people; books were turned out on their characters and needs; novelists depicted their sufferings, their difficulties; authors laid bare their own earliest years. All this has helped to build up an impression—but the impression may still be false. A fact newly noted may not be a new fact; likewise a practice which is suddenly deplored. The change may be less in the state of affairs than in the state of perception and judgement. In the treatment of children, we might usefully remember, the Victorian's failings were largely recorded by other Victorians.

Moreover, across the nineteenth century, the attitudes to parents and children changed: the change is engraved in literature, both fictional and factual. It is especially evident in children's literature, which altered far more in the nineteenth century, up to about 1880, than it has done since that time. After all, late Victorian children's books are still quite widely read and enjoyed. It was different with the earliest children's books: well before the end of the century they were dead and embalmed in derision. Thomas Day, so admired at the beginning of the century, was a figure of fun by the end; according to his modern biographer, 'Burnand's burlesque version of *Sandford and Merton* took the place of the original; then both of them vanished.' (Gignilliat, 1932.) Mrs Sherwood survived in bowdlerised versions, but after the middle of the century her work was quite often condemned. 'Pharisaical chatter . . . silly and nauseous . . . precocious canting . . . unwholesome . . . poisonous'—such was the opinion of *The Fairchild Family* served up in 1867 by the Chaplain of the Blind School, London (Johns, 1867). Mrs Trimmer was to suffer, from her own point of view, an even sorrier fate: remembered now and then for her implacable censure of the morality implicit in *Cinderella*, she was chiefly kept alive by a mocking allusion in Canto the First of *Don Juan*.

The account of children's literature in chapter III has been wholly confined to novels and stories, but in poetry, too, the same shift is apparent: a shift from the instructional, the punitive, the monitory to whimsy, entertainment and laughter. Lewis Carroll writes a parody of Isaac Watts and Belloc's hilarious *Cautionary Tales*, produced shortly after the century ended, are obviously send-ups of Ann and Jane Taylor, and perhaps of Elizabeth Turner. It is true that in poetry, as opposed to fiction, the classroom and pulpit were more quickly demolished—William Roscoe's *The Butterfly's Ball*, for example, was published as early as 1807. But on the whole the earliest poetry for children contained a good deal of instruction and warning—much of which was tacitly excised as the century went on. Modern selections from poets like the Taylors are frequently misleading. Nowadays their verse is normally cited as marking a break from the stern and didactic, as unveiling 'something novel and lightsome in the realm of literature for children' (Thwaite, 1972). Yet if we look at their earliest volumes, *Original Poems for Infant Minds* (1804–5), we find not only the lyrical and the tender—verses like the celebrated 'My Mother'—but productions of a somewhat fiercer kind. One poem by Jane is about a boy sadist who enjoyed going fishing because he was pleased when the fish 'writhed in agony' on the hook. Back at home, he is requited for his cruelty: as he jumps to reach a dish to put his victims in, he fails to notice 'a sharp meat-hook' which happens to be hanging close by. Caught under the chin, he dangles in the pantry, screaming, roaring, 'the crimson blood' pouring in torrents from his wound. The same volumes also include some poems by a certain Adelaide O'Keeffe. One of these, 'False Alarms', is on the same theme as Belloc's well-known 'Matilda'. A little girl's pranks are punished by fire: 'All burnt and all seamed is her once pretty face,/And terribly marked are her arms;/Her features, all scarred, leave a lasting disgrace/For giving Mamma false alarms.' Another lively offering from Adelaide concerns a young truant who, swimming in the river, has his body torn to pieces by a mill-wheel. Yet according to a recent book by Joyce Irene Whalley these volumes 'carried on the gentle tradition' begun by Isaac Watts (Whalley, 1974).

In attitudes to children 'the gentle tradition' was largely a Victorian creation; the earlier literature was either supplanted or significantly revised. Even the accepted text of 'My Mother' is not the original version. As we have it, the last stanza of this poem reads: 'For could our Father in the skies / Look down with pleased or loving eyes, / If ever I could dare despise / My Mother?' A gentle conclusion—but these sentiments were penned, not in 1804 but in 1866, by Ann Taylor in her eighty-fifth year, after someone had written to The Athenaeum to complain of the original version: 'For God, who lives above the skies / Would look with vengeance in His eyes / If I should ever dare despise / My Mother'. 'Vengeance', said the author, by way of explanation, 'is not a word I should now employ.' In this respect she was not alone: with the decline of Christianity the whole concept of vengeance was coming to be qualified or dropped—and especially vengeance on children. What popular preacher, for example, of the later nineteenth century, would have talked—as Jonathan Edwards had talked—of parents in heaven 'with holy joy upon their countenances' at the torment of their little ones? (Calhoun, 1917.) The attitudes changed—and not only to vengeance, but also to death, to transgression, to punishment, to what children might expect or deserve. Out of a multitude of possible examples, consider one particular contrast. Early in the century in a Manchester newspaper there appeared, under the heading 'Died', the following paragraph (de la Mare, 1935):

> On Tuesday, 5th instant, Mary Ann, daughter of John and Mary Weatherall, of this town, aged seven years. The deceased may be enumerated among those who in the dawn of life fall the victims of fire; and her troubled and disconsolate parents, ever tender and affectionate, clearly evince to all their acquaintance that parental love and solicitude should be invariably manifested in watching and reclaiming the giddiness of youth.

Clearly the attitudes of Adelaide O'Keeffe—or even of Mrs Sherwood—were not always confined to poetry and fiction; they lapped over into real life. Compare with this a late-century example of what it could mean to be, as a parent, 'ever tender and affectionate'—and also, after the death of one's child, 'troubled and disconsolate'. William Canton (1845–1926) was a poet and journalist whose daughter, in 1877, died in infancy. A few years later his wife died too, but he married again and in 1890 his second wife gave birth to a daughter, whom they christened Winifred Vida. But Canton had not forgotten his first child, and in 1894 he commemorated her with a book called *The Invisible Playmate*. The story concerns a man like himself who has lost one daughter but is bringing up another; however, at the end of the narrative this second child dies as well. The book proved extremely popular, and Canton was encouraged to write much more about the experience of parenthood and the ways of his second offspring. In 1896 he published a work called *W.V. Her Book*. This miscellany details almost everything about his five-year-old daughter: her games, her manners, her curious moods and her acquisition of language. Poems are included to evoke the rapport between the little girl and her parents. Her dialogues with the gardener are minutely recorded; so also is 'Her Bed-Time'. This kind of affection, this intensity of interest, were something quite recent in parent-child relations—and Canton is partially aware of the fact: he describes how, in one conversation with his daughter, he was 'telling her how sternly children were brought up fifty or sixty years ago'. Again the production was a great success and thousands of strangers became familiar with the life of 'W.V.' But in 1901 *The Invisible Playmate* caught up with William Canton: shortly before her eleventh birthday, his daughter, dearly loved by so many readers, died of peritonitis. Within months Canton published another book, *In Memory of W.V.* This time nothing at all was omitted: not only do we have an account of her illness, but also very full 'Recollections of her Schooldays', pieced together by her cousin Phyllis, to cover the periods when her father was not with her. Canton collects every possible memento, describes every relic of his daughter. He pores over Winifred's arithmetic books, examines her collections of wild flowers; he reproduces a play she wrote, gives extracts from a diary she kept at school: which sums she got right, which lessons she had had, which poems they recited in class. Dozens of people shared Canton's grief: they wrote him letters, proffered consolation; one reader sent a flower from New South Wales. We turn back to the obituary in the Manchester paper. Surely the difference between the two cases is not simply a matter of individual response. We are faced with a shift in domestic sensibility, a revolution in public taste. One view of children and of parent-child relations has been largely displaced by another.

These two views are, of course, in the broadest application,

the 'Puritan' and the 'Romantic': in nineteenth-century literature concerned with the family the trend was towards the latter.
The application has to be broad, for no one could rationally
maintain that all people of an evangelical disposition were unresponsive to childhood. Many of them were tirelessly philanthropic: to give but one example, Hesba Stretton, the enormously
influential evangelical novelist, was a founder of the N.S.P.C.C.
But on the whole one can scarcely avoid the conclusion that
throughout the nineteenth century a stricter view of children
was partly dependent on Christian teaching, and that many of the
less rigorous, 'Romantic' assumptions were more secular in origin.
Not only was there the doctrine of Original Sin; there was also
the analogy, frequently asserted, between the father's authority
and God's. As belief in Christianity began to crumble, patriarchy
was weakened too. Of course, it is possible to argue the opposite
—that as God departed from family relations, the parents became
supreme. In her recent book on Mrs Sherwood, a work of scholarly
apologetics, M. Nancy Cutt makes out this case. She points to
revisions of *The Fairchild Family* in which, as the religious framework was dismantled, 'the parent assumed disproportionate importance' and 'became the ultimate authority'. She also quotes
Chesterton on Victorian changes: 'Theirs was the first generation
that ever asked its children to worship the hearth without the
altar.' (Cutt, 1974.) One can see what she means—and Chesterton
too—yet the case is not finally convincing. It is true that in
Victorian fiction for children (and Victorian fiction generally) the
sentiment surrounding parents increased, but this was not the
same as the authority. No parents were ever more powerful than
the Fairchilds: they held sway over their children with an
absolute authority deputed to them by God. Their own subjection
was by contrast perfunctory: their sins, their 'struggles', occasionally mentioned, remained mere hollow assertions. The significance
of this goes beyond the Fairchilds. The point is that although, in
some later literature, children were expected to worship their
parents, to accord them a devotion which was formerly God's,
there was rarely any similar demand for His authority: as divine
authority evaporated, so too did that of parents. As far as one
can judge from Victorian literature, the 'Puritan' attitude to
parent-child relations was if not reliant on, greatly strengthened
by, the implications of Christian doctrine.

The 'Romantic' approach to children, on the other hand, despite

G*

having roots in Christianity, was encouraged by secularisation. In a sense Mrs Trimmer was quite correct: the democratic ideals of the French Revolution were potentially a threat not only to the monarchy, but also to the power of parents. Hannah More arrived at a similar conclusion. In her *Strictures on the Modern System of Female Education* (1799) she remarked that the child—or, as she said, 'the young probationer'—was increasingly lacking in obedience. This was because both sons and daughters had 'adopted something of that spirit of independence, and disdain of control, which characterise the times'. It was obvious, she claimed, that 'domestic manners' were affected by 'public principles':

> The *rights of man* have been discussed, till we are somewhat wearied with the discussion. To these have been opposed, with more presumption than prudence, the *rights of women*. It follows, according to the natural progression of human things, that the next stage of that irradiation which our enlighteners are pouring in upon us will produce grave descants on the *rights of children*.

But this, of course, is precisely what happened: Hannah More's sarcastic joke came true. The 'Romantic' view of children was concerned with their rights: insisting that in nature they were different from adults—in some ways they were even superior—it attempted to protect them, to condone their incapacities, to segregate young people from the adult world. And eventually children achieved their maturity: they won the right to be children.

A triumph—yet perhaps it was not such a triumph; from the children's point of view it was partially a loss. For although, with the waning of the 'Puritan' attitude, they were less often treated as miniature adults, the 'Romantic' approach had its dangers too; in the course of the twentieth century these dangers have become apparent. The 'Romantic' approach has entailed condescension: protecting children, acknowledging their weaknesses, it has lovingly robbed them of their independence, has tended to underrate them; the conviction that children are different from adults has led to their being cut off. As a result we have seen, in the later twentieth century, a startling change in the champions of children, a reversal in their arguments. Whereas in the past the most common objection was that children were being deprived of their childhood, the more usual complaint since about the 1950s has been rather the opposite of this. No longer are children being brought up too quickly: they are being held down too long. Moreover, what is needed is no longer segregation: it is the right to win freedom, to assume responsibility, to take part in the adult world.

Many of these proposals are highly understandable, given the nature of twentieth-century trends. Yet what all too often remains dubious about them is their hankering after the past. In the past, we are told, before the late eighteenth century, adults had a mutual understanding with children; in the modern world this has been lost. Possibly the first sustained statement of this viewpoint occurred in a work by a Dutch psychologist published in 1955. Childhood was not noticed before the eighteenth century because it did not exist: so we learn in J. H. van den Berg's *The Changing Nature of Man*. The complexity of modern civilisation, its 'multivalent pluralism', has altered the character of maturity and made it less accessible to children. As a consequence children are now different from adults; they need longer to mature. Formerly, it seems, this was not the case; fathers and children 'understood each other'; there were hardly any books on the training of children because parents 'did not need enlightenment, they knew how to act because they acted in a continuity; the child was right next to them, he was part of their mature world'. In adult-child relations, van den Berg concludes, 'we have made some good changes, but infinitely more bad ones'. This kind of analysis, comprehensive and nostalgic, has been highly influential. The ideas of Philippe Ariès have helped to support it; sociological lay-preachers have adopted it as their theme. We may hear it, for example, in *Escape From Childhood*, a recent work on the rights of children by a professed admirer of van den Berg, the anti-educationalist John Holt. At first sight Holt's proposals seem radical enough: children should have all the rights of adults— the right to vote, the right to sign contracts, to travel, to work, to have a guaranteed income, to take poisons (if properly labelled). Yet many of his suggestions, because of his assumption that children are really very similar to adults, have a strange air of *déjà vu*. 'If we gave up our vested interest', he says, 'in children's dependency and incompetence—would they not much more quickly become independent and competent?' The suggestion is reminiscent of Locke's: 'The sooner you treat him as a man, the sooner he will become one.' (Axtell, 1968.) Children are reasonable, says Holt; they should be allowed to be 'citizens'. But it was

Addison, in the eighteenth-century *Spectator*, who rejoiced in his children as 'reasonable creatures, citizens and Christians'. Holt's drift is repeatedly towards the past. It is scarcely surprising that, in his opinion, what we need, for the greater health of young people, 'is to re-create the extended family'.

The reaction against the 'Romantic' approach to children is beginning to come full circle. We are back with the notion that children are adults, and ought to be treated accordingly. Why should we chuckle at toddlers, asks Holt. We wouldn't at an adult in a similar condition: 'severely handicapped'. And what of our response to children's crying? Surely we should be 'frozen in wonder and terror'—as we would be, he says, if the sufferer were an adult. Of course, not all Holt's assertions are so wayward; nor those of other writers who share his conviction that children are nowadays over-restricted, too limitingly seen as both helpless and good. What, however, is finally of interest, for those concerned with Victorian literature, is how greatly such modern defences of children pay tribute to the past. Not only are they sometimes quite yearningly nostalgic (for the 'integrated', pre-industrial world), but they are also attacking a conception of childhood which was chiefly a nineteenth-century creation: the idealising, potent, 'Romantic' conception, which, as we have seen, gathered strength in the last century, largely displaced the more 'Puritan' outlook, and appears to have survived even into our own times. It may not survive much longer.

REFERENCES

This bibliography lists only books and articles which are cited or quoted in the text. With articles, the initial page number only is given. With books, the place of publication is London, except where otherwise stated.

Adye, Frederic, 'Old-Fashioned Children', *Macmillan's Magazine*, vol. 68 (1893), p. 286.

Anstey, F., *The Last Load* (1925).

Anstey, F., *A Long Retrospect* (Oxford, 1936).

Anstey, F., *The Talking Horse* (1892).

Anstey, F., *Vice Versa* (1882).

Ariès, Philippe, *Centuries of Childhood*, trans. Robert Baldick (1962).

Aristotle, *Nichomachean Ethics* (Loeb edition).

Austen, Jane, *The Novels of Jane Austen*, 6 vols., ed. R. W. Chapman (Oxford 1923–1954).

Austen-Leigh, J. E., *Memoir of Jane Austen* (Oxford, 1926).

Avery, Gillian, *Childhood's Pattern* (1975).

Avery, Gillian, and Bull, Angela, *Nineteenth-century Children* (1965).

Axtell, James L. (ed.), *The Educational Writings of John Locke* (Cambridge, 1968).

Balfour, Clara Lucas, *A Sketch of Mrs. Trimmer* (1854).

Barbauld, A. L., *Evenings at Home* (6 vols., 1792–6).

Barbauld, A. L., *Hymns in Prose* (1781, 1801).

Bartholomew, A. T. (ed.), *Further Extracts from the Notebooks of Samuel Butler* (1934).

Baxter, Richard, *Poetical Fragments*, 3rd ed. (1699).

Bayne-Powell, Rosamund, *The English Child in the Eighteenth Century* (1939).

Belloc, Hilaire, *Cautionary Tales for Children* (1907).

Berg, J. H. van den, *The Changing Nature of Man*, trans. H. F. Croes (1975).

Boas, George, *The Cult of Childhood* (1966).

Body, A. H., *John Wesley and Education* (1936).

Bolton, Mary, 'The Discipline of Children', *Sunday Magazine*, vol. 22 (1893), p. 762.

Boyd, A. K. H., 'Concerning the Sorrows of Childhood', *Fraser's Magazine*, vol. 65 (1862), p. 304.

Bunyan, John, *The Pilgrim's Progress* (Oxford, 1960).

Burnand, F. C., *The New History of Sandford and Merton* (1872).
Butler, Marilyn, *Jane Austen and the War of Ideas* (Oxford, 1975).
Butler, Samuel, *Erewhon* (1872).
Butler, Samuel, *Erewhon Revisited* (1901).
Butler, Samuel, *Ernest Pontifex, or The Way of All Flesh*, ed. Daniel F. Howard (1964).
Butler, Samuel, *The Fair Haven* (1873).
Butler, Samuel, *Life and Habit* (1916).
Butler, Samuel, *Shakespeare's Sonnets Reconsidered* (1899).
Calhoun, Arthur W., *A Social History of the American Family*, vol. 1 (1917).
Canton, William, *The Invisible Playmate* (1901).
Carey, John, *The Violent Effigy: a Study of Dickens' Imagination* (1973).
Carroll, Lewis, *Alice's Adventures in Wonderland* (1865).
Carroll, Lewis, *Through the Looking Glass* (1872).
Chambers, J. D., *Population, Economy, and Society in Pre-Industrial England* (1972).
Chapman, R. W. (ed.), *Jane Austen's Letters*, 2nd ed. (Oxford, 1952).
Chapman, R. W. (ed.), *Two Chapters of 'Persuasion'* (Oxford, 1926).
Charlesworth, Maria, *Ministering Children* (1854).
Charteris, Sir Evan, *The Life and Letters of Sir Edmund Gosse* (1931).
'Childhood', *Blackwood's Magazine*, vol. 12 (1822), p. 139.
'Childish Things', *Chambers's Journal*, vol. 64 (1887), p. 401.
'Children', *All the Year Round*, 3rd series, vol. 11 (1894), p. 584.
'Children', *Chambers's Journal*, vol. 19 (1863), p. 177.
'Children', *Fraser's Magazine*, vol. 26 (1842), p. 543.
'Children in the Church of England', *Christian Remembrances*, vol. 7 (1884), p. 1.
'Children Yesterday and Today', *Quarterly Review*, vol. 183 (1896), p. 374.
Chitty, Susan, *The Woman Who Wrote Black Beauty* (1971).
Christian Observer, vol. 56 (1856), p. 114.
Collins, Philip, *Dickens and Education* (1963).
Corelli, Marie, *Boy*, (1900).
Coveney, Peter, *The Image of Childhood* (1967).
Cruse, Amy, *The Victorians and Their Books* (1935).
Cutt, M. Nancy, *Mrs. Sherwood and Her Books for Children* (Oxford, 1974).
Darton, F. J. Harvey, *Children's Books in England*, 2nd ed. (Cambridge, 1958).
Day, Thomas, *Sandford and Merton*, 3 vols. (1791).
de la Mare, Walter, *Early One Morning in the Spring* (1935).
de Mause, Lloyd (ed.), *The History of Childhood* (New York, 1974).
Devlin, D. D., *Jane Austen and Education* (1975).
Dickens, Charles, *Complete Works* (Oxford Illustrated edition).
Documents, English Historical (1959), vol. xi (1788–1832).

Documents, English Historical (1956), vol. xii (1833–74).
Do Your Duty Come What Will (Edinburgh, 1871).
Earle, John, *Microcosmography* (1628).
Edgeworth, Maria, *Early Lessons* (1801).
Edgeworth, Maria, *The Parent's Assistant* (1796).
Edgeworth, R. L., *Memoirs of Richard Lovell Edgeworth*, 2 vols. (1821).
Edmonds, T. R., 'On the Mortality of Infants', *The Lancet*, 30 January 1836, p. 690.
'The Education of Children', *Christian Observer*, vol. 10 (1811), p. 622.
Evans, A. A., 'The Impact of Rousseau on English Education', *Researches and Studies*, The University of Leeds Institute of Education, No. 11 (1955), p. 15.
Ewing, J. H., *We and the World* (1881).
Farr, W., 'Health and Mortality of Children', *The Journal of the Statistical Society*, vol. 29 (1886), p. 1.
Farrar, F. D., *Eric, or Little by Little* (Edinburgh, 1858).
Field, E. M., *The Child and His Book* (1891).
Forster, John, *The Life of Charles Dickens* (1872–4), ed. J. W. T. Ley (1928).
'Funny Sayings and Answers by Children', *Chambers's Journal*, vol. 64 (1887), p. 699.
Garis, Robert, *The Dickens Theatre* (Oxford, 1965).
Garnett, R. S., *Samuel Butler and His Family Relations* (1926).
Gaskell, E., *The Life of Charlotte Brontë* (1857).
Gathorne-Hardy, Jonathan, *The Rise and Fall of the British Nanny* (1972).
Gatty, Mrs A., *The Mother's Book of Poetry* (1872).
Gignilliat, G. W., *The Author of Sandford and Merton* (New York, 1932).
Goodsell, W., *A History of Marriage and the Family* (New York, 1934).
Gosse, Edmund, *Aspects and Impressions* (1922).
Gosse, Edmund, *The Collected Poems of Edmund Gosse* (1911).
Gosse, Edmund, *Father and Son*, ed. James Hepburn (Oxford, 1974).
Gosse, Edmund, *The Life of Philip Henry Gosse, F.R.S.* (1890).
Gosse, Emily, *Abraham and His Children* (1855).
Gosse, Philip, *A Memorial of the Last Days on Earth of Emily Gosse* (1857).
Grahame, Kenneth, *The Golden Age* (1895).
Gwynn, Stephen, 'Modern Parents', *Cornhill Magazine*, N.S. vol. 8 (1900), p. 662.
Halévy, Elie, *A History of the English People in the Nineteenth Century* (1949).
Hill, Christopher, *Society and Puritanism in Pre-Revolutionary England* (1964).
Holroyd, Michael, *Lytton Strachey: a Critical Biography* (1968).
Holt, John, *Escape from Childhood* (1974).

Horton, R. F., 'Children and Parents', *Sunday Magazine*, vol. 23 (1894), p. 596.

Horton, R. F., 'On the Art of Living Together', *Sunday Magazine*, vol. 25 (1896), p. 145.

'The Happiness of Children', *Spectator*, vol. 68 (1892), p. 331.

Houghton, Walter E., *The Victorian Frame of Mind 1830–1870* (1957).

Howard, Daniel F. (ed.), *The Correspondence of Samuel Butler With His Sister May* (1962).

'The Idler's Club', *The Idler*, vol. 3 (1893), p. 229.

'The Instincts of Family', *Spectator*, vol. 59 (1886), p. 1110.

Jacox, Francis, 'About Goody Children', *Temple Bar*, vol. 24 (1868), p. 137.

Jaeger, Muriel, *Before Victoria* (1956).

Janeway, James, *A Token for Children* (1671–2).

Janney, F. L., *Childhood in English Non-Dramatic Literature from 1557–1798* (1924).

J. B. L., 'The Religious Education of Children', *Christian Instructor*, vol. 2 (1819), p. 278.

Johns, Bennet G., 'Books of Fiction for Children', *Quarterly Review*, vol. 122 (1867), p. 55.

Johnson, Edgar, *Charles Dickens: His Tragedy and Triumph*, 2 vols. (Toronto, 1952).

Jones, Henry Festing, *Samuel Butler, Author of Erewhon (1835–1902): a Memoir*, 2 vols. (1919).

Keynes, G., and Hill, B. (ed.), *Letters Between Samuel Butler and Miss E. M. A. Savage (1871–1885)* (1935).

Keynes, G., and Hill, B. (ed.), *Samuel Butler's Notebooks* (1951).

Kilner, Dorothy, *The Village School* (1828).

Kipling, Rudyard, *Stalky & Co.* (1899).

Laslett, Peter (ed.), *Household and Family in Past Time* (Cambridge, 1972).

Leavis, F. R. and Q. D., *Dickens the Novelist* (1970).

Macfarlane, Alan, *The Family Life of Ralph Josselin* (1970).

'Management of Children', *Hogg's Instructor*, vol. 9 (1852), p. 317.

Martin, L. C., 'Henry Vaughan and the Theme of Infancy', *Seventeenth-Century Studies Presented to Sir Herbert Grierson* (Oxford, 1938).

Martineau, Harriet, 'Herod in the Nineteenth Century', *Once a Week*, vol. 1 (1859), p. 195.

Mason, Charlotte M., 'Character in Children', *Murray's Magazine*, vol. 4 (1888), p. 765.

Mason, Charlotte M., 'Home Rule in the Nursery', *Murray's Magazine*, vol. 5 (1889), p. 516.

Mason, Charlotte M. (ed.), *The Parent's Review*, vol. 1 (1890), p. 574.

Mathers, Helen, *Comin' Thro' the Rye* (1875).

Maude, W. C., 'The Condition of Unbaptised Children After Death', *The Month*, vol. 77 (1893), p. 160.

Mazlish, Bruce, *James and John Stuart Mill* (1975).

Meredith, George, *The Ordeal of Richard Feverel* (1859).

Meynell, Alice, *The Second Person Singular* (1921).

Molesworth, M. L., *Carrots* (1891).

Montgomery, Florence, *Misunderstood* (1869).

'The Moral Culture of Children', *British Quarterly Review*, vol. 27 (1858), p. 383.

More, Hannah, *Strictures on the Modern System of Female Education* (1799).

Morgan, Edmund S., *The Puritan Family: Religion and Domestic Relations in Seventeenth-Century New England* (New York, 1966).

Muggeridge, Malcolm, *The Earnest Atheist: a Study of Samuel Butler* (1936).

Musgrove, Frank, *The Family, Education and Society* (1966).

Musgrove, Frank, *Youth and the Social Order* (1964).

Nicolson, Harold, *The Development of English Biography* (1927).

Norris, John, *Spiritual Counsel: or, the Father's Advice to his Children* (1694).

'On the Training of Children', *Methodist Magazine*, vol. 59 (1836), p. 751.

Palgrave, Mary E. (ed.), *The Fairchild Family* (1902).

'Parents and Children', *Quarterly Review*, vol. 39 (1829), p. 183.

Payn, James, 'Maxims on Children', *Chambers's Journal*, vol. 45 (1868), p. 161.

Pinchbeck, Ivy, and Hewitt, Margaret, *Children in English Society*, vol. 1 (1969).

Plumb, J. H., 'The New World of Children in Eighteenth-Century England', *Past and Present*, No. 67 (1975), p. 64.

Powell, C. L., *English Domestic Relations 1487–1653* (New York, 1917).

'Protection of Children', *Spectator*, vol. 57 (1884), p. 910.

Quinlan, Maurice J., *Victorian Prelude: a History of English Manners 1700–1830* (New York, 1941).

Rands, William Brighty, 'Honour to Parents', *Good Words*, vol. 14 (1873), p. 378.

'Religious Education of Children', *Christian Observer*, vol. 5 (1806), p. 337.

'Religious Education of Children', *Congregationalist*, vol. 3 (1874), p. 341.

'Religious Education of Children', *Westminster Review*, N.S. vol. 48 (1875), p. 374.

Rigby, Elizabeth, 'Children's Books', *Quarterly Review*, vol. 74 (1844), p. 1.

Roddier, H., *J. J. Rousseau en Angleterre au XVIIIᵉ siècle. L'oeuvre et l'homme* (Paris, 1950).

Rousseau, J. J. *Émile*, trans. Barbara Foxley (1955).

Salmon, A. L., 'The Love of Childhood', *Sunday Magazine*, vol. 19 (1890), p. 18.

Salmon, Edward, *Juvenile Literature As it is* (1888).

Sangster, Paul, *Pity My Simplicity* (1963).

'Scented with Lavender', *Once a Week*, N.S. vol. 13 (1874), p. 116.

Schücking, Levin L., *The Puritan Family* (1969).

Scudder, Horace E., *Childhood in Literature and Art* (New York, 1894).

Semmel, B., *The Methodist Revolution* (1974).

Sherwood, M. M., *The History of the Fairchild Family*, 3 vols. (1818, 1842, 1847).

Sherwood, M. M., *The Life and Times of Mrs. Sherwood* (1854).

Shorter, E., *The Making of the Modern Family* (1976).

Silver, Arnold (ed.), *The Family Letters of Samuel Butler, 1841–1886* (1962).

Sinclair, Catherine, *Holiday House* (Edinburgh, 1839).

Slater, M. (ed.), *Dickens 1970* (1970).

'The Society for the Prevention of Cruelty to Children', *Saturday Review*, vol. 55 (1883), p. 596.

Southey, Robert, *The Life and Correspondence of Robert Southey*, vol. 1 (1849).

Stephen, Leslie, *Hours in a Library*, vol. 1 (1892).

Stewart, J. I. M., *Rudyard Kipling* (1966).

Stewart, W. A. C., and McCann, W. P., *The Educational Innovators 1750–1880* (1967).

Stone, Lawrence, 'The Massacre of the Innocents', *The New York Review of Books*, 14 November 1974, p. 25.

Storr, Catherine, 'Freud and the Concept of Parental Guilt', *Freud: the Man, his Work, his Influence*, ed. Jonathan Miller (1972).

Sully, James, 'The Child in Recent English Literature', *Fortnightly Review*, vol. 61 (1897), p. 218.

Tadema, Laurence Alma, 'An Early Portrait of Edmund Gosse', *Cornhill Magazine*, vol. 67 (1929), p. 750.

Taylor, Ann and Jane, *Original Poems for Infant Minds* (1804–5).

'Tears of Parents', *Christian Observer*, vol. 32 (1832), p. 642.

Thwaite, Mary F., *From Primer to Pleasure in Reading* (1972).

'To Parents', *All the Year Round*, vol. 11 (1864), p. 512.

Townsend, John Rowe, *Written For Children*, 2nd ed. (1975).

Traherne, Thomas, *Poems, Centuries and Three Thanksgivings* (Oxford, 1966).

Trimmer, Sarah, *Fabulous Histories* (1786).

Trimmer, Sarah (ed.), *The Family Magazine* (1789).

Trimmer, Sarah (ed.), *The Guardian of Education* (1802–6).

Trimmer, Sarah, *Some Account of the Life and Writings of Mrs. Trimmer* (1814).

'The Troubles of Children', *Chambers's Journal*, vol. 54 (1877), p. 13.

Tytler, Sarah, *Childhood a Hundred Years Ago* (1877).

Vaughan, Henry, *The Works of Henry Vaughan* (Oxford, 1957).

Watson, John, 'Vexatious Children', *Sunday Magazine*, vol. 25 (1896), p. 405.

Watts, Isaac, *Divine and Moral Songs for the use of Children* (1812).

Waugh, B., and Manning, H. E., 'The Child of the English Savage', *Contemporary Review*, vol. 49 (1886), p. 687.

Whalley, Joyce Irene, *Cobwebs to Catch Flies* (1974).

Wilberforce, William, *A Practical View of the Prevailing Religious System* (1797).

Williamson, George C., 'Edmund Gosse as a Boy: a Reminiscence', *London Mercury*, vol. 18 (1928), p. 634.

Wilson, The Rev. Carus (ed.), *The Children's Friend* (1826).

Yonge, Charlotte, 'Children's Literature of the Last Century', *Macmillan's Magazine*, vol. 20 (1869), p. 448.

Young, G. M., *Victorian England: Portrait of an Age*, 2nd ed. (1966).

INDEX

(*Works are indexed under the name of the author*)